S0-AXJ-207

Advertising in the Age of Persuasion

Advertising in the Age of Persuasion

Building Brand America 1941–1961

Dawn Spring

palgrave
macmillan

ADVERTISING IN THE AGE OF PERSUASION
Copyright © Dawn Spring, 2011.

All rights reserved.

First published in 2011 by
PALGRAVE MACMILLAN®
in the United States—a division of St. Martin's Press LLC,
175 Fifth Avenue, New York, NY 10010.

Where this book is distributed in the UK, Europe and the rest of the World,
this is by Palgrave Macmillan, a division of Macmillan Publishers Limited,
registered in England, company number 785998, of Houndmills,
Basingstoke, Hampshire RG21 6XS.

Palgrave Macmillan is the global academic imprint of the above
companies and has companies and representatives throughout the world.

Palgrave® and Macmillan® are registered trademarks in the United
States, the United Kingdom, Europe and other countries.

ISBN: 978–0–230–11694–8

Library of Congress Cataloging-in-Publication Data

Spring, Dawn.
    Advertising in the age of persuasion : building brand America, 1941–1961 /
Dawn Spring.
        p.   cm.
    Includes bibliographical references.
    ISBN 978–0–230–11694–8
    1. Branding (Marketing)—United States—History—20th century.
    2. Consumption (Economics)—United States—History—20th century.
    3. Free enterprise—United States—History—20th century. I. Title.
    HF5415.1255.S67 2011
    659.10973'09045—dc22   2011015016

A catalogue record of the book is available from the British Library.

Design by Integra Software Services

First edition: November 2011

10 9 8 7 6 5 4 3 2 1

Printed in the United States of America.

Contents

Preface

Advertising in the Age of Persuasion documents and analyzes how American advertisers during the 1940s and 1950s worked to make themselves vital to businesses and government agencies and promote their version of free enterprise and how in doing so they made persuasive information vital to economic, politics, and international relations. Beginning with World War II, and girded by the Cold War, American advertisers, brand-name corporations, and federal government representatives institutionalized both the use of persuasive information for political and diplomatic reasons and the role that the advertising industry would play. Alongside the promotion of brand-name goods and consumer-driven economies, American advertisers helped formalize a peacetime structure for what would eventually become known as public diplomacy. During the 1940s and 1950s, they made themselves vital to business, media, government, and religious instruction and put forth a vision of democracies based on the mass consumption of brand-name goods, using advertising across all major media to sell products and distribute information. Many of the free enterprise evangelists believed free enterprise represented the fulfillment of America's god-ordained mission. They envisioned an American-led global consumer order supported by advertising-based media where the brand took precedence over the corporation that owned it and advertising, propaganda, and public relations were considered the same thing. To support these ideas and ensure that their services remained of value, they created a network and a process for disseminating persuasive information that have survived into the twenty-first century.

To these ends, nonprofit organizations such as the Advertising Council or the Ad Council (often I used interchangeably), famous for campaigns such as Smokey the Bear, McGruff the Crime Dog, and currently "Get Out and Play an Hour a Day" to fight childhood obesity, and the Brand Names Foundation created community activities and public service campaigns that brought together advertisers, business leaders, media moguls, politicians, and religious leaders. These campaigns, partnerships, and relationships standardized a methodology for the dissemination of persuasive information, promoted the idea of a consensus as to the American way of life and the American dream, helped modernize American politics in the age of television, and participated in the formation of the U.S. public diplomacy apparatus from Radio Free Europe/Radio Liberty to the United States Information Agency. The Advertising Council's post – World War II and early Cold War campaigns branded the United States and promoted free enterprise at home and abroad. From the creation and implementation of campaigns such as "The Freedom Train" and "The Crusade for Freedom," a network emerged that connected American advertising companies to the White House, the CIA, and other U.S. government agencies; to major broadcasters such as ABC, CBS, and NBC; to department stores and supermarkets; to popular magazines such as *Reader's Digest*, *Time*, and *Life*; to market research and psychological testing organizations such as A.C. Nielsen, the Gallup Poll, and the Psychological Corporation; and to brand-name corporations such as Coca-Cola, Ford, Kodak, Kraft Foods, Procter & Gamble, General Electric, General Foods, and General Motors. Collectively, these organizations pursued an economic and political strategy in which the United States would profit from leading the world in a geopolitical order based on the consumption of advertised brand-name goods. The presence and the extent of the network have been elusive, both in American history and in contemporary discourse until the twenty-first century, an invisible hand that influences consumer markets, contemporary politics, and public knowledge and masks the complexities of modern multinational megacorporations.

Advertising in the Age of Persuasion analyzes how advertising, business, and the federal government in America worked together to promote free enterprise capitalism at home and abroad during the 1940s and 1950s, as well as how they helped to develop long-term organizations to promote those goals. In doing so, it explores the crafting of American consumer culture by free enterprise supporters and with it an age in which persuasive information became an essential part of the American economy, politics, and foreign relations. It demonstrates that the free enterprise strategy and the idea of the consumer republic became a pervasive, yet unseen, part of the American political landscape into the twenty-first century. Organizations such as the Ad Council have survived into the twenty-first century, bringing together the country's major media organizations and brand-name manufactures, and promoting the free enterprise system within the United States and around the globe. This network of free enterprise supporters and their strategies for launching campaigns have supplanted Adam Smith's invisible hand of the market, replacing it with the invisible hand of persuasive information to guide brand-name consumer markets and shape public discourse.

Abbreviations

AAAA	Association of American Advertising Agencies
ACA	Advertising Council Archives
AEC	Atomic Energy Commission
BNF	Brand Names Foundation
BTC	Bancroft Textile Collection
CBS	Columbia Broadcasting System
CIA	Central Intelligence Agency
CIAA	Coordinator of Inter-American Affairs
EL	Eisenhower Library
FEC	Free Europe Committee
HCAMR	Hartman Center for Sales, Advertising, and Marketing Research, Duke University, Durham, North Carolina
HM&L	Hagley Museum and Library
HIWRP	Hoover Institution for War, Revolution, and Peace
HSTL	Harry S. Truman Library
JWT	J. Walter Thompson Company
JWTCA	J. Walter Thompson Company Archives
KHC	Kodak Historical Collection
NATO	North Atlantic Treaty Organization
NBC	National Broadcasting Company
NCFE	National Committee for a Free Europe
NDEA	National Defense Education Act
NSA	National Security Archive
NSC	National Security Council
NYPL	New York Public Library
OSA	Open Society Archives, Budapest, Hungary
OSS	Office of Strategic Services
OWI	Office of War Information
P & G	The Procter & Gamble Company
PPF	President's Personal File

PSB	Psychological Strategy Board
RFE	Radio Free Europe
RL	Radio Liberty
SMOF	Staff Member and Office Files
TPTL	Truman Papers, Harry S. Truman Library & Museum
UN	United Nations
USIA	United States Information Agency
USIS	United States Information Service
UWML	University of Wisconsin-Madison Library
VOA	Voice of America
WHCF	White House Central Files
WHO	White House Office

Introduction

And the people must either be compelled or persuaded
—there is no other way.

War Advertising Council, 1945

. . . in America advertising has become the greatest single means for mass communication, information, and persuasion which has ever been seen in any society, anywhere, at any time . . .

. . . advertising in America has available to it incomparable mechanical means for the distribution of messages, through newspapers, magazines, radio and television stations, outdoor signs, street car cards, and others . . . .

. . . Massed together, these are capable of an almost overpowering effect.

James Webb Young,
War Advertising Council
Advertising Council
J. Walter Thompson Company
March 11, 1949

. . . it is often assumed that there is some essential difference between ***advertising*** and its more modern counterparts: ***propaganda*** and ***public relations***. They differ only superficially; they are identical in kind. All three set out to influence public opinion.

A Technique of Planning Applied to Influencing Opinion and Behaviour
J. Walter Thompson Company Limited, London, 1948

Brand America

The age of persuasion finds its beginnings in the late 1800s, when free enterprise visionaries began imagining a world where everyone bought American brand-name goods.[1] In the early twentieth century, the use of advertising, market research, and global trade to advance American interests became a more widely accepted economic and political strategy, and advertisers sought to make themselves invaluable in the modern world. As advertising came into prominence, capitalism and the mechanism of the economy increasingly came to be about the ideas and messages about a product and no longer about the manufacturing of the product.

In 1941, the often referred to "grandfather" of the Ad Council, J. Walter Thompson executive James Webb Young, articulated a vision of a world where advertisers helped mass produced American brand names span the globe, one in which free enterprise meant advertising played a central role in culture, education, government, religion, and society, where brand-name products would dominate national and international markets and advertising money would support every major media from newspapers to radio to television. All men, women, and children, regardless of ethnicity, nationality, and religion would be potential consumers with advertising tailored to their demographic.

All over the world, countries would be shown the shining example offered by the United States and embrace the free enterprise system of advertising and brand names. Market research, targeted advertising, and commercial media would lead every nation to voluntarily adopt American leadership and a free enterprise consumer economy. Advertising and brand names would guarantee employment and enough money in the family budget to afford consumer items and entertainment. Happy consumers across the globe would exercise their freedom of choice by selecting from various brand-name goods and services. Advertising would be on a par with news, bringing vital information to the public. Advertising and brand-name political parties would streamline the political process, allowing citizens to choose from political brands. Free choice in consumer goods would ready people to participate in democratic politics, and thus world democracy would flourish.[2]

In the twenty-first century, American brands and the use of persuasive information in business, diplomacy, and politics spanned the globe as nations increasingly became enmeshed in the American consumer economy. By 2008, American consumer spending accounted for 60 percent of the American economy and helped make the United States the "engine of the global economy."[3] Advertising and branded consumer goods and services infused American culture and connected the world.

The "Campaign for Freedom"

Sixty years after the Young articulation and six days after 9/11 that same Ad Council, creator of Smokey the Bear and McGruff the Crime Dog, offered to help the White House and the State Department respond to the attack on the World Trade Center. The council coordinated over a $100 million in donated time and space to run the advertising campaigns "I am an American" and "Campaign for Freedom." Some called this type of persuasive information propaganda; others saw it as a return to the Ad Council's original mission. In 2002, the Ad council designed "Campaign for Freedom" to "fight the war on terrorism," coordinating a series of television commercials with the slogan "Freedom. Appreciate it. Cherish it. Protect it." One commercial showed a man arrested for having newspapers. Another showed a tree-lined residential street, a voice-over stating "On Sept. 11, terrorists tried to change America forever." The image then faded out, replaced with a new image of the street; this time every house had an American flag and the voice-over stated, "Well, they succeeded."[4]

Public Diplomacy

On November 1, 2001, the House of Representatives Committee on International Relations held hearings called "The Message is America: Rethinking U.S. Public Diplomacy" to which the Ad Council sent a representative. The U.S. government defined *public diplomacy* as "activities intended to understand, inform, and influence foreign publics." One of the committee's goals was to "make better use of the range of media available to us—such as radio, television, the Internet and other means of communication—to expand our potential audience."[5]

Bob Wehling, cochair of the Ad Council Advisory Committee, former chairman of the Ad Council, and retired marketing and advertising executive from Procter & Gamble, testified that his "experience with both P&G and the Ad Council proves conclusively that advertising can change attitudes and practices." He urged the use of public diplomacy in the Middle East and claimed to be "absolutely convinced that an advertising and communications program can be effective in the Middle East."[6]

Norman J. Pattiz, a Clinton and Bush appointee to the Broadcasting Board of Governors (BBG), "the independent federal agency responsible for all U.S. government and government sponsored, non-military, international broadcasting," and the founder and chairman of Westwood One, Inc., "America's largest radio network and provider of radio programming, serving over 7500 stations coast to coast," testified that

> U.S. International broadcasting has played a key role in every major world conflict and crisis in which the United States has been engaged over the last 60 years. In every one of these, World War II and the Cold War especially, our government-supported overseas broadcasting has been a major contributing factor in our country's success.[7]

On the basis of his experience at Westwood One distributing "music, entertainment, sports, and talk programming . . . news and information" to "CBS Radio News, Fox News Radio, CNN Radio News and the NBC Radio Network," Pattiz recommended "something well beyond anything U.S. International broadcasting has been able to do before, something that uses American commercial broadcasting techniques to attract the largest possible audience to advance U.S. public diplomacy."[8] In 2002, the U.S. public diplomacy broadcasting organization Radio Free Europe/Radio Liberty began broadcasting Radio Farda to Iran. After the 2003 invasion of Iraq, Pattiz worked with the BBG to develop Radio Sawa and Alhurra satellite television. This television complex went on to serve 22 Middle Eastern countries, while his company Westwood One produced news and information for many major American networks.[9] Like half a century before, Procter & Gamble executives and Ad Council members were called on to support the U.S. government for advertising and public relations to the other nations and forging strategies to create media networks to sell the United States around the world.

Advertising the *American Century*

In 1941, as *Time-Life* editor Henry Luce declared "the American Century," American advertisers took on a new role in American life and politics, forming a relationship with the White House, national security agencies, and overseas information services that remained into the twenty-first century.[10] Coming out of World War II, the United States remained the only industrial nation largely unscathed by the global conflicts of the early twentieth century, leaving American advertisers in a prime position to cement their status in the world economy and help govern the global flow of information. Throughout the 1940s and 1950s, prominent advertisers and their affiliates, in broadcasting, government, industry, and retail, promoted brand America and free enterprise capitalism within the United States and around the globe. Nonprofit organizations such as the Ad Council, the Brand Names Foundation, the American Heritage Foundation, and the Crusade for Freedom, made up of representatives from the private and public sectors, coordinated "public service" advertising campaigns across a vast network of American businesses, government and military agencies, media outlets, publishers, and schools. These campaigns were designed to create an appearance of consensus, yet they were tightly controlled from the top down and were carefully orchestrated at every level, from grassroots activities to print advertisement. For these campaigns, these organizations created billboards, guides for community activities, national activities, print advertisements, prepackaged news, public displays, radio and television commercials, school curriculum, and religious sermons. In addition to domestic campaigns, they created campaigns for foreign markets, ones largely hidden from the American public by the Smith-Mundt Act of 1948. The act remains in effect into the twenty-first century and prevents Americans from having access to much of the material produced by the government for foreign audiences due to the concern that the material would constitute the use of propaganda on the American people.[11]

From the 1940s into the twenty-first century, organizations such as the Advertising Council have served as a meeting ground for American advertisers, the media, brand-name corporations, labor unions, banks, the military, national security agencies, and the White House to develop the apparatus and techniques for using persuasive information at home and abroad. Their network for creating and disseminating information has remained largely unseen, yet collectively they have exerted an immeasurable influence on the economy. These persuasive information pioneers advocated what they called *free enterprise*. Not free enterprise in the sense of an unrestricted free flow of goods and services where quality and customer satisfaction determined success or failure. To the proponents of free enterprise, it represented more than just a lack of government interference in economic matters. Rather free enterprise meant a system based on the mass consumption and mass production of heavily advertised, brand-name goods and services, which were promoted across all major media and supported by consumer credit and the brand management system. A system in which communicating about a product or a service, the branding of a product or a service, the public relations of a company, and the advertising of a branded good or service took precedent over the actual product and the manufacturing of the product. In other words, the quality of the good or the service would have far less to do with it than how well the company convinced the consumer that the good or the service was worth purchasing. And since the free enterprise system required continually having consumers to buy new products to keep the economic engine turning, how the consumers felt about purchasing products took precedent.

Free enterprise meant a form of capitalism that utilized the advertising of brand-name goods across all available media to create mass consumption, expanding markets, and mass production. Whereas Adam Smith described capitalism as being guided by the "invisible hand" where every individual pursuing his own interest in a free market created good for the community, in this version of free enterprise, the invisible hand that guided the market included advertising, advertising-based media, and the brand management system.[12] They believed that a world of free enterprise - based republics would create peace and prosperity, and held that since free enterprise was a uniquely American form of capitalism, the United States should guide others in that global system.[13] To represent their vision, they pushed an American brand that incorporated ideas such as the American Dream and the American way of life.

Advertising in the Age of Persuasion analyzes the early campaigns and organizations that created the network for disseminating information and launching persuasive information campaigns during the 1940s and 1950s. In doing so, it demonstrates that by the end of President Eisenhower's administration, the invisible hand had become an American institution (which survived into the twenty-first century), one that brought together the country's major media and brand-name manufactures, and promoted the free enterprise system within the United States and around the globe. It shows how the network became a pervasive part of the American landscape, how it helped build diplomatic information services, how it advanced free enterprise capitalism, and how it helped usher in an age of persuasive information and public diplomacy.

Chapter 1 discusses the evolution of the strategy of free enterprise, beginning in the late 1800s; the companies and individuals who played major roles in its development; the idea of persuasive information and public interest campaigns; and the formation of the War Advertising Council and the modern day Advertising Council. Chapter 2 describes how the postwar campaigns "The Freedom Train" and "The Miracle of America" created a peacetime network of advertisers, business leaders, media moguls, and politicians and what process was used for launching campaigns. It also discusses how these campaigns were designed to create a brand for the nation and unify Americans around a common vision of American history, free enterprise, and civil rights. Chapter 3 looks at the rise of the brand as a mechanism for selling goods and the importance of the idea of the brand to creating effective persuasive information. It traces the development of brand management at Procter & Gamble in the 1930s. It also examines the Brand Names Foundation, an affiliate organization that promoted the use of brand-name goods and the brand management system as an essential part of free enterprise and freedom of speech. Chapter 4 examines the Smith-Mundt Act of 1948 and the Advertising Council's role in the international "war on ideas," as the council began working with the Department of State to brand and promote the United States overseas. Chapter 5 looks at the use of advertising and marketing techniques to promote religion through the "Religion in American Life Campaign" and the career of preacher Billy Graham. It explores the relationship between Christianity and free enterprise during the 1940s and 1950s and the sense of religious purpose regarding America's global mission held by many of the key participants. Chapter 6 describes the "Crusade for Freedom," a campaign that inspired Ronald Reagan and raised money to help the CIA send balloons to drop leaflets over Eastern Europe and develop Radio Free Europe and Radio Free Asia. Chapter 7 explores the role of television in expanding America's persuasive information capacity, the development of American television as a solely advertising-based medium, the use of television to promote civil rights, the early plans for television around the globe, and the beginning of television-based political campaigns. Chapter 8 shows that with Eisenhower's election, the "Atoms for Peace" and the "People's Capitalism" campaigns, and the appointment of Procter & Gamble advertising executive Neil McElroy to the position of secretary of defense, American advertisers had found a permanent place in the nation's economy, politics, and foreign relations among both major political parties. The conclusion explores how the strategies for promoting free enterprise in the 1940s and 1950s became institutionalized and largely remained a hidden part of American policy into the twenty-first century, evolving into contemporary practices such as nation branding and public diplomacy. It examines the continuity in the use of persuasive information by American politicians and political strategists, as well as how Ronald Reagan's administration helped the invisible hand outlive the Cold War and survive into the twenty-first century. It reviews the brands and media outlets that have remained, the ways brand management informed the rise of multinational megacorporations, and the invisible hand in the age of the internet.[14]

CHAPTER 1

"Persuaders in the Public Interest"*

Between the late 1800s and the 1940s, free enterprise capitalism and the persuasive information industry emerged in the United States and the companies whose representatives championed these causes in the 1940s and 1950s were some of the most important early practitioners. Free enterprise was born in the late nineteenth century with the sale of goods to mass national markets; the large-scale production of brand goods, such as Ivory soap by Procter & Gamble and the Kodak camera; and the development of the profession of advertising. Together, these advertising and brand-name companies crafted a version of capitalism dependent on the advertising of brand-name goods, mass consumption, mass media financed by advertising, mass production, and perpetually expanding markets. As free enterprise capitalism increasingly dominated American corporations, advertising went from being a questionable practice in the late 1800s to a place of prominence, assisting the American government win World War II.

After a fall from the boom period in the 1920s, by 1941, American advertisers faced mounting criticism about their value in American society. Advertising agencies, whose business had grown steadily since the 1870s, found revenue dropping throughout the 1930s. Historic agencies and companies that developed their business through the use of advertising and mass marketing found the value of that advertising challenged. The work of advertisers and public relations specialists in selling World War I faced attacks. Their work with President Wilson's Committee for Public Information during World War I had been heavily criticized as being propaganda, leaving industry participants such as public relations pioneer Edwards

* Jason Weems, "Persuaders in the Public Interest," Advertisement, *Time,* December 29, 1958, box 2, J. Walter Thompson. Howard Henderson Papers, Rare Book, Manuscript, and Special Collections Library, Duke University.

Bernays to suggest that advertising, government information and, public relations professions no longer use the term *propaganda* when describing persuasive information.[1] However, World War II and the era of American internationalism that it ushered in erased many of the concerns regarding the value of advertising in the United States. With the War Advertising Council during World War II, advertisers proved their usefulness to politicians, creating a permanent relationship with the White House and U.S. national security agencies.

Advertising and brand-name manufacturing developed during the late nineteenth century and laid the foundation for modern American free enterprise. While many American companies and politicians did not embrace free enterprise until after World War II, the ideas and techniques—advertising, brand management, commercial broadcasting, mass markets, and overseas expansion—were in place by the war. Fledgling advertising agencies like Cincinnati-based J. Walter Thompson and brand-name companies such as Procter & Gamble and Eastman Kodak used advertising to sell goods on a national level. From the end of the nineteenth century to the beginning of World War I, advertising went from being primarily a service that sold newspaper and magazine ads to providing full service marketing strategies.

During the 1920s, radio became commercial broadcasting, establishing the precedent for advertising to be the bedrock of radio and television. After rising to social acceptance, influence, and profits in the 1920s, advertising expenditures slid rapidly as the U.S. economy fell into depression and a new consumer movement pushed for the regulation of advertisers. As advertising prepared to defend itself in the early 1940s, America entered World War II, and a permanent relationship between American advertising and the American government was born. During World War II, advertisers and brand-name manufacturers proved their usefulness to the White House, and after the war the Advertising Council incorporated as a permanent nonprofit entity with bipartisan support.

Pioneers

Three companies played a unique role in the pioneering use of advertising and the brand structure: the Eastman Kodak Company, the J. Walter Thompson Company, and the Procter & Gamble Company. In the 1870s, Procter & Gamble began its first mass marketing of a brand good, Ivory soap. George Eastman began building his film and eventually camera business, Kodak.[2] And, in 1877, J. Walter Thompson bought the William J. Carlton agency from William James Carlton, changed the name to J. Walter Thompson, and began turning it into the country's leading advertising agency. While just a few of the many brand-name companies emerging at the turn of the century, these three companies played went on to play pivotal roles in developing advertising, branding, broadcasting, government partnerships, and public information campaigns.

Procter & Gamble's branding and marketing of Ivory soap quickly became a model of a mass produced, mass marketed brand-name good. Unlike other companies, P & G did all its advertising in-house and did not work with outside agencies until it hired J. Walter Thompson to do the Crisco campaign in 1911—putting itself in the position of being a leader in the twentieth century in terms of the range of goods produced, how they were researched, developed, and manufactured, and how advertising and brand names could be used to create new markets. Between the 1880s and 1900, Procter & Gamble also helped develop the American advertising profession.[3] It helped pioneer the idea of the brand, which began literally as a branding iron mark used on the outside of wood boxes to make them easily identifiable as Procter & Gamble Star candles.[4] Procter & Gamble branded its new soap product, Ivory, after a biblical passage and began a successful national marketing campaign. By the late nineteenth century, Procter & Gamble became one of the United States' largest advertisers.[5]

Kodak's Four Fundamentals

Within a decade of spending his own savings to start his camera business, George Eastman started doing Kodak business in England in 1885 and getting the company's first overseas patent there.[6] Kodak first advertised using the J. Walter Thompson agency in 1888, when the agency placed ads for Kodak in many of the major national magazines, including *Scientific America* and *Harper's*.[7] While over the decades J. Walter Thompson taught many companies how to market, they also learned marketing from Kodak. By the end of the nineteenth century, Kodak spent over three quarters of a million dollars, one of the biggest expenditures on advertising in the nation.[8] In 1878, George Eastman laid out his four fundamental business principles: mass production done by machinery, prices low enough so as to make the product useful, demonstration of the product combined with extensive advertising, and worldwide distribution. These principles represented some of the basic tenets behind free enterprise capitalism; however, while many companies in the United States undertook practices similar to Eastman's domestically, his final principle of expanding world markets remained contested until after World War II.[9]

World Markets

In 1898, the Spanish-American War sparked debates among American politicians and businessmen about expanding business overseas and using former Spanish holdings such as Cuba and the Philippines as a launching point for American business to have access to consumer markets in other countries. The Spanish-American War opened up new markets for both Kodak and J. Walter Thompson. As the new century began, Mr. Thompson claimed that J. Walter Thompson could operate in the world without restrictions—that "any spot on earth where goods are to be sold by advertising is inside the fence of the Thompson field." As American action overseas generated increased trade, Thompson declared: "Trade follows the flag. Where trade goes the J. Walter Thompson Agency is ready to go also."[10] Shortly after the Spanish-American War, J. Walter Thompson's New York office set up a Spanish department and began preparing advertising for Latin American countries and the Philippines. Within five years, J. Walter Thompson was placing ads in local publications in Hawaii, Latin America, and the Philippines. It opened its first overseas office in London in 1899. There, it worked to both provide advertising for companies and encourage American businesses to expand overseas, producing resources such as the "Thompson Blue Book of Advertising" in 1904 that described American export trade around the world.[11]

Stanley Resor and J. Walter Thompson

The early twentieth century witnessed the continued growth of all three companies and the techniques of advertising and brand-name marketing. The rise of the Hollywood movie industry brought additional business and influence for Kodak and advertisers benefited greatly from the exploding auto industry.[12] J. Walter Thompson continued to expand its domestic business. In 1911, Cincinnati-based Procter & Gamble hired the local agency to market its new product made out of cotton by-products. J. Walter Thompson executive and testimonial advertising specialist Stanley Resor changed the name of the product from Krispo to Crisco, creating another of Procter & Gamble's famous brands.[13] As manager of the Cincinnati office, Resor made the fateful decision to persuade James Webb Young to give up his career as a Bible and religious book salesman to work writing advertising copy for the J. Walter Thompson Company.[14] In 1916, Resor; his wife, Helen Resor; and several associates bought the J. Walter Thompson Company from Mr. Thompson, making the Cincinnati office of J. Walter Thompson one of the most important offices and Resor one of the country's most powerful advertising executives. He exerted considerable influence in expanding both the company and the profession, helping to found the American Association of Advertising Agencies (AAAA) in 1917 and building the company into the "world's biggest agency."[15]

World War I and the Crusade for Democracy

World War I marked the first foray of advertisers and public relations experts into government information campaigns. In April 1917, President Wilson created the executive order 2594 that established the Committee for Public Information (CPI). Since he appointed George Creel as head the CPI also came to be known as the Creel Committee. The federal agency worked with advertising and public relations executives to create campaigns to advertise America The Creel Committee developed the Crusade for Democracy campaign with slogans such as "the war to end all wars" and "the war to make the world safe for democracy" and produced such famous campaigns as the Uncle Sam poster—"I want you"—for army recruiting. It created multi-platform campaigns that ranged from print advertisements, posters, and cartoons to the 4 Minute Men speakers, who gave four minute speeches across the country. In 1918, James Webb Young was "drafted by the first World War Creel Committee for Public information, to develop a plan for propaganda on the western front."[16] Young provided recommendations for the creation of wartime propaganda, preparing a report for the Creel Commission entitled "Enemy Country Propaganda from an Advertising Viewpoint." The Creel Commission remained only a wartime entity and was disbanded after World War I amidst criticisms of propaganda, leaving Young and others to return for the moment to advertising for business purposes.[17]

Postwar Years

The 1920s brought a booming free enterprise economy and prosperous times for advertising. Advertisers left the propaganda business and focused on expanding across the nation and overseas and developing the radio into a commercial advertising medium. Buoyed in part by Young's 1919 advertising copy for deodorant—"Within the curve of a woman's arm" for Cincinnati-based Odorono—which dramatically increased sales and brought industry attention to Young's techniques, J. Walter Thompson helped lead advertising to its first phase of major growth in the twentieth century. The 1920s saw further international expansion by both Kodak and J. Walter Thompson. By that decade, Kodak did business in Switzerland, New Zealand, Denmark, Egypt, India, the Netherlands, South Africa, Spain, Argentina, Singapore, and Portugal and the J. Walter Thompson London office produced advertising for American and British clients across Europe.[18] Throughout the 1920s, Kodak also continued its expansion into Brazil, Mexico, Lebanon, Uruguay, Chile, Greece, Hong Kong, Kenya, Panama, Peru, and the Philippines, while J. Walter Thompson helped General Motors grow its business overseas.[19] In 1927, J. Walter Thompson as part of its contract with General Motors International opened an office in every nation that General Motors had an assembly or manufacturing plant. To establish these offices Young traveled across Europe with J. Walter Thompson staff, resulting in offices being created in Germany, Belgium, Denmark, Spain, and Egypt.[20]

During this period several important mechanisms and methods of advertising and public relations developed, such as the use of psychology and market research to study the effectiveness of advertising. During this period, the Psychological Corporation, which also did educational testing in the twentieth century, began working with advertising agencies. In the 1920s Raymond Rubicam hired George Gallup to conduct opinion polls. In 1924, Procter & Gamble created one of the first "market research departments" in order "to study consumer preferences and buying habits."[21] During the 1920s, Young also spent time developing further skills for market research and persuading consumers. He pursued the study of psychology with Dr. John Watson, "originator of 'behaviour psychology," and worked at the University of Chicago with Dr. Anton Carlson. Young, who technically retired from JWT in 1928, went on to teach advertising at the School of Business at the University of Chicago in the 1930s, helping to train a new generation of advertisers and gain legitimacy for the profession.

Radio and Commercial Advertising

Advertising's growth occurred not just in offices and print campaigns, but also across mediums as radio quickly became an ideal advertising medium. While the Happiness Candy Company sponsored a series show on the AT &T network in 1923, advertising agencies did not embrace the radio until the mid-1920s. In 1922 in New York City, AT & T created the first commercial radio broadcasting, as radio began transitioning from a hodgepodge of local stations to a national commercial media.[22] Procter & Gamble was one of the earliest innovators in commercial radio broadcasting and by the 1930s was one of the "biggest advertisers on the airwaves." In 1923, Procter & Gamble began sponsoring radio cooking shows on behalf of Crisco, and during that period sponsored radio programs began with companies such as Goodrich Tires sponsoring shows. Procter & Gamble also created the first radio "soap opera" in the 1930s.[23] In 1926, the Radio Corporation of America (RCA) launched the National Broadcasting Company (NBC) and began selling the idea of radio advertising to advertising companies. In 1927, the federal government established the Federal Radio Commission, creating a permanent system of commercial broadcast within the United States.[24] While advertisers took to the airwaves throughout the 1920s, JWT did not utilize the radio until 1929. Like JWT, once engaged in the medium radio advertising and commercial broadcasting quickly became well established.[25]

Advertising during the Depression

Throughout the 1930s, advertisers sought to grow business despite an unfriendly climate. During the Depression, politicians, academics, and consumer activists challenged the necessity of advertising for the economy. They challenged its potential for deception and the cost it created for consumers. More regulation was attempted against advertisers than any other time in American history. The annual volume of advertising dropped from $3.4 billion in 1929 to $2.3 billion in 1931 and reached $1.3 billion (its lowest volume) in 1933.[26] Yet, at the same time, advertisers and brand-name manufacturers continued to develop their businesses through innovations in marketing techniques, as well as expanding the role of advertising, radio, and new foreign markets.

The marketing power of radio grew, eventually informing the development of television, as advertisers and corporations broadened their capacity for producing commercial programming. As well as advertisements for radio, both JWT and Procter & Gamble developed programming and programming sponsorships. In doing so, they helped establish American commercial entertainment. Entertainment programming made for the purpose of attracting audiences to encourage brand loyalty and sell goods.

Throughout the 1930s, both companies developed commercial radio programming. JWT produced its first two-hour commercial radio program in 1933 for Kraft Miracle Whip.[27] Also in 1933, Procter & Gamble started producing radio soap operas when "Ma Perkins," a radio serial program sponsored by P&G's Oxydol soap powder, aired nationally. Its popularity led P&G brands to sponsor numerous new "soap operas." Faithful listeners become loyal buyers of P&G brands at the grocery. "Radio advertising techniques were quickly applied to the early days of the television. In 1939, months after television broadcasting began, P&G aired its first television commercial. The commercial for Ivory soap aired during the "first televised major league baseball game" and helped establish the value of advertising during televised sporting events.[28]

While the types of persuasive information expanded, so did the major advertising companies. By the mid-1930s, J. Walter Thompson claimed to be the "world's largest agency." In 1932, J. Walter Thompson opened its public relations department, "JWT News Bureau," to develop "editorial publicity" for Kodak.[29] At this point in the persuasive information business there was still a divide between public relations and advertising. Public relations pioneer Edward Bernays described public relations as the cultivation of public opinion, whereas advertising broadcast messages about a product.[30] So, the addition of a public relations department at a firm as prominent and far-reaching as JWT shifted the function of advertisers from merely being broadcasters and announcers of products to cultivating associations, loyalties, and opinions about a topic at hand.

Brand Management

In 1931, Procter & Gamble's Neil McElroy wrote a revolutionary memo about marketing Camay soap. The memo formed the basis for the business and marketing strategy of brand management and put McElroy on the road to becoming Secretary of Defense. The memo suggested a corporate structure whereby each brand would be marketed as its own company, competing with other brands owned by the corporation. In other words, Camay soap and Ivory soap though the same product (soap) and though manufactured by the same corporation (P&G) would complete against each other with unique marketing strategies. The brand of the product would take precedence over the corporate ownership of the product. This way a company could own multiple types of the same product, but the range of brand names the product was marketed under would give the appearance of being multiple competing companies. McElroy's brand management of Camay propelled him up the executive ladder at P&G and further advanced the brand management system.[31]

Though it would take Neil McElroy's memo to formalize the corporate brand management system, throughout the tens and twenties, Procter & Gamble developed the instruments of "brand making." Building a successful national brand included conducting extensive research and development, refining marketing campaigns, and refashioning the distribution infrastructure to reflect products in the same market. In 1923, Procter & Gamble established an "economic research department" to further expand the capacity of advertising and market research to create mass production and mass consumption. In May 1931, Procter & Gamble's man in charge of Camay soap, Neil McElroy, wrote a memo about the "duties and responsibilities of brand men" that formalized the brand management system. McElroy came to be considered one of the most important people in defining the use of brands and the brand management system. The memo suggested a corporate structure whereby each brand was marketed as its own company, allowing for each brand to have a unique marketing strategy. This eventually created the brand management system in which a corporation could own limitless brands and competing brands.[32]

In 1930, when Procter & Gamble sought to use the same brand marketing techniques to capture markets in China, Mexico, and the Philippines, it opened a Long Beach, California, plant to expedite distribution. The ceremonies included the launching of a four-foot bar of Ivory soap. By the late 1930s, P&G had become one of the biggest brand advertisers on radio, and radio soap operas had become a "centerpiece of P&G's marketing campaign." By 1939, when Procter & Gamble first ventured into televised baseball with a Brooklyn Dodgers and Cincinnati Reds doubleheader, the company owned hundreds of brands, many of which, like Ivory and Camay, competed against each other. In 1946, Procter & Gamble named brand pioneer Neil McElroy vice president and general manager. By then, he had helped Procter & Gamble turn radio and early television into media designed around the delivery of advertising by major brand manufacturers.[33]

Foreign Markets

Despite economies weakened by a global depression, advertisers and manufacturers who invested in advertising were still able to continue growing overseas. By the late 1930s, J. Walter Thompson had 22 offices throughout the world and staffs throughout the British Empire (Australia, Canada, India, South Africa), in Europe (France, Germany, Spain, Sweden, Belgium), and in South America (Argentina and Brazil). In some countries, J. Walter Thompson helped create local publications; for instance, in Australia, a year after opening there, it helped create *Women's Weekly*.[34] By 1931, J. Walter Thompson had also grown into one of the largest advertising agencies in Britain. It opened its first office in Berlin in 1928; however, due to the Nazis the office was closed in 1934 and it did not reopen an office in Germany until 1952.[35] During the 1930s, Kodak expanded into Hawaii, China, and Japan.[36] Unlike Eastman at Kodak and Stanley Resor at J. Walter Thompson, the executives at Procter & Gamble were more cautious about setting up "worldwide operations." However, during the 1930s Procter & Gamble expanded into Britain and in 1935 into the Philippines before World War II.[37] By the mid-1930s, J. Walter Thompson claimed to be the "world's largest agency."[38]

World War II

Though war in Europe started bringing the American economy out of the Depression in 1939, advertising still found itself under attack. Debates raged in the country about whether America should enter the war in Europe. Though advertising faced mounting criticism, President Roosevelt quickly called on the service of advertising. James Webb Young once again played a role in creating wartime propaganda when in 1939 Roosevelt appointed him director of the Bureau of Foreign & Domestic Commerce in the Department of Commerce. In 1941 he resigned to assist Nelson Rockefeller organize his staff as coordinator of Inter-American Affairs and that he same year he was also elected to the Business Advisory Council to the Department of Commerce.[39] During this period, Young declared advertising an integral part of America's freedoms. Advertising provided Americans with what Young called America's fifth freedom in response to President Franklin D. Roosevelt's speech about America's four freedoms—"freedom of speech," "freedom of religion," "freedom from want," and "freedom from fear." Young declared the fifth freedom to be the "free choice of goods and services which can be supplied only by free enterprise."[40]

The Hot Springs Conference and the Blueprint for the Invisible Hand

On November 13, 1941, 700 American advertisers converged on the Homestead, a 17,000-acre hot springs resort in Virginia's Alleghany Mountains where America's wealthy and influential had met since the days of George Washington's visits.[41] To face the threats of New Deal restrictions on advertising and the possibility that World War II would render advertising further unnecessary, the AAAA and the Association of National Advertisers (ANA) had called a conference. The conference had been called to bring together media groups, advertising agencies, and in-house corporate advertisers in order to form "a united front of those who have a common concern in advertising." Thus, ending the war and human suffering was not a concern; rather, as Paul West of the ANA explained, there was "grave concern about advertising and what may happen to the business which is largely dependent on manifesting itself daily in many quarters" and "a growing alarm that advertising is going to be throttled by whatever method, for whatever purpose and with whatever motive." Advertising's opponents were not the Nazis, but rather the "high officials in government" who felt that the advertising of "trademarks and brands" represented a "waste" and "added cost to the consumer." Specifically, West warned that if left unchecked government officials would succeed in their "push for mandatory standardization and government grade labeling," and severely restrict advertising revenue, jeopardizing not only national brand-name manufacturers and advertising agencies but also one of America's fundamental freedoms, the freedom of press. The tax bill under consideration by Congress in 1941, creating taxes on "radio and outdoor advertising and electric advertising signs," threatened "the national media whose very freedom depends on a large and continuous flow of national advertising revenue." On November 14, 1941, William L. Batt (director of the Materials Division of the Office of Price Management) urged advertisers to start working for the war effort. During the morning sessions "advertisers and media men met to map out a self preservation program for advertising," and at times, the entire audience rose in response to calls for an "organized program to sell advertising to the public."[42] Years later, James Webb Young described the crisis as advertisers "literally on trial for its life," because "violent attacks were being made upon it in every branch of government—executive, legislative, and judicial. Educators and publicists berated it without mercy—and often without facts. Publications were founded on the boast of freedom from its pernicious influence. And an anti-advertising 'consumer movement' of sizeable proportions was giving many earnest souls the jitters."[43]

On November 14, 1941, James Webb Young gave one of the most under recognized speeches of the twentieth century. He laid out a plan for advertisers to launch a self-promotion campaign, citing three major obstacles for American advertising. The first was that important and "influential" segments of the American public found advertising repugnant. Second, no major training opportunities existed for advertisers. And, finally, many people in the federal government wanted to create an American economic system in which advertising played a less "integral" role.[44] He and others warned that any threat on advertising also represented a threat against a free press, and thus, free speech. He told advertisers that by serving the public, advertising could improve its reputation; they were "in an era of soul-searching" where advertising existing only as a capitalist enterprise, designed to make money for itself and for the businesses that advertised, was longer enough for the public to accept advertising. The threats on advertising created "a demand to justify advertising now as a social force."[45] Young argued that advertising had "potentialities for use far beyond its present levels." He asserted that "advertising is the most modern, streamlined, high-speed means of communication plus persuasion yet invented by man." As such, he called for it to be used by the government, "labor unions," "farm organizations," "philanthropic organizations," "churches," and "universities." He insisted that "it ought to be used by political parties, not just in elections, but continuously." He argued that it be used "extensively by governments," including "for open propaganda in international relations, to create understanding and reduce friction."

Young's remarks eventually earned him the title "grandfather" of the Advertising Council, and created a strategy for free enterprise practitioners to use in persuading the public. His speech immediately prompted pledges by advertising executives, including Walter D. Fuller, president of the National Publishing Association; Niles Trammell, president of the National Broadcasting Company; Frank Dunigan, president of the National Outdoor Advertising Association of America; Frank Trippe, chairman of the Bureau of Advertising, American Newspaper Publishers Association; and Frank Braucher, president of the Periodical Publishers Association. The pledge dedicated advertising to work in order to create "an understanding that advertising is an important part of American business—that attacks on advertising are attacks on business." To protect themselves, advertisers pledged "that the best defense" included "better taste in copy and commercial," "dissemination of facts on the function and effects of advertising," and "reteaching a belief in a dynamic economy."[46] Less than a month later, on December 7, 1941, the Japanese air strike on Pearl Harbor, Hawaii, brought the United States into the war and created a permanent place for advertising in American government.

The War Advertising Council

Advertisers quickly offered their services to the Roosevelt administration to help with the war effort and formed the War Advertising Council. The war created a network of American advertisers, broadcasters, and brand-name manufacturers working together to advance all their self-interests and agendas. Twenty-two people signed the bylaws for the War Advertising Council, including Procter & Gamble's Neil H. McElroy and James Webb Young. The bylaws read "it shall be the purpose of the Advertising Council, Inc., to provide a means for marshalling the forces of advertising so that they may be of maximum aid in successful prosecution of the war." The purpose was to create "one division to become responsible for the overall psychological aspects of the public relations job." The War Advertising Council worked with the Office of War Information. It represented a "fusion of all elements of the advertising industry, including media."[47] As the council later described the War Advertising Council "for the first time advertisers, agencies and the four major media—magazines, newspapers, outdoor and radio put aside their specialized interests in the interest of the nation at large."[48] In addition, AAAA requested that American advertisers sign a pledge to support "war-theme advertising and to showing clients wherever possible how war themes could be included in their advertising."[49] According to the War Advertising Council members, during the war they "circulated millions of war messages, through every medium of mass communications, to every nook and cranny in the land." They described themselves as "collectively, the group represents the spearhead of what is perhaps the greatest single means of mass communication—the weight and power of advertising." They created editorial and advertising facilities to distribute "war information" on "more than 100 wartime problems."[50] During World War II, the council rallied American businesses to conduct over 100 campaigns, developing programs in cooperation with the Office of War Information, the Department of Agriculture, the Office of Price Administration, and the War Manpower Commission. The War Advertising Council called January 15, 1942, and August 14, 1945, the "1307 of the most crucial days in American history." The council established the network of advertisers, media, newspapers, business, and government. It also established the precedent for private/public partnerships, standardized methodologies for campaigns and for advertising partnering with the government in the dissemination of information. For campaigns supporting causes, the War Advertising Council made copy and advertising mats for newspapers and magazines in which each company could simply fill in its own name.[51] In 1942, J. Walter Thompson created a radio allocation plan with the War Advertising Council and the Office of War Information. The War Advertising Council was entrusted with "the job of telling the American people what needed to be done to speed Victory." This meant addressing the practical issues, such as fat salvage, recruiting woman for work, saving paper and rubber, as well as creating overall themes to frame the war for the public. The War Advertising Council did find itself at odds with other governmental information organizations. The Office of War Information objected to what it viewed as the council overreaching its purpose to sell free enterprise.[52]

During the war the overarching agenda of the War Advertising Council was to demonstrate "the nature of the conspiracy against us and our way of life," by "showing that this war is a fight against a revolution which seeks to crush liberty" and "explaining what the militarism of the Axis would mean in terms of every day American life." The War Advertising Council material also projected a larger international mission by "showing that by winning this war the United States will share the freedoms precious to men." The advertising copy aimed at expressing "in simple, every day terms the meaning of the four freedoms" and at "proving the values of the four freedoms by accurate portrayals of life in the Axis nations and in the subjugated countries."[53]

The campaigns written by the War Advertising Council raised money, organized resources, and stabilized the wartime production. The campaigns included War Bonds, Food, Armed Services, Civilian Nurse, Conservation and Salvage, Manpower, Fund-Raising, Civilian Services, Security of War Information, and Homes for War Workers.[54] They featured nutrition, venereal disease, treasury bonds, payroll savings, "womanpower campaigns," Victory Gardens, fuel conservation, iron, steel, rope, rubber, and fat salvage.

The War Advertising Council also conducted anti-inflation test campaigns in Richmond, Charlotte, and Indianapolis. On behalf of the War Advertising Council, J. Walter Thompson handled the Red Cross campaigns, the Office of War Information, and "the second war-bond drive." The campaigns helped save tire rubber, and paper, and conserve coals, as well as recruit nurses, fight inflation, and organize a national health campaign. J. Walter Thompson helped raise financing for the war by creating campaigns for Treasury Bonds, including preparing a movie script for the Treasury. It produced war themed advertisements for Shell Industrial Lubricants, Kellogg, Kraft, French's Mustard, Fanny Farmer, Libby's, Northrop Aircraft, Inc., and the Radio Corporation of America. It helped the Petroleum Industry War Council handle wartime gas shortages. In order to mobilize women into industry, women's armed service, and nursing, J. Walter Thompson helped the War Advertising Council prepare advertisements for the War Manpower Commission and the Office of War Information. J. Walter Thompson also helped create some of the most iconic campaigns of World War II, the image "We can do it" associated with Rosie the Riveter, and "Loose Lips Sink Ships."[55] After the Allied victory in Europe, the War Advertising Council turned American attention toward the "Job Ahead—Japan," and started a campaign to achieve "complete victory" over Japan that presented Americans with "facts about Japanese fanaticism." At the same time, James Webb Young ran a "Problems of Peace" campaign "to focus public attention on the urgent need for U.S. cooperation with other nations in a program to insure future peace."[56]

The War Advertising Council formed a national network for disseminating information from the federal government to the American people. James Webb Young served as chairman of the War Advertising Council alongside Paul West, president of the ANA, Charles Mortimer from General Foods, and Theodore Repplier, future president of the Advertising Council.[57] The War Advertising Council included representatives from "radio, newspapers, magazines, outdoor, and display advertising." This network included the major advertising agencies and industry organizations such as McCann-Erickson, Inc., Young & Rubicam, Inc., and J. Walter Thompson Company; the trade publication *Advertising Age;* the billboard advertiser Outdoor Advertising Incorporated; and the major advertising associations such as the Outdoor Advertising Association of America, the AAAA, the National Industrial Advertisers Association, the Advertising Federation of America, Direct Mail Advertising Association, National Association of Transportation Advertising, and the Association of National Advertisers (ANA). Publishing was represented by McGraw-Hill Publishing Company and Curtis Publishing and the National Publishers Association. Magazine industry representatives included Hearst Magazines, Time and Life, Inc., and the Periodical

Publishers Association. Newspaper publishing representatives included the New York Herald Tribune, Negro Newspapers Publishers Association, the Allied Newspaper Council, American Newspaper Publishers Association, and National Business Papers Association. Industry representatives included General Foods, the McCall Corporation, Vick Chemical Company, Shell Oil Company, Inc., and the Bristol-Myers Company. NBC, Columbia Broadcasting System, the American Broadcasting, Co., and the National Association of Broadcasters represented national broadcasting.

The network coordinated by the War Advertising Council also included the military. In March 1944, the War Advertising Council and the Office of War Information brought 200 of the country's most prominent advertising and business executives to Washington for meetings, including briefings by the army and the navy at the Pentagon.[58] Also in March 1944, President Roosevelt spoke to the War Advertising Council, praising its efforts in the war. Roosevelt told the council members that the White House was relying on them to educate the people that winning the war required their assistance, and he discussed with them that he wanted the campaigns to be education programs so that their work could be clearly differentiated from Nazi propaganda.

In addition to working with the War Advertising Council, advertisers and brand- name manufacturers contributed to diplomatic and military efforts. The J. Walter Thompson Company helped the Coordinator of Inter American Affairs (CIAA) from 1942 to 1945 develop newspapers and magazines in Latin America that supported the Allies. It also helped the CIAA arrange for American companies to advertise in Latin America. It helped arrange for shortwave radio programs to be broadcast in Latin America. During the war American businesses worked with the defense industry, in addition to Ford, GM and GE producing for the war effort. While J. Walter Thompson employees took the lead in the War Advertising Council, P & G and Eastman Kodak played more direct roles in the military. In late 1940, the U.S. Army asked Procter & Gamble to run ordnance plants in Tennessee and Mississippi.[59] Kodak participated in vital war services on several fronts. It made microfilms of soldiers' letters (called V-Mail), helped the air force take photographs for mapping, and made military training films.[60] Kodak made products for X-rays and photographic paper, as well as participated in the Manhattan Project. The Tennessee Eastman Corporation in Kingsport, Tennessee, made "acetate-rayon products" and "cellulose esters." Kodak also "operated the uranium isotope plant at Oak Ridge which during the war employed 26,000 people as part of the Manhattan Project." At year's end in 1946, the "Tennessee Eastman Corporation continued to operate for the Government the Y-12 atomic bomb material plant at Oak

Ridge, Tennessee." As the president of the Tennessee Eastman Corporation, Perley Smith Wilcox described their wartime activities Kodak ran "two enormous—and enormously important—undertakings for the government. One, near Kingsport, produced a new, but relatively conventional high explosive called R.D.X. And another, at Oak Ridge, involved Kodak in something so top secret that only the ultimate release of the first atomic bomb explained it all."[61]

Proving Advertising's Value

The War Advertising Council gave advertisers the boost that Young had hoped for at the Hot Spring conference. The wartime advertising had shown the industry that "the best public relations advertising is public service advertising," and the industry had proven its capacity to launch large-scale, multimedia, multiplatform persuasive information campaigns. One of the most important things learned during the war, according to Young, was that "from the largest national ones to the smallest local ones, the advertising agencies of every kind and size, the thousands of media owners of every kind, and all the affiliated industries and suppliers" could work together on campaigns. Young also felt that the war had brought advertisers in step regarding the importance of combining research into consumer opinions, a well-planned, multitiered "program of attack," and regarding the presentation of facts in a simple and interesting manner. Young claimed that World War II had empowered advertising executives. They gained confidence in their ability to persuade Americans. During the war, Young said that "we found that advertising's ability to repeat these facts until they stuck, a power which made news releases seem like a puff of wind."[62] Future president of the Advertising Council, Theodore Repplier said that one of the most valuable things about the council was that "for the first time advertisers, agencies and the four major media—magazines, newspapers, outdoor and radio put aside their specialized interests in the interest of the nation at large." Advertisers streamlined the process of carrying out a national campaign involving hundreds of businesses and utilized all public media. They learned how to create national campaigns with information developed and disseminated by the council.

Advertisers were also able to increase their perceived monetary value, as they could set their own price estimates of the value of their time and labor. The War Advertising Council estimated that it spent $4 million in "payroll" and "$60 million" in "space and time"—first year, "$250,000,000" in 1943 and "$400,000,000 in 1944." The council claimed that the best way to measure the results achieved in "home front programs" was to look at the number of war bonds sold. It claimed that 85,000,000 individual owners had purchased 800 million war bonds. American companies "devoted more than $1 billion worth of time and space" working on "more than 100 public service campaigns."[63]

The Advertising Council

Unlike its World War I predecessor, which was quickly dismantled after the war, the War Advertising Council became a permanent peacetime institution, the Advertising Council. As Young had envisioned, advertising had found its place as persuaders in the public interest with the capacity to be "the greatest single means of mass communication." After World War II, President Truman supported the creation of a permanent peacetime Advertising Council that would work with the American government. By November 1944, the council had rallied support, and all the groups involved in the War Advertising Council ratified a plan for the peacetime council.[64] Truman authorized John W. Snyder, director of War Mobilization and Reconversion, to "establish a unit in his office to serve as liaison between government agencies and the Advertising Council," and on October 29, 1945, Snyder created a Media Programming Division to serve as the federal government's liaison with the Advertising Council.[65]

On November 2, 1945, the War Advertising Council started using the peacetime name "Advertising Council." The War Advertising Council announced that as a peacetime advertising council it hoped to have $30,000,000 worth of public service advertising a year.[66] In 1946, the Advertising Council established its peacetime structure and network for campaigns. Theodore Repplier became the Advertising Council's first president. The council formed a unit for working with the government, an Industries Advisory Committee under the leadership of Charles E. Wilson, president of General Electric; and a Public Policy Committee to determine which causes to take on.

As with the War Advertising Council, membership of the Advertising Council included major advertisers, media, newspapers, magazines, brand-name manufacturers, educational institutions, and the government. Early members came from General Electric, Radio Corporation of America, Procter & Gamble (including Neil McElroy), Harvard, General Foods, Gillette, BF Goodrich, and Eastman Kodak, as well as leading advertising agencies and their trade organizations.[67] The list of newspaper and magazine publishers included Hearst Magazines, Time-Life Inc., and the Washington Post. Also, all the major radio and television companies—ABC, NBC, and CBS—signed on. Gallup and Nielsen represented the market research firms and testing organizations.[68]

White House Conferences

Once established as a permanent peacetime entity, the Advertising Council began hosting annual White House conferences to bring together the media, advertisers, business, and the government for "off-the-record" discussions about America politics and foreign policy. In September 1946, the conference brought together the council and federal officials for "an informal review of major international problems." Over the years, these meetings would continue to present "off-the-record views and opinions of important Federal Government officials to the advertising and business men most closely associated with the work of The Advertising Council." These meetings were pointed to by the Advertising Council as proof that "the attitude which existed in Washington toward advertising a few years ago" had disappeared and that the government recognized the value of advertising.

In spite of its many successes during the war, the council had to continue selling its value to advertising agencies and the media. The council encouraged advertising agencies to support the council because public service advertising represented "good advertising based on the principle of enlightened self-interest." To businesses, the council claimed that public service advertising would "stimulate new uses of their product" and to the media the council suggested that public service advertising would demonstrate its sense of "moral responsibility to the public," thusly serving as excellent public relations.[69]

Advertisers and brand-name companies also continued to face concerns over Office of Price Administration (OPA) restrictions on manufacturers' brands; advertising experts asserted that OPA restrictions interfered with free enterprise. Criticism of business included the idea "that business is concerned only with profits." The council called the critics "enemies of our system." Young claimed that to combat anti-advertising forces a study at Harvard School of Business Administration regarding the "economic consequences of advertising" should include a unit to study "consumer education in advertising." According to Young, a leading publishing house assigned "a woman editor to devote her full time to expending the social benefits of advertising before women's clubs." Because, in spite of its lofty goals, the Advertising Council believed that "the battle for markets is now on, and advertising must resume its star role as a profitable seller of goods."[70]

That battle for markets extended around the globe. While other countries were in dire shape after the war, the United States had profited during the war and emerged an economic powerhouse. The war ended the idea that America should not engage itself in the affairs of the world, and internationalists and free enterprise capitalists set out to capture foreign markets. The Advertising Council saw the new "course of internationalism" resulting from the "international monetary funds, its world charter, its new pattern of 'working together.' " In 1944, the Bretton Woods Agreements established the International Bank for Reconstruction and Development. Members agreed to facilitate "the investment of capital for productive purposes" through international monetary funds. Most significantly, for American business, the agreements based the international monetary system on the dollar standard. While all member states contributed a share of capital, the "authorized capital stock of the Bank" converted to 10,000,000,000 in U.S. dollars.[71] Most of the foreign markets where Advertising Council members marketed their products during the 1950s were countries that signed the original Bretton Woods Agreement.[72]

John W. Snyder told the council that the next few years were crucial on the world stage. He saw the period as putting "free enterprise on trial." He questioned whether the country could "convince the world that the private enterprise system works," and claimed that "the entire world watches us as we grapple with reconversion to see whether we can make our system work." To contribute to the country's new course of internationalism, the council created six advertisements for the United Nations. It also urged businesses operating overseas to counter any "misconception abroad as to our intentions."[73] The need for selling America and American products overseas increased as wartime alliances gave way to the Cold War.

By 1946, the same year that Procter & Gamble introduced Tide laundry detergent, fighting communism had become part of the Advertising Council's agenda. In February 1946, George Kennan sent his long telegram calling for the containment of communism, and in March 1946, Winston Churchill famously declared that an "iron curtain" had descended. At the September 1946 Advertising Council White House conference, Secretary of State William Clayton claimed that the " 'government's foreign trade policy' " would encourage " 'all measures that will result in an improved economy and higher standard of living for all people everywhere.' " He asked for advertising, business, and government to work together to shape "free markets for all people" that involved "multi-lateral rather than bi-lateral trade agreements" and "the reduction of tariffs." The expansion of American companies around the globe emerged as a vital part of American foreign policy. Considered crucial in the battle against global communism, the Advertising Council declared itself an important means "of winning the 'undeclared war against communism' which we are living through today."[74] This conference and the Cold War concerns it raised shaped the Advertising Council's first major peacetime campaigns.

Everything was in place by World War II regarding the ideas, mechanism, and methods of free enterprise, but it was not until after the war that

American politicians and business executives implemented the ideas. The war allowed advertisers to prove their usefulness to the government. It allowed them to establish an extensive national network of business, media, advertisers, government, schools, churches, and community groups. It helped them reinforce their goal of making broadcast media dependent on advertising revenue. The success the War Advertising Council had in organizing the American public legitimized the use of persuasion. Regardless of the use of psychology and market research to achieve maximum persuasion, it was considered democratic because it involved a free choice made by an individual. This belief allowed the Advertising Council and its network to begin campaigns of persuasion on the American public and develop the foundations of American public diplomacy.

CHAPTER 2

"Miracle, U.S.A."

Two of the major campaigns after World War II, the Freedom Train and "The Miracle of America," established a peacetime network between advertising, the media, and the federal government.[1] This network formed the invisible hand of persuasion that came to guide American free enterprise. These campaigns also helped create a brand identity, a positive essence associated with the brand and visual symbols that represented the brand for the United States. With these campaigns, the Advertising Council members helped free enterprise supporters situate advertising and free enterprise into the history of the United States. They attempted to convey to the public an unbreakable bond between democracy, free enterprise, and America's mission. They hoped to inspire patriotism and demonstrate the advertising industry's patriotism. They wanted to rally Americans behind the idea that American businesses should expand around the globe and also wanted to show other nations a positive image of the country's civil rights record.

Participants in the Advertising Council's September 1946 White House conference left with the resolve to create a large-scale national campaign. Concerned with civil rights, communism, crime, poor voter turn-out, and strikes, they wanted to unify Americans around a common vision of the country. To this end, they created the Freedom Train to define the history and significance of the country as inoffensively as possible, and the American Economic System campaign to define the country's economy. The Freedom Train crisscrossed the United States from September 1947 to January 1949, displaying 127 historical documents. The American Economic System taught Americans about free enterprise through a series of advertisements, billboards, and the brochure "The Miracle of America." The Freedom Train, the Rededication Weeks, and the Advertising Council's "Miracle of America" campaign created a brand identity for the nation. Participants created an abstract symbol for all that the United States represented, a symbol that would evoke all that the United States had to offer to its own people and to the world. The goal was to be as inclusive as possible. Since every citizen represented a potential consumer, the effort needed to remain bipartisan and not appear to be politically motivated; those involved developed the Freedom Train campaign to be as inoffensive as possible.[2]

While the Advertising Council played a vital role in the Freedom Train tour, members created a nonprofit organization, the American Heritage Foundation, to manage the project. For the train's arrival, the American Heritage Foundation helped communities organize "Rededication Weeks" and encouraged citizens to take the "Freedom Pledge." The Freedom Train, accompanied by Rededication Weeks, the signing of a freedom pledge, and "The Miracle of America," demonstrated the brand identity that free enterprise proponents wanted Americans to embrace, one in which red, white, and blue, and stars and stripes represented their version of American history, economics, and politics and in which social class and racial conflict disappeared amidst a nation of happy consumers and producers, an American model for the world. The Freedom Train also helped the Advertising Council maintain the strategy of campaign development, dissemination, and management established by the War Advertising Council. The train established a permanent peacetime structure and methodology for advertising, brand manufacture, the media, nonprofit organizations, and the federal government to work together. It allowed the network to slip virtually unnoticed, and with minimal public objections, into the background as it distributed ideological material across the nation.

The idea for the traveling exhibit originated with Attorney General Tom C. Clark as the Bill of Rights Exhibit tour. As would often prove an effective strategy for the Advertising Council and others over the years, they latched onto a project that served their agenda. Concerned with "the increase in lawlessness, the development of a tacit acceptance of American institutions, and the threatening danger of subversive activity," Clark felt a national tour of the U.S. Constitution and the Bill of Rights would both combat communism in America and teach "good citizenship." At the same time that Attorney General Clark was meeting with the National Archives and executives from Paramount Pictures, members of the Advertising Council were calling for a "campaign to sell America to Americans."[3] Collectively, they created the American Heritage Foundation to organize and run the Freedom Train.

In April 1947, Truman praised the Advertising Council and endorsed its continuation into peacetime. Truman called the council "a highly significant new development in American life." He said that council advertising "is a greater force for informing the public than the editorial columns of newspapers." He claimed this represented an important example of American democracy, since it brought together "the voluntary cooperation of thousands of American firms, from large concerns to stores, banks and merchants in the smallest towns." Truman also saw it as evidence that American businesses embraced "social responsibility."[4] The same month Attorney General Clark announced the project and stated its purpose was to "reawaken in the American people the loyalty it is known they have for the American way of life." In May, he sent out invitations for a "White House conference, May 22, 1947." The invitations stated that the conference concerned a "national public service project to be sponsored by Department of Justice with endorsement of the President of the United States." The invitations stressed to invitees that "these critical times on domestic and world scene require intensive dramatic and militant programs to reassert the emphatic advantages of American democracy," as well as President Truman's participation in these projects. From these meetings, the Freedom Train developed into one part of a three-part plan that included Rededication Weeks and the Freedom Pledge. Like campaigns conducted by the War Advertising Council, the campaign would utilize "all media of communication, education, and community action." The National Archives and the Library of Congress put together the documents. The Advertising Council put together the campaign literature and advertisements. The council also organized the radio advertisements and newspaper articles and cartoons.[5]

Allegedly, what bothered Attorney General Clark was that "most of the moral breakdown could not be handled by the federal, state or municipal courts," and he felt only the "spread of information and knowledge" could "combat" it. In addition to the perception of a moral breakdown in the country, a 1945 National Opinion Research Center poll raised alarms when only 31 percent of those surveyed had heard of the Bill of Rights. The parties at the meeting were also concerned with the general political apathy, since in the 1944 elections 48,100,000 people voted, but 40,000,000 of voting age did not vote. Furthermore, all parties involved feared the spread of communism and viewed the Freedom Train as a vital part of helping "to strengthen the nation against Communist propaganda."[6] They viewed creating "a strong and unified America" as vital because they saw communism as putting "our democratic way of life to a critical test." Communism created what they called "the threat of totalitarianism of the left," and caused the "shrinking on the global map" of "the areas of democratic government." They also wanted Americans to believe that the country had a global mission to spread its political and economic system throughout the world.[7]

The Freedom Train reinforced the wartime network created by the War Advertising Council. It allowed the companies involved in the Advertising Council to establish an extensive network connecting advertisers, major corporations, banks, retailers, schools, religious institutions, and governments (local, state, and federal). The campaigns also allowed them to establish a permanent network among advertisers, Hollywood, newspapers, the publishing industry, and major broadcasters. Many of the same people and organizations that were part of the Advertising Council or participated in Advertising Council events made up the America Heritage Foundation. The Board of Trustees for the American Heritage Foundation included Henry Luce, editor of *Time-Life*, financier Winthrop Aldrich, James W. Young, John D. Rockefeller, John Foster Dulles, and Charles E. Wilson of General Electric.[8] The Board also included Paul G. Hoffman, who was picked by Truman to head the Economic Cooperation Administration, the Marshall Plan. W.B. Potter of Eastman Kodak coordinated the country's ten major advertising agencies in a full-time campaign.[9] The Ad Council's Communications Committee included the Periodical Publishers Association of America, Western Newspaper Union, Newspaper Enterprise Association, American Newspaper Publishers Association, Mutual Broadcasting Company, National Association of Broadcasters, United Features Syndicate, Columbia Broadcasting Company, National Broadcasting Company, and American Broadcasting Company. The Motion Picture Committee included Universal, RKO, 20th Century Fox, Warner Bros., Screen Actors Guild, the Motion Picture Association, National Association of Visual Education Dealers, and the Encyclopedia Britannica Films.[10] In addition to magazine publishers, the McGraw-Hill Book Company, Inc., participated in the American Heritage Foundation. In keeping with the hope that using adverting would solve the country's ongoing labor disputes and strikes, the planning for the Freedom Train and the American Heritage Foundation included labor leaders William Green of the American Federation of Labor and Philip Murray of the Congress of Industrial Organizations (CIO).[11]

This national network enabled the Advertising Council to launch a uniform campaign across the nation. In addition to sending out complete packets with premade advertising mats, it disseminated program guides for a week's worth of community activities, films, radio scripts, and a collection of newspaper articles and editorials, all of which helped create a cohesive branding for what the United States of America had to offer its citizens and the world.

In order to run the Freedom Train campaign, Advertising Council members created a nonprofit organization devoted solely to promoting the history of America. Named the American Heritage Foundation, the membership roster overlapped with the Advertising Council and the council prepared the foundation's campaign literature and advertising copy. As a nonprofit organization, the purpose of the American Heritage Foundation was "to institute a broad national educational program seeking to emphasize the blessings of our American heritage."[12] Not only did this keep the campaign process from being transparent, it established the precedent of the Advertising Council playing a major role in conducting campaigns, but with another organization's name out front. It also further established the peacetime precedent of the council serving as the clearinghouse to coordinate the creation of information and the top dissemination of the materials necessary for a campaign.

Once involved, the American Heritage Foundation created a call to arms for companies and politicians to participate in the Freedom Train. It argued that in the years following the war the country was "at a cross-roads of its history," facing the threat of communism and "moral and spiritual illness." The "military victory," it argued, "brought only a breathing space in our quest for peace . . . economic despair, has turned to the panacea of state control." World War II created a country where "Americans accept wartime controls, obey the laws, respect their fellowmen, appreciate their democracy," and are otherwise "good citizens." However, the peacetime transition brought citizen apathy, "cynicism," "lawlessness," and "voices of discord." Crime, the American Heritage Foundation claimed, had increased 13.6 percent from 1946 to 1947, evidence of lawless path the country could take.[13]

Brand America

The Freedom Train served as a perfect means to unify Americans around a set of symbols, ideas, feelings, associations, and meanings that they wanted Americans and those overseas to equate with the United States. In other words, the Freedom Train offered the perfect means to unify Americans around brand America. With the use of historical documents, organizers sought to craft a unified American history—a history that framed America as an exceptional nation without gross inequities, labor strife, civil rights problems, or religious intolerance, a nation whose unique political structure allowed for the growth of the most prosperous nation on earth. A nation whose unique history had created a system of government and economics that could guarantee any nation peace and prosperity. These qualities made it America's destiny to lead the world.

The overarching campaign goal was to create "a continuous program of education" to "remind our people of the American heritage which they enjoy."

The Freedom Train became one part of "a comprehensive program of education in the ideals and practices of American democracy." The Rededication
Week programs would "give meaning to the American heritage, vitality to
its spirit, and validity to its historic mission." Combined, they would teach
Americans that "the sanctity of the individual" represents "the essence of
democracy" and that "freedom of enterprise, protection of minorities, rights
of labor—and all the rights and liberties we enjoy under the Constitution and
Bill of Rights—rest upon this doctrine." In particular, the programs would
target children with activities and educational programs, because "above
all, there is the constant necessity to inculcate in the youth of America a
full appreciation of the heritage of which they will be the trustees tomorrow." The council viewed communism as presenting the United States with
"a critical test," which in order for the country to survive "the American people must know, understand, and appreciate the system of government which
has bestowed its blessings upon them." The Freedom Train represented "our
American heritage."[14]

Visually, the train itself was a logo that created instant brand recognition
as it crisscrossed the nation. The painting of the train white with blue and
red stripes made those colors in and of themselves a logo for the nation.
Even seen at a great distance the train colors could create instant visual
recognition as the train crossed the nation. The diesel engine, named the
"spirit of 1776," helped to further the brand association, linking the red,
white, and blue of the train with the history of the nation. Indicative of
this association is the *New York Times* caption on the Freedom Train that
read, "In an era of uncertainty, Americans of 1948 feel a strong link with
the spirit of 1776." The "spirit of 1776," a diesel engine, built and donated
by the American Locomotive Company and General Electric, pulled six cars,
three for display and three for staff and security.[15] With "Freedom Train"
embossed on every car, the train covered over 35,000 miles of track, and
visiting over 320 cities, allowing much of the nation the experience of the
patriotic display.

On September 16, 1947, radio stations began playing the Ira Berlin, Bing
Crosby song "The Freedom Train." The next day, the Freedom Train got its
start in Philadelphia. Then it went on to New Jersey and on September 24,
1947, arrived in New York City. It traveled through New England, before
heading south to Washington, D.C., in late November 1947. It continued
south through Virginia, the Carolinas, and Georgia and into Florida right
before Christmas. It visited Mobile, Alabama, through Christmas and spent
New Year's in Atlanta, Georgia, Throughout January the train crossed the
South, ending up in Texas by late January. After a two week tour of Texas

the train headed west, stopping in New Mexico and Arizona before arriving in California. After a month-long tour of California, the train spent the spring visiting the northwestern states, before heading toward the Midwest in June 1948. Traveling east, the train visited the Great Lakes and Midwest region throughout the early fall, then traveled back to New Jersey. It spent the remainder of the tour in Pennsylvania, New Jersey, and New York before ending the tour in Washington, D.C., in January 1949. Possibly as many as 50 million, one in three Americans, attended Rededication Week events, over three and a half million toured the train, and six million signed the Freedom Pledge. In terms of reaching the American public, for the Advertising Council, it was a resounding success.[16]

Community Rededication

As the Freedom Train traveled the nation, the American Heritage Foundation members helped communities organize "Rededication Weeks," programs for radio, film, and education, and encouraged citizens to take the "Freedom Pledge." They helped civic leaders to chair and organize "patriotic programs" and "good-citizenship programs" by creating a national campaign guide called "The American Heritage Program for Your Community." The model community program included instructions for contacting the local mayor, a local preparation schedule, and advanced copy promotion. To local leaders, the American Heritage Foundation argued that success in the program would result from community leaders understanding "that rededication to the principles essential to the preservation of our form of government is vitally important in maintaining a strong America." The guide included a prewritten proclamation "the mayor of the City" with fill in the blanks that stated "these times call for loyalty to American tradition and faith in their enduring character." The proclamation then declared that the mayor "hereby urge all citizens and organizations in the City of (fill in name of city) to participate in the ceremonies and events constituting (fill in name of city) REDEDICATION WEEK." The guide provided diagrams for the bureaucratic organization of the mayor's committee and plans for two weeks of events, including suggestions for daily events such as "School Day," "Women's Day," and "Freedom of Religion Day." The booklet also included mats of Freedom Train photos for local newspapers as well as the text for a newspaper article entitled "Longest Train tour Marks Rededication to Liberty." For events, the booklet also provided prewritten speeches that could be ordered from the American Heritage Foundation.

During the Rededication Weeks, Americans were encouraged to sign the Freedom Pledge:

> The Freedom Pledge
> I am an American. A free American
> Free to speak—without fear
> Free to worship God in my own way
> Free to stand for what I think right
> Free to oppose what I believe wrong
> Free to choose those who govern my country
> This heritage of Freedom I pledge to uphold
> For myself and all mankind[17]

In addition to suggestions for civic activities, the community guide included instructions for religious organizations to work on the rededication events and included freedom of religion as one of the Rededication Week themes.[18] Documents on the Freedom Train and in the campaign literature stressed the freedom of religion. They framed the country as "a religious Nation," rather than as a nation that allows freedom of consciousness. The *Reader's Digest* Program Services prepared "Sermon Notes" on "Religious Foundations of our American Heritage" for the American Heritage Foundation. The introduction stated, "It has been suggested that during the week of national rededication, coinciding with the visit of the Freedom Train, sermons might be preached to show how closely related are our religious ideals and the American form of freedom."[19] During Rededication Weeks, many cities, such as Philadelphia and New York, included a freedom of Religion Day. Freedom of Religion Day opened the ceremonies, and both churches and synagogues participated in the rededication programs, also discussing the Freedom Train during religious services. The Synagogue Council of America congregations observed Freedom Sabbath.[20] Freedom of Religion Day opened Manhattan Freedom Week. On the Sunday before the Freedom Train exhibit opened, "pastoral letters" were written by several religious leaders, including Cardinal Spellman and Rev. Charles Gilbert, Protestant Episcopal Bishop of New York.

Education

The American Heritage Foundation believed that children must be reached because "loyalties and ideals built during the impressionable years of childhood often thrive for a lifetime." It prepared a complete school plan, including decorations, free copies of documents, and activities. It called the plan "one of the most important activities in the entire American Heritage program" because it "affects one out of every five Americans—namely, the 30,000,000 pupils and teachers," and it "affects students' families—approximately 100,000,000." Quiz-kids radio show, a popular children's show, held an essay competition for high school seniors for $20,000 in scholarship money. Twelve thousand students submitted essays on "What America Means" to me, and 550 received scholarship money. Events across the nation were hosted by parent-teacher groups, assemblies were held in schools, and a companion study guide prepared by the American Heritage Foundation and copies of "Good Citizen" were distributed throughout the country. According to the American Heritage Foundation, the public school systems of Cincinnati, Ann Arbor, Grand Rapids, Kalamazoo, Sandusky, Terre Haute, Lansing, Jackson, and Pontiac were incorporating the study guide and "Good Citizenship" into the curriculum.[21]

The American Heritage Foundation created study guides with a "Your Heritage of Freedom" curriculum for teachers that included an open letter, a description of the documents, and social studies and English units. It addressed the letter to "the English and Social Studies teachers of The United States"; the letter was signed by John Studebaker, U.S. Commissioner of Education. The letter stated that "the time is here when in the interest of national strength and security we must make a more determined and successful effort than ever before to inculcate in the minds and hearts of our American youth the basic principles and the fundamental ideals for our American way of life, to create zeal for American democracy." It also distributed a film, *Our American Heritage,* and a " 'scroll containing the foundation's freedom pledge and the nine promises of a good citizen' to be placed in every public school."[22]

In 1947, Princeton University Press in cooperation with the American Heritage Foundation published a companion guide to the Freedom Train exhibit. Entitled *Heritage of Freedom: The History and Significance of the Basic Documents of American Liberty,* the book, written by historian Frank Monaghan, contained detailed descriptions of the documents in the exhibit.[23] The overall theme of the book stressed a history of the progressive development of political and religious freedom. The American Heritage Foundation also published a 72 page brochure entitled *Good Citizenship, the Rights and Duties of an American* as part of the Freedom Train program. It dealt directly with the concerns about voter turn-out and sought to engage American citizens more directly at every stage of government. It provided information regarding why Americans should vote and how to vote. As such, it sought to eliminate the inherent contradiction between the lack of voter turn-out and the definition of American democracy. While it never directly discussed the differences between communism and American democracy, it addressed criticism leveled at the United States. It described American democracy as a "system of government . . . that derives its power from the bottom up rather than from the top down," thus making those of voting age the "ruling classes—the one and only ruling class of this country." This contrasted with critics both inside and outside the United States who asserted that a ruling class of wealthy business owners and politicians existed in the United States. The brochure described in detail the voting process, from registration to marking a ballot. It placed special emphasis on the two-party system in the United States, claiming that "candidates without parties would be responsible to no group, subject to no check or discipline."[24]

A Citizen Movement

The American Heritage Foundation claimed that it had created a "Citizens' Movement" not only in the Rededication Week events surrounding the Freedom Train, but in the distribution of numerous pamphlets and guides supporting the program. In the first year, it claimed to have distributed 1,350,000 copies of "Good Citizen," 1,600,000,000 copies of "the Documents of the Freedom Train," 200,000 copies of "We, the people" (an "inspirational leaflet"), 135,000 study guides for teachers, 30,000 copies of "Heritage of Freedom," 650,000 copies of *Our American Heritage*, and 3,000,000 copies of the Bill of Rights reprinted by *Reader's Digest*. As many as six million Americans signed the Freedom Pledge.[25]

Part of the "citizens' movement" encouraged Americans to fund the project. The Freedom Train also established a pattern of getting American citizens to pay out of pocket for admission. At each stop of the Freedom Train, the American Heritage Foundation solicited donations, leaving Americans to pay for the project at every level. They bought the brand-name products of the sponsors, paid taxes used to fund project services, and gave public donations. Cities hosting a stop were expected to contribute two cents per resident. Collection bowls used to gather donations from the public averaged from $200 to $500 per day. Costs for running the Freedom Train were estimated at a million a year.[26]

Freedom Follows the Flag

The Advertising Council and the American Heritage Foundation wanted to stress to Americans their new role in the world. They believed that the "menace of totalitarianism of the right" had been "succeeded by the threat of totalitarianism of the left." As a result of communism spreading throughout the world, "the areas of democratic government have been perceptibility shrinking on the global map." To combat this threat and encourage Americans to view the fight against communism as essential to their way of life, they promoted the idea that "Freedom Follows the Flag." Community activities were included under the banner of "Freedom Follows the Flag." It also comprised a display aboard the train with the same name that featured President Truman's July 4, 1946, signing of the proclamation that recognized the Philippine Islands as a self-governing nation and not a holding of the United States.[27]

Civil Rights

The Advertising Council and the American Heritage Foundation also hoped that the Freedom Train could help with the country's unresolved labor and civil rights issues, particularly since these conflicts were used internationally to discredit the United States. American brand-name manufacturers and the Advertising Council had been plagued by civil rights issues in the global war of ideas. In 1944, the Carnegie Corporation commissioned Swedish economist Gunnar Myrdal to study race relations within the United States. Mydral's 2,000 plus page report, *An American Dilemma,* described the state of American race relations as the complete antithesis of the principles of the country. This report reached an international audience and provided fuel for Soviet propaganda, and other critics of the United States. American advertisers and brand-name manufacturers were in an awkward position regarding civil rights, especially with the advent of television. They did not want to alienate any potential market, so they needed to attract and include African American audiences without offending and upsetting white Americans used to a country segregated either officially by Jim Crow laws or unofficially by neighborhood and vocation. Internationally, American companies wanted to expand into South America, the Middle East, and the Far East and did not want to lose potential markets due to the belief that the United States represented discrimination, racial violence, and segregation.[28]

In February 1946, race riots in Columbia, Tennessee, reinforced the negative image the United States had on the international stage regarding race relations. In 1945, a strike by the United Auto Workers against Advertising Council member General Motors shut down the company for 113 days and led to other strikes across the nation with upwards of five million Americans on strike in 1946.[29] In addition to including William Green of the American Federation of Labor and Philip Murray of the CIO in the American Heritage Foundation, the literature it produced stressed that they received the endorsement of labor and management, and labor and management participated in activities together. To address civil rights concerns, they included the NAACP in the planning process and created an official policy regarding discrimination. The policy passed unanimously at the July 9, 1947, meeting of the American Heritage Foundation. It stated that the American Heritage Foundation "resolved that no segregation of any individuals or groups of any kind on the basis of race or religion be allowed at any exhibition of the Freedom Train held anywhere." Winthrop Aldrich told the *New York Times*, "It is our firm determination that the American Heritage program shall be an instrumentality for strengthening the freedoms and liberties of all Americans, regardless of race, creed or color." At the same time the Advertising Council ran a "United America" campaign to address "racial and religious antagonisms." While the campaigns did not end segregation in Southern cities, they "did score a moral victory" for the NAACP by embarrassing cities that were denied the opportunity to host a patriotic event. The American Heritage Foundation received an award from the NAACP for its policy of nonsegregation.[30]

On Christmas 1947, the front page headline of the *New York Times* read, "Many in South Lift 'Jim Crowism,' " "The big Southern cities in the main have abandoned 'Jim Crowism' to allow citizens of all races, creeds and colors to welcome the Freedom Train together as it rolls through Dixie." In Birmingham, officials planned to segregate, but the African American community set in motion a "threat of a black boycott" so the plans were canceled. On Christmas Eve 1947, Birmingham, Alabama, authorities banned the visit of the Freedom Train because of the city's racial segregation law and the train went to Mobile instead. The train toured Virginia, the Carolinas, Georgia, and Florida with no incidents, and visits occurred in Montgomery, Alabama; Chattanooga, Tennessee; and New Orleans, Louisiana, without segregation. In Savannah and Brunswick, Georgia, organizers used two separate lines and viewed the exhibit in groups of 25, alternating by race.[31] The American Heritage Foundation canceled a showing of the Freedom Train in Memphis, Tennessee, and Hattiesburg, Mississippi, due to plans for racial segregation. Atlanta mayor William Hartfield made a public statement announcing that there would be no segregation when Atlanta hosted the train. His statement included, "I am willing to stand beside any American citizen, regardless of race or creed, in mutual admiration and respect for those great historical charters of American freedom."[32]

The Advertising Council and the American Heritage Foundation also created promotional material regarding civil rights and the Freedom Train. One of the major events planned with the Freedom Train was a reenactment in Gettysburg, Pennsylvania, of the reading of Lincoln's Gettysburg address, one of the documents included on the train, with Attorney General Clark featured as a primary speaker. Brooklyn, New York, held ceremonies for "Freedom from Fear Day" at which the fire commissioner spoke out for civil rights, stating that his department rescued people "regardless of their race, color, or creed, so must the rest of the world." Promotional inserts in the *New York Times* boasted that the Freedom Train was "helping break down barriers of racial discrimination that some of its documents declare do not exist under law." The advertisements claimed that "white man and colored man met for the first time at the Freedom Train on the basis of equality to which our Declaration of Independence says we were born." They also stated that "if the Freedom Train serves to awaken the conscience of areas where racial discrimination is practiced and to point out the essential un-Americanism of such attitudes to the people and to the leaders of those areas, then its 33,000-mile journey will have, indeed, been worthwhile."[33]

The Miracle of America

In 1948 the Advertising Council launched a free enterprise campaign called the American Economic System to "show that economic freedom and political freedom are dependent upon each other." The campaign ran from 1948 to 1951 and consisted of advertisements and billboards that discussed the American economy, and urged Americans to order a brochure called "The Miracle of America." While the American Economic System did not have the extensive reach that the Freedom Train did, it spelled out the Advertising Council's vision for the nation's economy and its implicit definition of free enterprise. The American Heritage Foundation rejected it as a campaign under its organization because it feared it would be too controversial, though many of the American Heritage Foundation members endorsed or worked on the project. The campaign, like the Freedom Train, was designed to include newspapers, magazines, outdoor advertising billboards, car cards, and the radio. All magazine advertisements included "a coupon offering the 'Miracle of America' free of charge." Billboards throughout the nation included Uncle Sam and the statement, "The better we produce the better we live." In order to help unify labor and management, the campaign also included an "in-plant and community campaign."[34]

The committee that worked on the campaign included executives from the General Electric Company, Eastman Kodak Company, General Foods Corporation, U.S. Rubber Company, Aluminum Co. of America, and the same advertising companies that worked on the Freedom Train. Advertisements carried the signatures of Paul Hoffman, former president of Studebaker Corporation and administrator of the Economic Cooperation Administration (Marshall Plan administrator); Boris Shishkin, economist for the American Federation of Labor; and Evans Clark, executive director of the Twentieth Century Fund. Contributions from General Electric and General Foods helped finance the campaign. In October 1948, *Time* magazine printed 17,500 copies of "Miracle of America." In November, 134 national publications, "two Sunday supplements," 58 business publications, and "hundreds of company magazines," a collective circulation of 80,000,000, ran full-page advertisements with the slogan "Sure, America's going Ahead If We All Pull Together." Through the first six months of the campaign, the council claimed that the campaign made 1,134,000,000 "radio listener impressions" and countless impressions through the 4,000 billboards across the nation. The Psychological Corporation, the testing service that worked with advertising previously, conducted studies in conjunction with *Reader's Digest*. The aim was to determine the interest level of the digest's readers in the campaign.[35]

Like the Freedom Train, the American Economic System campaign connected to international relations. In a letter to Charles E. Wilson, General Electric Company, Paul G. Hoffman endorsed the campaign. The former Studebaker Corporation executive had recently been appointed the Marshall Plan administrator to manage the rebuilding of the Western European economy, allowing for the Advertising Council to help in the selling of the Marshall Plan in Europe.[36] Hoffman wrote: "You are, I am sure, aware of how strongly I believe in the—Advertising Council's campaign for economic understanding." He emphasized America's unique form of capitalism, stating that not only is it "in fundamental opposition to Marxism, but it differs sharply in many ways from Old World capitalism." Hoffman felt that "if it was understood by people throughout the world, it would I believe, be widely adopted." He also held the opinion that before the rest of the world could adopt America's unique form of capitalism, "we ourselves must understand it." He called the advertisements for the American Economic System campaign "better calculated to bring these about than any I have ever seen."[37]

To address both international public relations issues and the domestic tensions, the campaign again focused on labor and civil rights. The Public Policy Committee for the campaign included representatives from the American Federation of Labor (AFL), the Congress of Industrial Organizations (CIO), the Railway Labor Executives, and the National Association for the Advancement of Colored People. Where the Freedom Train emphasized civil rights, the American Economic System campaign directly addressed labor unrest. The American Economic System campaign had "a plan to improve labor-management and plant-community relations" that it claimed was "already at work in many market areas." The Advertising Council wanted to create an atmosphere whereby labor and management imagined themselves on the same team. In order to do this, the campaign had to "show that management, labor and all other groups agree that our system has one purpose—to strive for a better living for all," and "drive home that with management, labor and the public working together, everyone will continue to enjoy to the fullest degree all the best our system offers."[38]

First, the Advertising Council created a campaign brochure, "A Campaign to Explain the American Economic System," to sell the idea to American businesses. Produced as a "program of economic education for all people," the brochure sold the idea to businesses to get them to run the advertisements for the campaign. The council wanted to distinguish American capitalism from European capitalism. The first page of the brochure stated that "this campaign fills a vital need," claiming that "our American economic system is gravely threatened—by ignorance." The brochure said that Americans "cannot appreciate our System because they do not understand the basic fundamentals of how the system functions." It said that the American public had been "misled" by "labels and 'causes' " such as "redistributing wealth," and "planned production."[39] The council urged business leaders to take full advantage of the free advertisements to help with relations between labor and management and to help combat the spread of communism.

The Advertising Council created a scripted public campaign that included a year's worth of advertisements. It insisted that the campaign would be the most effective if it followed the exact order laid out in the campaign guidelines. The council outlined a "10-point platform" of what it wanted Americans to feel about the country. The list included how it wanted Americans to view "freedom," including "freedom of the individual to work in the callings and localities of his choice," "freedom of the individual to contract about his affairs," and "freedom of individual ownership." The goal of the platform was that all Americans should see "expanding productivity as a national necessity." The campaign consisted of full-page magazine advertisements with coupons that could be mailed in to get free Miracle of America. Each month featured a different campaign theme, and the ads included a spot to put the name of the business sponsoring them. The campaign began with a November advertisement that read "Sure America's going ahead, if we all pull together," which emphasized management and labor working together.[40]

The advertisements for February and May picked up the anticommunist, international emphasis. They framed the United States in terms of political and economic revolution. The banner read "Comes the Revolution!" and called Americans "the greatest revolutionist in history." They claimed that since "right now the people of many nations are faced with a choice—between dictatorship and a free economy," Americans had to be a model for the world. For that, they needed to be "constantly turning out more for every hour we put in," so that "our free, dynamic American system runs so well at home that others will want to follow the example"; then the United States would provide "new hope to millions everywhere." The May advertisement was a letter addressed to "Dear Soviet teacher" from "John Q. Public" that contained a list of things about Americans that Soviet teachers should not tell their students. The list included "don't refer to a dynamic way of life that keeps turning out more and better goods," and "we don't say our way is perfect . . . change is our middle name. And in the long run, our system always changes for the better." The March ad, "What happens to your job—if we get atomic energy to drive our machines?" framed atomic energy in a positive light and claimed that the American system had survived the change from coal to electricity and would adjust to atomic energy. The June advertisement described "Our right to choose." It emphasized the right of Americans to choose professions, the "free market and competition," and "labor's right to organize and bargain." It also stressed the right to choose "more goods of better quality at lower costs," which in turn created more jobs "paying higher wages."[41] Each of the advertisements contained a coupon to order the Miracle of America brochure free of charge.

Produced by McCann-Erickson, the Miracle of America boasted of America's economic successes. It claimed that "with only one-fifteenth of the world's population, and about the same proportion of the world's land area and natural resources, the United States—produces about half the world's manufactured goods." In spite of the population, the United States had "more than half the world's telephones, telegraph and radio networks, more than a third of the RR's- more than three-quarters of the world's automobiles-almost half the world's radio." The brochure called American capitalism the miracle, because American capitalism created a "better standard of living" than "Old World" capitalism. This miracle occurred because in American capitalism labor and management worked together to compete against other manufacturers. This competition in turn stimulated "constant research" and innovation.[42] In spite of the American Economic System campaign running nationally, substantial numbers of the Miracle of America brochures were never ordered.

The council wanted to create the appearance of success in any campaign it produced or in any information about the campaigns. Without any major efforts being made at the time to counter the council's estimates of its own success, the true effect on American opinions remains difficult to determine. While there were a few small demonstrations and acts of protest across the nation regarding the Freedom Train, the campaign left advertisers feeling they were the most persuasive force around, and reaffirmed to them the idea that Americans needed to be persuaded to participate and to understand the national goals. Yet, they viewed this persuasion as part of the democratic process. For instance, Charles Mortimer of General Foods claimed that "the essence of democracy is that it puts its faith in individual opinion; and it depends upon its information processes to carry the basic facts to the people."[43] While "The Miracle of America" campaign failed to live up to the hopes and expectations of its authors, the Freedom Train and the Rededication Weeks proved a success, and both campaigns aided the development of the nation's public diplomacy apparatus.

CHAPTER 3

The Brand Names Foundation's "Worthwhile Community Activity"*

While the Advertising Council and the American Heritage Foundation organized the Freedom Train, the Brand Names Foundation advocated the use of advertising, brand names, and brand-based media. The Brand Names Foundation called brands "the manufacturer's symbol of responsibility for his product and his pledge of quality and value" and argued that "brand names knowledge, learned through advertising, saves time and money."[1] Building on the early Cold War sense of nation and community, the foundation launched campaigns and research projects that promoted the concept of the brand name. Throughout the mid-1940s, it organized conferences and events promoting the centrality of the brand to free enterprise capitalism. Targeting the American public and small business owners, the Brand Names Foundation linked brand-name goods and the choice between consumer goods with democracy. The foundation worked to convince small-scale retailers and store owners to use national brand-name goods instead of locally produced goods, and made the consumption of brand-name goods a community experience. Participation in the foundation overlapped with participation in the Advertising Council and the American Heritage Foundation, and included the standard host of major brand-name manufacturers, media outlets, advertising agencies, polling organizations, public relations experts, national testing companies, and trade organizations. Significantly, among the foundation participants was the brand pioneer Procter & Gamble Company, whose success was in part dependent on its innovations in using the brand to cultivate markets.[2]

---

* Brand Names Foundation, "How Greenfield Did It...A Comprehensive Guide to a Worthwhile Community Activity" (New York: Brand Names Foundation, Incorporated, 1947).

The foundation originally formed in 1944, as the Brand Names Research Foundation to combat the Office of Price Administration's (OPA) proposed system of grade labeling.[3] Two year later, it changed its name to the Brand Names Foundation and expanded its mission from research into the use of brand names for the extensive promotion of brand names and the brand management system.[4] Like the Advertising Council, the Brand Names Foundation presented the American economy as being at a crossroads regarding the use of advertising and brand-name goods. In 1946, the closing of the OPA, which had been managing wartime consumption, prompted an outcry by consumer activist and labor organizations. The foundation interpreted these suggestions for continued regulation as a "battle for our lives" and a struggle over "the political system which guarantees the American way of doing business."[5] Through a series of speeches and award ceremonies across the nation in 1945 and 1946, members of the foundation made the case against government standards and for a brand-based free enterprise system.[6] They called trademarks and brand names the core of the American economic system and urged "every manufacturer and advertiser of a branded product . . . to join in a program to convince the people of America that their own best welfare lies in support of the system of brand-name identification." They complained that of "twenty-nine consumer education books" in the New York public library, none were "on the side of business." They urged advertisers not to be discouraged by the image portrayed in the 1946 novel *The Hucksters* of advertising manipulating people for profit. Rather, they urged advertisers to take credit for creating the country's high standard of living.[7]

The foundation officially called itself an "educational organization," whose goal was to bring about "a clearer understanding of the roles which brand names and advertising play in the daily lives of the American people." It argued that the unregulated advertising of brand-name goods through mass media was the American economic system and "destroying advertising" would "destroy the whole American economic system." The foundation defended advertising and brand names claiming that "creating new wants, stimulating demand and giving information . . . brought mass production to its fullest achievements under our competitive economy." In addition to linking brand names and advertising to the preservation of American democracy, Brand Names Foundation spokesmen insisted that a system based on advertising and brand names was what the term "free enterprise" meant. According to the Brand Names Foundation " . . . people in this country live under the brand name system. It is part and parcel of the American economy." While many organizations, such as the Association of National Advertisers and the Trademark Association, connected and supported advertising agencies, manufacturers, and the media, the Brand Names Foundation served uniquely in an educational capacity.[8] According to its president, Henry Abt, it represented "the voice of those who believe that the way to create the mass demand America needs is to build up confidence in well-known products." The voices that the foundation represented included "manufacturers, advertising specialists, and media of information," who funded the organization through an annual subscription.

The overarching goal of the foundation was to get all of America to speak "the Brand Names language" and to get Americans to understand "the social and economic significance of trade-marks and advertising."[9] As the nation faced labor problems and the highly contested Taft-Hartley Bill (Labor-Management Relations Act), which restricted the rights of workers, worked its way through the new majority Republican Congress, the foundation wanted the public to believe that a brand-based system would solve all labor problems by ensuring continual production. It wanted the public to believe that advertising about brands names and the brand-name system would "stabilize and increase employment," "provide maximum opportunity for free choice," and allow "the satisfaction of individual tastes."[10] Foundation members also argued that advertising and brand names ensured that the country maintained freedom of the press. They warned that "an attack on advertising is an indirect blow at a free press" and that if revenue from "brand-name advertising" did not support newspapers, then the press would have to rely on government subsidies.[11] They argued that a brand-name system would help with labor unrest by stimulating production. The foundation also focused much of its attention on children and women. It wanted brand loyalty to be conflated with family tradition. The foundation argued that "there are brand names which have served many successive generations as a means of expressing product preferences. Taught by parents to their children, and thence to their grandchildren and to their offspring, these names have been subject in each generation to the possibility of rejection." Since the nineteenth century, advertisers had targeted women as the primary household consumers. The foundation reinforced this notion by working with women's clubs and targeting the bulk of brand-name advertising toward women, whether they worked outside the home or not.[12]

In February 1946, the foundation received Republican backing. Twelve hundred advertising and corporate professionals attended a Foundation dinner in which 200 brand-name manufacturers received "Certificates of Public Service." The featured speaker, Senator Albert W. Hawkes, Republican from New Jersey, warned that dubious factions within the United States opposed the brand-name system, creating a "powder chest" of "social unrest" with the potential of causing an "economic revolution." According to Hawkes, "the brand names system is keystone" to the American economy and any criticism of it represented an "attack on freedom itself." Unnamed "factions" within the United States threatened to "destroy the great American business system." To combat these forces, asserted Alfred Buckingham, newly elected chairman of the foundation, "every manufacturer and advertiser of a branded product" needed "to join in a program to convince the people of America that their own best welfare lies in support of the system of brand-name identification."[13]

Prior to the major initiatives of 1947, the Brand Names Foundation sponsored several smaller campaigns. It launched a newspaper campaign in Coldwater, Michigan, a town with a population of 7,500. Henry Abt called it the "first concerted attempt of consumer goods manufacturers to foster better relations between industry and the community." After the local campaign, it ran a statewide campaign in Michigan organized by the Michigan League of Home Dailies. One of the major concerns of brand-name manufacturers was that supermarkets and department stores would sell in-house brands and not national brand names. The foundation worked with local businesses to engage customers in buying national mass produced brand-name goods. For instance, with hardware stores, the Brand Names Foundation sponsored a contest designed to make sure customers saw their "local store as a headquarters for quality hardware brands."[14] To support national brands over local production, it worked with industries to develop material about brands, such as a "promotional manual for daytime frocks" with the National Association of House Dress Manufacturers that promoted not only "trade-marked apparel," but the idea that brand-name goods would create "faster turnover for the retailer."[15] The Brand Names Foundation handed out awards and certificates across the nation as one of the methods for engaging companies in its mission. It published a roster of historic American brands and issued special certificates honoring brands 50 years old or older. The foundation also gave out "certificates of merit" to local retailers who created local newspaper ads that featured the 'benefits of manufacturers' brand names." Over the next few years, they distributed these awards monthly.[16]

Brand Celebrations

In 1947, the Brand Names Foundation held two pivotal events: one to sell brand-based free enterprise to industry executives, and the other to engage the American public wholeheartedly in brand-name consumption. In April, the foundation hosted hundreds of advertising, media, and retail executives for a "Brand Names Day" at the Waldorf-Astoria in New York City. The following October, it prototyped a large-scale community program in Greenfield, Massachusetts. For two weeks, Greenfield (population 15,000; shopping center for 55,000 suburban and rural customers) celebrated the glories of the American system of brand management by hosting a "Brand Names Celebration."[17] The foundation published the results as *How Greenfield Did It . . . A Comprehensive Guide to Worthwhile Community Activity.* Though they distributed the guides throughout the nation, the cities that adopted the program never embraced its grand scale.

The Waldorf Conference

In April 1947, the Brand Names Foundation hosted an industry conference at New York's Waldorf-Astoria Hotel. The Brand Names Day program brought together advertising, corporate, and media executives to discuss the importance of the brand-name free enterprise system in America and the threat of restrictions on advertisers, as well as strategies for teaching free enterprise to the public. The Brand Names Foundation divided the conference into a series of clinics designed specifically for advertising, retail, manufacturing, and media executives. In doing so, it created a vast network encompassing virtually every aspect of possible consumer activity. During the conference, speakers addressed criticism of advertising and brand names and made the case for them One of the major purposes of the conference was to extend the network of those in American business supporting the use of brand-name goods.

Brand name certificates were awarded at the Waldorf Conference luncheon of 600 executives. At the luncheon, speakers warned that "demagogues" throughout the country were attempting to "discredit" the advertising of brand-name goods. They claimed that if these forces succeeded in reducing the influence of brand-name advertising, "free press, free radio and free choice" would come under attack. The luncheon included the election of Brand Names Foundation officers such as Paul West, president of the Association of National Advertisers (ANA), and Brigadier General Julius Ochs Adler, vice president and general manager of the *New York Times.* Theophil H. Mueller, chairman of the executive committee, spoke about the outcry over the closing of the OPA. He suggested that an organization such as the OPA would create a monopoly situation and expressed concern over the number of women who had been "taken in by the honeyed doctrine these people advanced." In defending brands, he emphatically stated that they represented the antithesis of monopoly, guaranteeing "free and active competition," as well as "a free press, a free radio and the system of free choice." Edward Rogers of Sterling Drug was elected chairman. During his speech, Rogers referred to brands as the "keystone of a competitive economy" and guaranteed to his audience that with the support of business and advertising and the "direct educational work" of the foundation, the public would accept that brand names represented the cornerstone of America's economy.

Throughout the day's clinics, speakers took on criticism of advertising and brand names and the consumer movement that embraced grade labeling. One of the major criticisms leveled against advertising was that it was an "economic waste."[18] Speakers expressed concern over academic and popular cultural criticism directed toward advertising and brand names. Throughout the day, they complained that "too many tainted text books are already redolent with spurious and unsupported allegations that brand names and trademarks make for monopolies" and "that advertising increases distribution costs." "Anti-brand charges in text or reference books" far outweighed any positive references. One advertising executive claimed that "twenty-six of twenty-nine reference books on economic consumption contend that advertising burdens consumer costs." Speakers also viewed themselves as under attack in popular culture by "novels full of vivid imagination which relate the hypothetical excesses of advertising men." They argued that grade labeling, such as that supported by OPA advocates, would "eventually destroy" the American system and that any attack on advertising represented a "sinister propaganda tactic" designed to create "government control."

Proper education regarding brand-name goods would ensure that the public understood that any attack on advertising and brand-name goods represented an attack on the American economic system. Operating under the premise that "the hidden secret is the happiness of possession," the Brand Names Foundation sought to ensure that the public "understand as much as possible about how the American economic system works." These ideas formed the basis of the "experiment" at Greenfield and a mass education campaign developed to convert the American public to the brand names system. Once converted, the American public would sell the brand names system, if "the brand names story should be told either in terms of benefit to the user or it should express a cogent, biting thought that will give ammunition to somebody who wants to argue our cause for us. There are hundreds and thousands and millions of such people in this country. Give them the ammunition and they will defend our cause." Speakers stressed to advertisers the importance of capturing the loyalty of children.[19] They argued that brand loyalty and the "habit of buying many nationally known brands" began in childhood and was often instilled by mothers. They asserted that "there were millions of new families founded in the war years" who could be enticed into supporting the brand-name system. They believed that "each individual's preferences among the many products offered by industry begins in childhood" and must be "steadily augmented during maturing years through attention to advertising and through accumulated experience."[20]

In the Public Relations Clinic, George McMillan, secretary, Bristol-Myers Company, spelled out how the foundation sought to spread the gospel of the brand name system. Based on meetings brand advocates held throughout the nation during the 1940s, the Brand Names Foundation had created a multi-pronged program that created a "pattern" to foster "a climate and atmosphere, an attitude of mind if you will, that is conducive to pleasant and efficient production and distribution in business." On this note he addressed one issue rarely discussed by free enterprise supporters, the question of whether advertising of the brand name system constituted propaganda. He argued that if industry across political lines worked together in promoting the brand name system, it would not be propaganda; only if business lacked a united front then "the signature of one firm or of a manufacturer in itself might indicate an attempt to propagandize." McMillan also stressed that companies should teach their employees about the brand name system. This group, he argued, represented the bulk of America's consumers and workers and "the core of our whole competitive enterprise system."[21]

The Advertising Council provided one of the keynote speakers, Paul Ellison, who worked on the council's Red Cross campaign. Ellison minced no words in stating that free enterprise served business interests and that industry leaders needed to convince the American public that it served them. He described a battle on the horizon. One that in order to win businesses they would need to continue using "economic power to further its own ends." However, in his opinion, business still failed on one crucial front, "the important battle for the political system which guarantees the American way of doing business." Ellison warned that if the American public lost "faith in either brand names or advertising," they would lose faith "in the free enterprise system."[22]

The logic behind the idea that advertising revenue would guarantee a free press resonated with Cold War anxieties about state controlled media. The Brand Names Foundation insisted that the use of advertising and brand names to financially support the media ensured that the country retained freedom of speech. The media in the United States remained free "because advertising revenue supports them," and "because the educational process of advertising brands and their distinctive features yields independent revenue to channels of information, the brand names language helps to guarantee to press and radio freedom from government domination."

However, in spite of lofty arguments about constitutional freedoms, the foundation offered no other justification other than the creation of revenue. They also did not address any possibility that if the media remained completely dependent on brand-name advertising revenue, advertisers and brand-name manufacturers would have an inordinate amount of influence over the media since they had the power to withdraw financial support. The Brand Names Foundation stressed that advertisers and the media were all part of a network whose very existence was dependent on advertising and brand names: "radio, magazines, our cars and billboards, all are working partners with newspapers in creating and enlarging public demand for brand products, and in building and supporting our top standard of living, and our still free economy." It presented this network as a core component in maintaining American democracy, insisting that democracy went hand in hand with advertising and brand names and that "media are thus vitally interested in protecting the brand names system from attacks by the enemies of democracy." Brand names, advertising, and the media were dependent on each other and "the future of advertising media is closely intertwined with that of the brand names system." If they continued to work together, they would be successful "in fighting off socialist mediocrity."[23]

At the Advertising Media Clinic, National Broadcasting Company (NBC) executive George W. Wallace reminded his audience of media and advertising executives that the American media played a vital role in facilitating the brand-name system. Media, magazines, newspapers, radio, and the emerging potential of television, needed to "promote the Brand Names story." For survival "mass media" must lead the battle to keep "a disillusioned, cynical public, such as we have today" from taking "the plausible bait of brand elimination." While he said that he thought advertisers understood the importance of brand-name advertising to themselves and to the American economy, he said that the media could invest more in encouraging "the Brand Names philosophy in advertising." One way he felt it could be done was by "indicating what the media itself is doing to promote the Brand Names story." According to Wallace, the NBC worked closely with the Brand Names Foundation. Together, they created a record series about the brand-name philosophy. Done in 13 records, the NBC offered the series free to radio stations across the nation. According to Wallace, as of April 1947, 138 stations had accepted the NBC's offer. He encouraged radio stations to use "publicity and exploitation stunts in helping to promote Brand Names." He praised Baltimore, Maryland's WBAL for hosting a "Brand Names Week," and encouraged other radio stations to follow suit. To convert the nation to the brand name system of free enterprise, the media needed to launch an "all-out attack." To expand on the tenets' ideology behind the attack he turned the floor over to Hearst executive, H.J. Gediman.

H.J. Gediman, regional manager from Hearst Advertising Service, of Hearst Publishing, described the need to support brand names to keep the American economy working. Gediman's speech demonstrated that those espousing the free enterprise ideology feared that some business executives still did not believe in free enterprise. Brand names alone, he argued, created America's economic and political success. Gediman asserted that "the regular consumption of branded products has not only created but also supports our great manufacturing status of today." He also acknowledged the strictly self-serving purpose of supporting brand-name free enterprise: "the future of advertising media is closely intertwined with that of the brand names system."[24]

Gediman stressed the parallel between American consumerism and democracy. Gediman told his audience that "democracy as we know it must be closely linked to the development of better products for the American consumer." In terms of American democracy, "we can all agree that the brand names system has proven to be the best way of approaching this ideal."[25] Choosing between brand names represented democracy, because "the perpetual concentration of this system on pleasing the individual buyer, and the acknowledgment of his freedom to choose or reject, is democracy incarnate." Consumers needed to be treated as citizens; " . . . it is sound policy for the advertiser to include in his advertising the facts and philosophies of the brand names system so that the public will understand. In connection let me make it clear that I am talking about the public, not only as consumers and customers, but as citizens and voters."[26]

At Hearst, Gediman stated, a three-point treatment had been created to make sure that everyone clearly understood free enterprise and understood that the American way of life brought the greatest satisfaction to the greatest number of people. First, Hearst endeavors sought to bring about a "reaffirmation of the belief that our kind of economic system and our kind of government is the kind that yields the most material and spiritual benefits for the most people." Second, if one believed in "our kind of economic system and our kind of government," then one needed to "accept free enterprise as an inseparable part of that system." The final tenet asserted that keeping America running required advertising, claiming that "if we accept free enterprise then we must accept advertising as a proved means of promoting the efficient operation of that system, a mechanism for selling more and better goods at lower cost to the consumer."[27]

At the conference, the Brand Names Foundation targeted department and grocery stores. By securing the allegiance of local sellers, small-scale retailers could remain seemingly autonomous, yet still fully endorse the brand-name system. Advertisers and major brand-name manufacturers feared national chain stores would have in-house labels that could undermine the use of national brand names. They hoped that stores would see that "the national brand is a necessity for volume and for profit." The national brand-name producer creates "demand and goodwill" through "merchandize that is consistently advertised by a reliable manufacturer under his own brand names in magazines, newspapers, radio and/or billboards." This would make the job of the department stores easier, because national companies provided them with advertising and display copy and stores would benefit from the "demand and goodwill already created by the manufacturer through his national advertising."[28]

While the direct influence of the Waldorf conference on the opinions and actions of participants cannot be determined, it unified retailers, manufacturers, advertisers, and the media around the use of brand names. The Brand Names Foundation urged executives to spread word across the nation and to focus on giving speeches at women's clubs and at local Chambers of Commerce. This urging helped give rise to Greenfield's Brand Names Celebration and helped finance other foundation initiatives. The autumn after the Waldorf conference, the foundation launched a major initiative to promote brand names and the brand name system to Americans. Latching on to an event proposed by the Chamber of Commerce in Greenfield, Massachusetts, the Brand Names Foundation created a template for a grassroots campaign designed to convince Americans to use brand name goods. Feeling the public still lacked full knowledge of what brands were and the role they played in the nation's economy, the Brand Names Foundation wanted to ensure that Americans understood "the meaning of the word 'brand', and the benefits to the consumer of competition between brands."[29]

Greenfield

Originally, the Greenfield Chamber of Commerce wanted to promote Greenfield business throughout the local region. It contacted the Brand Names Foundation, which quickly turned the project into a prototype for community education. While it had sponsored small events, the Greenfield project represented the first major test of the "consumer reaction to promotion of brand-name goods." The foundation called the two weeks of events a "cooperative interpretation of the brand competitive system," based on the belief that the way to avoid another Depression was "to sell on an unprecedented scale." Population 15,000, Greenfield served as a shopping center for 55,000 suburban and rural customers.[30] Greenfield's Brand Names Celebration consisted of 15 days of events, from October 20 through November 5, 1947, all organized around mass produced brand-name goods. The celebration included fashion shows, sales classes for retailers, contests for women and children, cooking demonstrations with new electronic gadgets, a consumer school, and a day of celebrating the deep connections between the history of the country and the history of brand names.[31]

The Brand Names Foundation called Greenfield a success, claiming that 90 percent of the local stores participated and over 96 percent of the community were "aware" of the program. For the foundation, the purpose of the program was to "impress on Greenfield's shoppers—the meaning of the word 'brand,' and the benefits to the consumer of competition between brand names." It hoped that through "the experiment," it could create "community education" regarding "the full meaning of a brand name" and "the function of advertising." The goal of the program was to educate citizens at all levels—from the consumer to the retailer to local manufacturers—about "the brand competitive system, and what it means to Greenfield." The two weeks of events were designed "to tell the 55,000 consumers in the Greenfield shopping area in every way possible why it is better to buy products bearing brand names." The foundation saw in Greenfield the "possibility of blue printing the entire program for the benefit of other communities throughout the country," as well as the "opportunity to test the effectiveness of all our educational materials in one area, for a specific period of time."[32]

The brand-name activities, the advertisements, and the participant responses were carefully documented and studied. The foundation also filmed the week's events. It, however, did not use the opinion of consumers to determine the success of the program or to determine whether consumers believed in the use of brand name goods. Instead, in order to judge the effectiveness, it had local retailers keep records on how the events affected their business. This also served to further engage retailers in the week's events.[33]

After analyzing and improving on the weeks in Greenfield, the foundation put together a guide for other communities to implement similar campaigns. It claimed that Greenfield "pioneered a community project which average American towns from Maine to California can follow with wholly beneficial results." Published as *How Greenfield Did It . . . A Comprehensive Guide to Worthwhile Community Activity,* the guide was distributed throughout the nation by the foundation. In the guidebook, the foundation claimed that "Greenfield set out to declare certain principles," foremost among them the "fact that workers, management, retailers and salesman were actually partners, united in a common effort to bring the American consumer the highest standard of living in the world." The guide described the events as "an intensive community relations program built around the meaning of America's well-known brand names." It claimed the foundation chose to create activities around the use of brand-name goods because "every merchant and every consumer had a stake in this aspect of American industry." Part of the package for creating your own local event included a promotional brochure, entitled "A Comprehensive Guide to a Worthwhile Community Activity . . . by the Consumers, Merchants, Manufacturers of an Average Town." In spite of the Brand Names Foundation distributing *How Greenfield Did It* nationally, other communities did not launch campaigns on the scale of the one in Greenfield. However, the Greenfield "experiment" did prompt many communities to host smaller brand-name events.[34]

The project was sold to the citizens of Greenfield as one of national scope and significance. For the town, the 15 days of "interesting and exciting events" were heralded by the local paper (*Greenfield Recorder-Gazette*) as "Greenfield's Brand Names Celebration, That Will Make Greenfield Famous Throughout the Country." The local paper claimed that "the Eyes of the Nation Are on You" because "what you people in Greenfield are doing is inspiration for thousands of communities across the nation." Like the Advertising Council's "Miracle of America," the Brand Names Foundation claimed labor and management were not at odds and could find further agreement and cooperation by embracing free enterprise. Local ads stated that successful national brand names result from "the faith of millions who trust these symbols has been won through the efforts of management and workers alike." Regarding the use of brands, the local paper stressed that "the challenge to every individual in Greenfield is to keep the pledges expressed by these symbols; and as we assure citizens of other communities of ever-better workmanship, we assure ourselves of steady employment, happy homes, good schools, and a good community in which to live and work."[35]

Between the community organizers in Greenfield and the Brand Names Foundation, 600 invitations went out across the nation, of which 300 "representatives of national publications, advertisers, wholesalers and manufacturers" were expected for the first week. According to the foundation, "350 national advertisers" sent "special display material" and "living trademarks." This material ranged from speakers to films to other promotional activities solicited through letters sent out by the Brand Names Foundation and local Greenfield retailers. Local organizers and the foundation also sent out press releases to national newspapers and magazines. The Brand Names Foundation told the national business community that through the program "the foundation will learn the best methods of making brand name products popular." Leading executives in sales and advertising went from New York to Greenfield for the purpose of evaluating "the effectiveness of the program to stimulate larger scales and profits for merchants, lower inventories but faster turnover for business generally." Upwards of 300 "representatives of national publications, advertisers, wholesalers and manufacturers" came into Greenfield during the first week of the Brand Names Celebration to study the community activities and participate in activities.[36]

Like the Advertising Council, the Brand Names Foundation helped create a full template of prepackaged advertising. The advertising manager of the local paper worked with the Brand Names Foundation "in preparing copy and layout." Throughout the two weeks, the local paper and radio advertised the daily events. The local radio station, WHAI, ran "news broadcasts" with "up-to-the minute information" on the program. It also ran musical programs called "Brand Names in Music" and "Folk Music Festival" that connected brand names with popular music. The local radio also promoted several contests.[37]

The local newspaper helped coordinate the events by carrying advertisements, articles, and event schedules and printing up over "2,000 form letters." For every day of the program, the *Greenfield Recorder-Gazette* ran the slogan "Greenfield Sponsors America's Brand Names" on the masthead and covered all the events. All advertisements for the events were required to carry the slogan "Greenfield Sponsors America's Brand Names." Advertisements running in the newspaper stressed the national and international connections the brand names created, with slogans such as "millions of people throughout the world buy Greenfield Brand Names because these products are important to their welfare, comfort, and happiness." The advertisements put forth the free enterprise idea that advertising and brand names were the route to national prosperity."[38]

The advertising campaign also rooted brand names deep in American history; one ad ran with the title "Backed by 155 Years of Service." It reminded audiences that the "Greenfield Recorder-Gazette Is a Brand Name" and that "almost anything worthwhile has a Brand Name." The ad conveyed America's historic spirit of individualism, stressed the importance of advertising and brands for employment, and equated them with freedom. Part of the copy claimed "that brands and advertising stabilize employment—the Brand system and advertising provide maximum opportunity for free choice and the satisfaction of individual choice." Some ads depicted the consumer republic. They framed the consumer and the citizen as one and the same and equated democracy with purchase power. When the *Greenfield Recorder-Gazette* ran the ad, it also had text that asserted that brand names get elected on a more regular basis than politicians. In politics, the ad claimed, "candidates come up for election every 2, 4, or 6 years," whereas "brand names are up for election every hour every day." The ads also reinforced the theme running through Brand Names Foundation and Advertising Council events throughout the mid-1940s that advertising and brand name goods would eliminate labor disputes, with statements such as "the faith of millions who trust these symbols had been won through the efforts of management and workers alike."[39]

The local paper also emphasized the global significance and global connections of American brand-name goods, for instance, the advertisement "Millions of people throughout the world buy Greenfield Brand Names" emphasizes the connections between the consumers of Greenfield and the consumers around the world. One of the advertisements run by the Greenfield paper showed the citizens of Greenfield how mass produced goods connected them to the world. The copy read, "When Greenfield Goes Traveling." It stated that "many of us don't get out of town very much" and internationally distributed brand names allowed "a little of us is on the shelves of stores, in the shops and in the homes in all the states and in many countries." This process connected individuals around the globe, because "regardless of the kind of work we do, these names are our symbols tying us to the daily lives of all the world." The brand goods produced by local residents helped make the world a better place because "wherever these names go, they stand for the best in all of us. In places thousands of miles away, they are Greenfield doing its proud part in the service of human needs and happiness."[40]

To engage local industry leaders, the Brand Names Foundation gave awards, "Certificates of Public Service," to brand-name manufacturers throughout Greenfield's Franklin County. In June 1947, the foundation issued a list of America's historic brands called "43,000 Years of Public Service: A Roster of Product-identifying Names Used by the American Public for 50 Consecutive Years or More." The list situated the brand name in the landscape of American history, claiming that American brand names predated the nation. It listed six brands that predated the nation—Cherry Richer, 1705; Crosse & Blackwell, 1706; Royal Worchester, 1751; Wedgwood, 1759; Britannica, 1768; and Spade, 1770. The same year the Brand Names Foundation awarded "Certificates of Public Service" to American companies with brand names of "50 years or more." The certificate recognized both individual brand names and the entire system of brands, which the foundation claimed had served the American people since colonial times. The certificate stated, "In Recognition of Continuous Service to the American People since 1705."[41]

Like the Waldorf Conference, Brand Names Foundation considered retailers a vital part of the brand-name mission. Retailers not only kept detailed records for the Brand Names Foundation to use for analysis after the events, but they also hosted displays by national manufacturers. During the last three days of Greenfield's Brand Names Celebration, 22 manufacturers set up window displays in Greenfield's retail shops. This proved to be so successful that the retailers and the national manufacturers planned to do the window displays annually. For Greenfield's Brand Names week, the foundation "advised national advertisers, advertising agencies and media of Greenfield's plan and suggested they cooperate with their most effective merchandising aids." The foundation served as a "liaison" between Greenfield and "national advertisers and media and the outside press." The foundation organized training sessions for retail clerks called "Salesmanship School" prior to the events to train them for the activities. Local retail stores also competed in "window display contests" judged by Brand Names Foundation representatives. Henry Abt, Brand Names Foundation president, told retail store clerks, "You are the American system," because they were in a direct position to convince a customer to purchase a brand-name good or a non-branded good.[42] He also told retailers that how they approached female customers was crucial for the brand-names system because "What she thinks of the American system depends to a considerable degree on what sales personnel do behind the counter." The final day of the Brand Names Week ended with 300 retailers receiving awards.

Like other campaigns for a system of free enterprise based on advertising and brand names, the Greenfield celebration rooted brands and advertising in the history of the nation through "Old Home Day." The day celebrated the town of Greenfield before "industrial development and modern brand competition began to change the life of this country."[43] The foundation also attempted to incorporate positive race relations through brand names. As part of the Old Home Day's events, it invited the African American spokesperson for Aunt Jemima syrup to come into town. Advertisements for the events urged audiences to "see Aunt Jemima arrive in an ancient motor vehicle on Friday and Saturday morning." The description, however, reinforced racial stereotypes of the time: "Aunt Jemima of pancake fame is the genial, jolly mammy who for years had cooked up the best dog gone pancakes and buckwheat cakes ever set on the table."[44] The foundation's attempt fell far short of that done by the Advertising Council with the Freedom Train.

Demographically, the primary focus for the Brand Names Foundation education programs was women and children. The foundation wanted to reach young children and "impress them with the importance of brand names."[45] It primarily targeted women, because of the belief that women did most of the household shopping. The foundation called women the "family purchasing agent," and events were gender specific. Activities were structured around the idea of a gendered economy. For men, the events included two auto shows of new cars, one "Ancient Auto Show," and General Motor's "Preview of Progress" that featured "a demonstration of electronic cooking and explanations of atomic energy, jet propulsion, infra-red lighting and butyl rubber manufacture."[46] For women, there were fashion shows, "electric cooking demonstrations," "consumer schools," and gender-specific contests.[47]

Targeting women was such a significant part of the Brand Names Foundation that it created "The Women's Club Division of the Brand Names

Foundation." This division helped prepare the literature that went out to women's clubs and to school home economics departments. The foundation also developed "wall charts, one-act plays and folders on the economics of today's buying" and provided educational material for women's clubs and libraries such as charts and study material about the "economics of today's buying."[48] Since the late nineteenth century, *Good Housekeeping,* the women's magazine, helped introduce mass production to American women throughout the country. It was also a member of the Brand Names Foundation. One ad for women in the *Greenfield Recorder-Gazette* headlined with the copy, "To Justify Your Faith." Its message to the women of Greenfield was to trust only the nationally advertised brand names because "Brand Name Merchandise is investigated or 'pre-used' so that you may buy with confidence those products which have earned the famous Good Housekeeping Guarantee Seal."[49]

Two of the major events for women were the Brand Names Queen contest and the consumer school.[50] The contest featured five days of elimination quizzes. The winner represented the "woman who was most alert to the progress of American industry as presented in local and national advertising." The newspaper ran the title, "You Can Be Greenfield's Brand Names Queen," and called the event the "grand climax to Greenfield sponsors America's Brand Names." Contestants answered questions about brand names in a succession of elimination rounds. The panels of judges asked questions such as " 'The flavor lasts' is the slogan of what product?" "What are 'Keds'?" The foundation crowned the winner "Brand Queen" and gave her $1,500 worth of national brand-name retail goods.[51]

The adult consumer school was held during the day making those in attendance far more likely to be women. The goal of the adult education program was "to provide the consumers of Greenfield up-to-the-minute information on buying in fields of merchandising which affected the home." Though the event was held at the Chamber of Commerce, the Brand Names Foundation completely organized it. It claimed the average daily attendance was "over 900," at the four day, two hour a day classes.[52] The local paper reported the attendance at 650 for the first two days. To attract people the foundation used the popular advertising technique, the free give away—"5 prizes awarded" at the end of each session; everyone who attended received a "bag of 'give-away' " that included "soap flakes, foods, cereals, and advertising matter." The classes were taught by employees of major national brand manufacturers and publishers, emblematic of the network surrounding advertising and brand names. For example, Ruth Casa-Emellos, assistant food editor from the *New York Times,* taught "Patriotic and Practical Meal Planning." Alyce Dunshee, resident stylist at the McCall Corporation, hosted a "Happy Holidays—Fabric

Fashion Show." La Verne Johnson, director of field activities, Revlon Products Corporation, taught "Individualization in Your Make-Up." A.J. Norris Hill from the Retail Trade Extension of Hearst Magazine discussed "What the Good Housekeeping Seal Means." One of the few sessions not solely targeting women featured a discussion on "Home Insulation" by Robert V. Donnelly of the Wood Conversion Company who promoted press-board.[53]

The literature directed at children also taught the gendered economy. Activities for children represented one of the most important parts of the Greenfield campaign. The ability to reach young consumers and shape their taste and their desire for brand-name goods from a very young age was considered a vital part of the future of brand-name goods. The superintendent of the Greenfield schools worked closely with the Brand Names Foundation and required students to participate in Brand Names Week programs. The foundation provided educational kits for the local schools. These were targeted primarily at home economics classes, since the foundation was operating under the premise that girls would be the ones in charge of most household production. The kits included "buymanship charts" and "study material" for high school home economics classes and "marks of merit" for elementary students. The kits included 25 by 41 inch wall charts that illustrated "the meaning of brand names, how they help people to shop, principles of good budgeting and other essentials which are requisite to intelligent buying." Junior high and high school girls participated in classes about "good buymanship."

The school activities and kits, however, did not target teenage girls exclusively and provided activities for school children of all ages. Foremost, the kits were designed to teach all school age children the meaning of brands. "What is a brand name?" the literature rhetorically asked the children, providing the answer as "the word or symbol a manufacturer places on his product. You identify this product by that word or symbol." One hundred and fifty home economics students between the ages of 13 and 17 used foundation charts and "other educational materials on brands." They also participated in discussion groups such as "how competition between brands helps the consumers." Over 1,000 students saw the Brand Names Foundation film, *Marks of Merit*, which demonstrated the virtues of brand names in America. *Marks of Merit* targeted social science students, drawing an analogy between the heraldry of knighthood and the trademarks of industry. Outside of the schools, the Brand Names Foundation reached children through the library and through contests. To educate adults and children, the Brand Names Foundation set up an exhibit at the local library of "charts and other educational material."[54] Children under the age of 13 participated in a contest called "Round the Clock with Rocky and Ruthie." The foundation called the book a "playbook," in which children collected advertisements and trademarks from magazines and newspapers and pasted them in the books. The local newspaper also included cartoons for children featuring "Billy Brand."[55]

The Brand Names Foundation viewed the week of events in Greenfield to be a success. The *New York Times* reported it increased sales at least 30 percent and as much as 100 percent. The paper reported the event was "more successful than anticipated." Surveys conducted before and after the program by Fact Finders Associates reported that "before the program started 32.2 percent" of those interviewed "believed that advertising increased the cost of goods." This figure dropped to 23.5 percent by the end of program. Before the program 37 percent of those questioned "believed mandatory grade labeling of goods by the government would benefit the consumer." After the program, it was down to 23.5 percent. "The frequent allegation that advertising confuses customers" dropped from 26 percent to 16.9 percent. However, more significant than public opinion the "national brand proportion of over-the-counter retail sales" increased "from an average of 68% to an average of 84%." The Brand Names Foundation included its "critical appraisal" of the Greenfield events in the guidebook *How Greenfield Did It . . . A Comprehensive Guide to Worthwhile Community Activity.* It determined that the week's events should begin with a "well-publicized parade" or a "giant mass meeting." The local town leaders and politicians should make a "community-wide proclamation." The foundation also determined that local campaigns needed more effective or "accurate" campaigns. It concluded that "Greenfield Sponsor's America's Brand Names" proved too confining and did not reflect the "broad, educational purposes of the program." As a result, the Brand Names Foundation chose the slogan "Parade of Progress" for other events and included it on all material the Brand Names Foundation provided other towns.[56]

The Brand Names Foundation distributed *How Greenfield Did It* to "chambers of commerce, publishing and advertising groups" across the country. In order to help other communities prepare local events, it provided a complete chart of all the planning stages, "educational materials, publicity and visual aids," as well as helped with "booking speakers for sales instruction classes" and arranging "suitable programs for consumer classes, style shows, product demonstrations, special exhibits and lectures on home economics and home decorating." The Brand Names Foundation provided all event planning and materials free of charge. It also distributed the films taken of the "Greenfield test." The first screening of the documentary occurred in January 1948.[57]

Together with advertisers and manufacturers, the foundation also created "cooperative institutional advertising," six full-page ads about the virtues of brand names, placing the "value of the brand competitive system in hometown terms" to create "better informed consumers." The Brand Names Foundation also prepared radio broadcasts, short segments about "brand names and today's shopping." It distributed free educational material. The foundation provided home economics classes throughout the nation an eight-page folder entitled "Review of Good Buymanship Principles." It described the "steps in good buymanship" and "how the brand competitive system operates to aid the consumer, outlines the principles of good budgeting, and in general provides much useful data for the future homemaker."[58] For younger children, the foundation gave away free copies of "Around the Clock with Rocky and Ruthie." For older students, it provided the "Review of Good Buymanship Principles" and the film "Marks of Merit." For women's clubs, it provided a special package to help them put together "programs dealing with the economics of today's buying," because "among your community's important opinion forming groups are the members of your women's organizations." For the press, it would provide a sample press release, and a series of historical cartoons called "The Brand Family," describing "the development of American industry."

For retailers and department stores it provided guides (called "Plus Profit Power—In Your Brand Names Policy" to help them advertise national name brands) and sample posters. The window posters created by the foundation reinforced the theme that brand-name goods connect small town Americans with people all over the nation and the world. One poster stated that "millions of people throughout the world use these brand names to ask for products important to their welfare, comfort and happiness." The posters stressed that the only way for consumers to receive accurate information about products was through advertising and they also stressed that the brand name represented both the company and all those who worked for it. The posters reflected the foundation's goal as being to create "A United Community" around the common consumption and production of brand-name goods. The posters claimed that brand loyalty was the duty of every American and every American institution. The foundation provided a file in the blank pledge for local officials and argued that "the broad civic partnership" forged by the brand-based event in Greenfield demonstrated "a new sound and objective comprehension of the value in our system of free, competitive enterprise."[59]

The foundation claimed that the citizens of Greenfield were now "Better Informed Consumers" and "common economic fallacies and misconceptions have less credence in Greenfield now. For this program has given shoppers a head start toward a keener insight into the values of the brand competitive system and advertising." The program in Greenfield did more than just promote advertising and brand names, it created a sense of civic and community pride.

According to the Brand Names Foundation, Greenfield became a "United Community," and "a town in which every group recognizes the value of teamwork." Most significantly, it was a community based on free enterprise being a system of advertising and brand-name goods. As the guidebook stated, "This broad civic partnership is based on a new sound and objective comprehension of the values in our system of free, competitive enterprise."

As the Freedom Train crossed the nation, American towns and small cities followed Greenfield's example and hosted brand-name events. The Brand Names Foundation reported 25 communities that created brand events, including Falmouth, Massachusetts; White Plains, New York; and New Brunswick, New Jersey. The first major event based on the Greenfield experiment occurred in White Plains, New York, and was announced by Henry Abt in February 1948. The ten-day program scheduled for May 1948 used the slogan "Best in the Land When You Buy a Brand."[60] At the Second Annual Brand Names Day in March 1948, again held at the Waldorf, hundreds of advertising, media, and public relations executives listened as L.R. Boulware from the General Electric Company raised the call to use the "principles and practices" used "in building faith in brand names" to convince employees to be enthusiastic and productive. In April 1948, 200 "variety chain store companies," which owned upwards of 6,000 stores nationally, held "national brands week." The same month "thousands of stores" across the country ran campaigns promoting national brands. The campaigns emphasized that national brand names lowered the cost to the consumer.[61]

For the following decade, the Brand Names Foundation continued to place brand names within an international context and connect advertisers, brand-name manufacturers, and major media outlets. In 1949, the vice president of *The New York Times,* Major General Julius Ochs Adler, was elected vice chairman of the board for the Brand Names Foundation.[62] The same year John Foster Dulles spoke at the Brand Names Foundation luncheon on April 12. He discussed the problems faced by the United Nations because it had not properly branded itself.[63] In 1950, a study conducted by the National Family Opinion, Incorporated, concluded that the work of the Brand Names Foundation had created "brand loyalty," and the "reliability, authenticity, conditions favorable to high inherent value, and the convenience of naming the brand become more and more generally appreciated by the general public as a result of the program of Brand Names Foundation."[64] The foundation helped cities set up Brand Names Weeks throughout the 1950s. Henry Abt personally helped Burlington, North Carolina, prepare one for the fall of 1950. By the late 1950s, 100,000 stores had participated in Brand Names Weeks. All the promotion material was still prepared by the Brand Names Foundation and distributed through its network of advertisers and media.

The Brand Names Foundation's campaigns remained continuous and year round well into the 1950s, as did its expansion of the network through the giving of awards.[65]

In 1956, the foundation published a "Roster of the Sponsors of Brand Names Foundation, Incorporated, Their Brands, Products and Services" that contained names of all the important American brands and the companies that manufactured them. In addition, it provided a summary of the foundation's organizational structure. On the state level, the foundation included representatives from almost every state in a retail advisory council. The national Board of Directors and officers included executives from the Columbia Broadcasting System, Mutual Broadcasting System, Motorola, Inc., the Curtis Publishing Group, the Coca Cola Company, the National Association of Radio and Television Broadcasters, and the major advertising companies and organizations, such as Young and Rubicam, McCann-Erickson, the Association of National Advertisers (ANA), the American Association of Advertising Agencies (AAAA), and the National Association of Transportation Advertisers. The publication demonstrated that while the organization had national support from American manufacturers, the media, and advertising agencies, it still needed to create national advertising and broadcasting. Almost ten years after Greenfield, the perpetual campaigning suggested that the use of brand names had not become universal.[66] In the 1960s, thousands of companies belonged to or supported the Brand Names Foundation. However, the foundation continued to run ads teaching that "a brand name is a maker's reputation" and "practical folks buy brand name products."[67]

Selling the value of the brand name to the American people represented a significant step in the adoption of free enterprise capitalism. The experiment in Greenfield provided an opportunity to shape a community and create common bonds around brand names. The Brand Names Foundation conferences for retailers and executives countered the idea that the success of American capitalism lay with individual small business owners. Instead, brand management allowed for large corporations to create lower-cost goods, which helped local retailers and the public. The Brand Names Foundation, like its counterparts, the Advertising Council and the American Heritage Foundation, hoped that use of brand names and the principles of brand management would unite America to the world through brand-name goods. As the Freedom Train crossed the nation and the Brand Names Foundation attempted to turn brand-name buying into a national community activity, the council helped the Truman administration incorporate advertising and public relations techniques into the Cold War struggle.

CHAPTER 4

"Advertising—A New Weapon in the Worldwide Fight for Freedom"

As the Cold War progressed through the late 1940s, the containment of communism became the focus of U.S. foreign policy. Cold War policies favored the expansion of American businesses and the advertising-based model of free enterprise as envisioned by the Advertising Council, and both became increasingly more intertwined with American foreign policy and the national security apparatus. The council's "invisible hand," the bipartisan coalition of businessmen and politicians, extended into American foreign policy, helping to form the basis of what would come to be labeled as public diplomacy decades later, and helping brand the nation around the globe.[1] Many council members wanted to grow their businesses and the system of free enterprise capitalism around the globe before World War II, and the image of the Iron Curtain descending upon the world's markets preventing that growth gave new urgency to their goals.

After the war, council members lost no time looking to expand business overseas with a world trade campaign coordinated with the government. As Congress and the Truman administration implemented Cold War legislation and policy throughout the 1940s, the council continued as the American government's primary advertising agency. When the United States gave aid to war-torn Europe through the Marshall Plan, the council helped create a brand for American foreign aid. When the National Security Act restructured the U.S. Armed Forces and created the National Security Council, the Advertising Council helped explain the restructuring to the American public. When the overseas information act, the Smith-Mundt Act of 1948, provided a permanent federal structure to overseas broadcasting, such as the Voice of America (VOA), and overseas information, and expanded education exchanges under the Fulbright Act of 1946, the Advertising Council worked with the Department of State to help business overseas advertise the United States.[2]

Free enterprise advocates and Advertising Council participants such as J. Walter Thompson, Eastman Kodak, and *Time-Life,* supported the expansion of American business overseas long before World War II. They continued urging American businesses to expand overseas throughout World War II. As the war ravaged Europe, *Time-Life* editor Henry Luce declared the twentieth century the American Century. Luce boasted of being "a Protestant, a Republican and a free enterpriser," and ardently supported "free enterprise and internationalism." Luce's *Fortune* magazine promoted "open door" policies that linked "economic growth and overseas markets."[3] This sentiment underpinned the World Trade campaign and companies as they expanded overseas. He insisted that the United States was the political and economic model other nations should follow and urged Americans to provide economic and political leadership to the world. By the mid-1940s, the containment of communism provided new urgency to that expansion.

In a confidential 1945 report, "The International Operations of the J. Walter Thompson Company, Analysis of an Expanding Venture with Policy Recommendations," Carroll Wilson of the J. Walter Thompson Company detailed ways to expand its advertising business into more foreign markets as nations recovered from World War II. Wilson concluded that the J. Walter Thompson Company had "attractive opportunities to build a stronger agency, through the mass-marketing of its services in foreign countries." The report urged the company to continue training "foreign managers" in "American advertising methods," but it should also employ American citizens. According to Wilson, "the underlying trends affecting advertising—trends in population, literacy, and buying power—are probably more favorable in most of the Company's present international markets than they are in the United States."[4]

After the war, J. Walter Thompson nurtured radio and the development of television in Mexico, Central, South America, and the Caribbean.[5] In 1946, Procter & Gamble introduced the laundry detergent Tide, its "most important new product since Ivory," and one of the products that helped Procter & Gamble establish new markets around the globe. In 1948, brand management creator, Neil McElroy, became the head of Procter & Gamble and the company established an Overseas Division. It created its "first subsidiary in Latin America" in Mexico and the first on the "South American continent" in 1950 in Venezuela. By the mid-1940s, Kraft, Kellogg, Kodak, Pan American Airlines, Delmonte, General Foods, Colgate-Palmolive, Standard Brands, International General Electric, and Libby were doing business in South America and the Caribbean.[6] J. Walter Thompson also worked with the Reader's Digest Spanish publication *SELECCIONES* and Ford Motor in Peru, Colombia, Venezuela, Puerto Rico, Cuba, Mexico, and Argentina, and the company sold tractors in Guatemala City.[7] By 1950, J. Walter Thompson's clients in South America included Procter & Gamble, Ford, Chesebrough, Pepsi-Cola, Rolex, Reader's Digest, Kodak, Standard Brands, Kraft, Kellogg, Goodrich, and Parker Pens. Not only did companies expand into South America and Europe, with the help of the Marshall Plan, but they also expanded into Africa, the Middle East, India, and the Far East. By 1948, American companies invested approximately $1.5 billion in other countries with the oil industry representing one of the major industries in which they invested.[8]

At the same time that American businesses renewed their expansion into foreign markets, the federal government continued providing information about the United States in other countries. During World War II, to counter Axis propaganda, the United States dropped leaflets and created posters, cartoons, newsreels, and radio broadcasts. After World War II started in Europe, President Roosevelt created agencies to counteract Axis propaganda. These included the Coordinator of Inter-American Affairs (CIAA), the Office of Facts and Figures, the Office of Government Reports, and the Coordinator of Information (COI). In 1941, the CIAA leased radio broadcast towers in South America. During World War II, President Roosevelt created the VOA to broadcast radio in Europe. Beginning in February 1942, the United States broadcast the VOA to Europe in French, Italian, and English. From 1942 through 1945, James Webb Young and the J. Walter Thompson Company worked with newspapers, magazines, and radio broadcasters in Latin America to "counteract Axis propaganda." Working with the CIAA, J. Walter Thompson helped American businesses advertise across these media throughout Latin America. In December 1945, the CIAA broadcast services and the VOA became a part of the Department of State.[9]

In June 1946, the State Department issued a manual about the "Operations for the Division of Libraries and Institutes," which stated, "The objective of the United States Information Libraries is to provide foreign communities and solidly documented explanations of the United States, its people, geography, culture, science, government, institutions, industries and thinking: in short the American scene." In August 1946, President Truman signed the Fulbright Act, which formed the Fulbright Program of international education exchanges.[10] Created by Senator James Fulbright (Democrat from Arkansas), the Fulbright Program initially created grants and scholarships for educational exchanges between the United States and its World War II allies.

Later the same month, *Time-Life* executives, Advertising Council members, and Department of Commerce and Department of State representatives conducted a series of meetings to organize a "World Trade" campaign. Among those present at the meetings were Charles D. Jackson, Henry Luce confidant and *Fortune* editor; Theodore Repplier, Advertising Council president; and Charles W. Jackson from the War Mobilization and Reconversion office. Repplier insisted that the campaign "demonstrate that world trade is vitally important in the lives of the average citizen."[11] From the meetings, they reached the common goals of making sure that Americans believe that "their futures will be better with more world trade," that Americans support "the steps essential to this development," and that overall the campaign would create "a crusading zeal in many quarters for development of world trade." Dr. George Gallup, of the famed Gallup poll, offered to "conduct public opinion polls on world trade" before the campaign started.[12] They chose as a campaign slogan, "Our Future Will Be Better with World Trade" and set out to conquer "2 billion new, potential customers over the world." The Advertising Council created a "campaign guide" with "sample ads," "sample posters," and "advice on radio cooperation." In 1947–1948, full-page ads ran in 23 magazines, including *Time, Life, Fortune,* and the "international editions of *Time-Life* and *Newsweek*."[13]

C.D. Jackson of *Time-Life* coordinated the campaign with the help of Compton Advertising, Inc. The council described the campaign as based "in the belief that expanded foreign trade is essential to American prosperity and that world prosperity is largely dependent on the prosperity of the United States." The campaign poster featured the globe with an exaggeratedly large, but typical small town American Main Street wrapped around the globe. The text with the image projects a global economic vision exclaiming "look . . . how Main Street Has Grown! . . . Part of Every Dollar You Get Comes From World Trade!" The council organized the publication and distribution of 20,000 campaign guides that explained "why business should support the World Trade Campaign not only in the interest of the world but of business itself."[14]

As the decade progressed, the Cold World created greater urgency for expanding American businesses overseas. The council described communism in Eastern Europe as "a threat to the world's security that became clearer with every passing month." Advertising industry trade press, *Tide,* covered a campaign conducted by Westinghouse on "selling the U.S. system abroad," and urged advertisers to sell the system at home and abroad. By 1948, the council argued, Americans recognized their need to be part of a global mission. In the council's report for March 1947 to March 1948, "What Helps People Helps Business," the council said that "it dawned slowly on the people of the United States that help for Europe was no longer Santa Claus stuff, but a grim matter of our own self-interest." As a result, the council claimed that "all these tensions—economic, ideological and emotional—were reflected in the campaigns."[15]

Increasingly, American policymakers viewed the spread of the American economic system of consumer capitalism as vital to American security. In March 1947, President Truman announced that the United States would provide assistance to countries threatened by communism (the Truman Doctrine). The president made his first request on behalf of Greece and Turkey. In the Truman Doctrine, "Recommendations on Greece and Turkey," Truman urged the nation to accept that "at the present moment in world history nearly every nation must choose between alternative ways of life." He argued that the "evil soul of poverty" nurtured totalitarianism and that the United States should assist nations in choosing democracy "primarily through economic and financial aid."[16]

In 1947, the Advertising Council took on several international projects. Council members began meeting with the State Department to create an overseas information program.[17] The council also began using foreign aid as larger public relations for American business and the American system of advertising-based capitalism. It launched the foreign aid campaign on behalf of CARE. The nonprofit Cooperative for American Remittances to Europe, Inc. (CARE) represented 27 agencies involved in foreign aid. CARE raised money from the American public to send boxes of clothes and food to Europe. The organization and the council's campaign received endorsements from the Department of State and the White House. The council claimed that in the first year of the campaign, CARE packages shipped increased from 175,000 packages per month to 300,000. The council continued to promote CARE until 1957, claiming increases in donations throughout the 1950s.[18]

At the same time that the Advertising Council worked on the CARE campaign, the legislation that became the Marshall Plan and the National Security Act worked their way through Congress. In June 1947, Secretary of State George Marshall delivered a speech at Harvard University that described a plan for the United States to assist Europe in recovering from the war. By 1948, Marshall's plan had been formalized as the Organization for European Economic Co-operation (OEEC) under the administration of the European Cooperation Administration (ECA). Under the Marshall Plan, the United States gave economic and technical aid to Europe and helped American businesses invest in Marshall Plan countries. The Advertising Council helped by branding goods provided by the ECA. The "stars and stripes emblems" also had the phrase "for European Recovery: Supplied by the United States of America," and the brand was emblazoned on all containers. Also, in 1947, Truman signed the National Security Act, "a comprehensive program for the future security of the United States"[19] The act established the Central Intelligence Agency (CIA), created the National Security Council, and reorganized the armed services. In response to the Soviet Union, for the first time in U.S. history, President Truman had created a permanent peacetime agency for gathering foreign intelligence.

In the fall of 1947, the Advertising Council held a "'Secret' Confab" with the federal government. Over 100 American advertising and business executives met with federal officials at the White House for "off-the-record" discussions regarding the Marshall Plan. The council conducted a study on behalf of the State Department regarding the overseas information aspects of the Marshall Plan. Not only was the Department of State concerned about how Europeans perceived the aid, it wanted to ensure that Americans could help keep "brand names alive in territories that cannot currently be served." The council especially studied the Friendship Trains that delivered American food assistance to Western Europe and employed visual branding similar to the Freedom Train. Clearly marked as from the United States, as the Friendship Trains crossed Europe, they created the impression of goodwill. The council studied the response in France, which it declared a "warm reception" and found encouraging. It concluded that the State Department should help maintain "a continuous flow of facts to Europe showing the scope and importance of American aid."[20]

In 1948, advertising and brand names became a vital part of the Cold War and American foreign policy. The Advertising Council became "the liaison organization between the Department of State and those American advertisers with contacts overseas."[21] The overarching theme for the 57 projects that the council implemented for 1948 "increased public knowledge of the American economic system and counter-action of anti-American propaganda overseas." According to the *New York Times,* "decisive gains in the 'cold war' were made in 1948 through the voluntary action of American business in using weapons of ideas developed by Advertising Council, Inc." Newspapers ordered 476,867 Ad Council advertisements versus 222, 837 in 1947, an "increase of 110 per cent." Radio participated in "more than fifty campaigns through the council's allocation plan with announcements and special productions." In 1948, television also became a part of the Ad Council's network. Along public roads and walkways, Ad Council outdoor advertising increased "48 percent" to "75,302 twenty-four sheet posters." On public transportation "348 transportation advertising companies," increased the number of "car cards" by 139,755–1,133,719.[22]

The Smith-Mundt Act

In 1948, the Smith-Mundt Act, also known as the United States Information and Educational Exchange Act of 1948, made overseas broadcasting and information a permanent part of American foreign policy. The purpose of the act was to create "better understanding of the United States among the peoples of the world and the strengthening of cooperative international relations."[23] The act included educational exchanges with other nations. It established information centers, such as libraries, that provided citizens of other countries free information about the United States. It created a permanent system of American radio broadcasting, and eventually television, beginning with VOA, which provided free entertainment and information about the United States to other nations. The Smith-Mundt Act also blocked the distribution of the same information and broadcasting to American citizens due to concerns that the information could be construed or used as propaganda.[24]

The Smith-Mundt Act resulted from a joint Senate-House Committee spear-headed by Republican Senator Alexander Smith of New Jersey and Republican Representative Karl Mundt of South Dakota. In 1947, a joint Senate-House Committee led by Smith and Mundt conducted an investigation of the "information and propaganda in Europe." Committee members took a two month tour of Europe with Advertising Council associates; the manager of Firestone Tire and Rubber Company and the president of Ford Motor Company; Walter Lippman (columnist); and several film stars. Senator Smith reported that the United States "must help now to prevent communist rule," and pointed out to the press that Britain spent 45 million a year "on a propaganda program" and the United States spent only 12 million. Mundt studied "more than 20 countries" and reported to the press in 1947 that all the communists were working together. He reported that "hostile propaganda" in many European countries "was noticeable" since his visit in 1945 by the "decreased friendliness toward America."[25]

The act, which remains official U.S. policy, was established "to promote the better understanding of the United States among the peoples of the world and to strengthen cooperative international relations." The act created "an information service to disseminate abroad information about the United States, its people and policies promulgated by the Congress, the President, the Secretary of State and other responsible officials of Government having to do with matters affecting foreign affairs." In other words, it created a U.S. public relations body, similar to corporate public relations. In addition to disseminating information, the act included "an educational exchange service to cooperate with other nations in—the interchange of persons, knowledge, and skills; the rendering of technical and other services; the interchange of developments in the field of education, the arts, and sciences." It provided assistance to "schools, libraries and community centers in foreign countries." The act authorized the secretary of state to "provide for the preparation, and dissemination abroad, of information about the

United States, its people and its policies, through press, publication, radio motion pictures, and other information media, and through information centers and instructors abroad." The act states that if "private information dissemination is found to be adequate," the Department of State would not need to run programs. The act recommended that the State Department not have "a monopoly in the predication or sponsorship" of any "medium of information." The act required "a loyalty check on personnel"; anyone employed under the act needed to be investigated by the FBI, and all information needed to be reported to the State Department, the only exception being for Presidential appointments, approved by the Senate. The act also required that the State Department use "private agencies, including existing American press, publishing, radio, motion picture, and other agencies, through contractual arrangements or otherwise."[26] The Smith-Mundt Act ensured that any information created and disseminated under it be banned from the United States unless authorized by Congress. The reason for banning information from being distributed within the United States was a concern that the information could be used for either propaganda or partisan purposes.[27]

Within a short period of time, the Smith-Mundt Act helped expand the Fulbright Act, bringing almost 20,000 individuals from overseas to study at American colleges and universities. The act expanded the Fulbright Act from 1946 that provided grants for educational exchanges between the United States and the Lend Lease nations, and it expanded the Fulbright Act to include more nations. The Smith-Mundt Act also covered the VOA, the radio station that started broadcasting to counteract Axis propaganda during World War II and exposed millions around the globe to American culture, particularly music such as jazz and rock-n-roll. Under Truman, not only did the VOA expand, but information centers were established throughout Africa and the Middle East. The first ones opened in 1944 in Baghdad, Iraq, and Beirut, Lebanon, followed by Cairo in 1945. By 1951, before many of the countries had U.S. embassies open, Algeria, Jordan, Lebanon, Libya, Syria, and Tunisia all had U.S. information centers. By 1949, the VOA claimed to have an audience of several million listeners.[28]

Overseas Information and the Brookings Institute

The Brookings Institution, a think tank incorporated in 1927 to "aid constructively in the development of sound national policies" and "to offer training of a supergraduate character to students of social sciences," issued recommendations regarding international information services. In 1948, it published an analysis of American overseas information services. Noting

Truman's approval of the Smith-Mundt Act—"for the first time in our history committed our government, in time of peace, to conduct international information and educational exchange activities on a world-wide, long-term scale"—the Brookings Institute assessed this new aspect of the federal government. The purpose of the analysis was to determine whether the United States needed "to deal systematically and seriously with the overseas information function." It noted that the Advertising Council contributed significantly to the cause by "getting U.S. export firms to adjust their public relations and advertising programs abroad, where feasible, to implement national objectives."

The Brookings Institute claimed that overseas information was necessary for American interests and recommended that it continue. It claimed that American information service was not propaganda, but simultaneously referred to those involved in overseas information as "the American propagandist." The institute recommended that goods given to Europe for recovery have slogans such as "For European Recovery, from the United States." It recommended that radio broadcasts, such as VOA, continue and expand, as well as publications, filmstrips, and photographic exhibits for foreign markets. It also advised screening motion pictures overseas that showed "typical daily life in the United States with emphasis on such basic characteristics as: importance of individual effort, initiative, resourcefulness and cooperation; the high standard of living in this country and the opportunity of the individual citizen for economic advancement." Information should demonstrate "the inherent strength of representative government," "the concern of the Government for the welfare of its citizens," and "the rich diversity of the country—its size, physical characteristics, traditions, industries, resources and people." The information should also showcase "the educational facilities and opportunities in the United States and the cultural and creative achievements of the people and institutions of this country," and "modern American techniques in agriculture, industry, public health, medicine, dentistry, etc., which portray the technical competence of our professional men and women."[29] In spite of viewing the overseas information as propaganda, the Brookings Institute endorsed the expansive use of advertising, business, entertainment, and media to promote U.S. interests around the globe.

The Advertisement Council and the Department of State

The council called 1948–1949 a "year of intensified Cold War." The final year of the Freedom Train ended in January 1949. At the same time, the council continued to help the American Heritage Foundation work domestically in the battle for men's minds. W. B. Potter of the Eastman Kodak Company coordinated ten advertising agencies, including Leo Burnett, McCann-Erickson, Inc., and the J. Walter Thompson Company, in a "campaign to raise the level of active citizenship in America." The Leo Burnett Company "planned and produced" the "Good Citizen" booklet. The council claimed that 1,491,000 booklets were distributed and six billion radio listener impressions were made. In 1948, the Advertising Council became the "liaison organization" between American businesses advertising overseas and the Department of State. In this capacity, it produced "Advertising a New Weapon in the Worldwide Fight for Freedom."[30]

The "Armed Forces Prestige" campaign during the 1948–1949 council year was designed to both raise the image of the military and explain the restructuring of the military. Within the Department of Defense the council helped establish "an advertising committee composed of representatives from each of the Armed Forces." Coordinated by H.M Warren of National Carbon Company and advertising agencies J. Walter Thompson, N.W. Ayer & Son, Inc, and the Gardner Advertising Company, the committee worked with the White House, the Navy, the Air Force, the Marine Corps, and the Coast Guard. Committee wanted to raise the status of servicemen and women, as well as to explain to the public that the Armed Forces were unified under the Department of Defense, and "that the work of servicemen protects our national security and contributes to better peacetime living." CARE, during the same year, was coordinated by A.R. Stevens, American Tobacco Co. and N. W. Ayer & Son, Inc.[31]

"In 1948, the Advertising Council became the "liaison organization" between American businesses advertising overseas and the Department of State In this capacity the Advertising Council worked with the Department of State, to create "Advertising—A New Weapon in the Worldwide Fight for Freedom—A Guide for American Business Firms Advertising in Foreign Countries." In 1948, the 13-page brochure went out to business leaders across the United States. Done "in consultation with the United States Information Services of the Department of State," it explained to American advertisers how their overseas business could fulfill American propaganda needs.[32] In explaining to American businesses how to use advertising overseas, the booklet sold to the businesses both the importance of advertising and the idea that their pursuit of business overseas played a role in American foreign policy. Like many of the early campaigns sponsored by or promoting brand-name advertising, the council brochure justified the involvement of advertising in both foreign relations and the expansion of businesses overseas. The council feared that the spread of communism would threaten its version of free enterprise. In the brochure, the council detailed the criticism leveled at the

United States and American businesses overseas. It focused on how to advertise American products and simultaneously fight communism. It spelled out the specifics of how to advertise America and the specifics of what America should mean. It called on all American businesses and advertisers working overseas to participate not just to expand business, but to preserve America.

Instead of providing copy and advertising mats, like most of the council campaigns, the brochure explained what the advertising should say. The council described advertising as the "newest weapon of democracy" and tried to rally business by insisting that "your foreign advertising can greatly strengthen liberty-loving people overseas who are struggling against those who would destroy their freedom." The council pointed out to businesses that their "overseas advertising" could help by devoting "some of its product copy or institutional copy to removing misconceptions and telling some of the important facts about the United States, our way of life, or our foreign policy." The council recommended that for these ads businesses should use "both foreign publications and foreign editions of American publications." American businesses advertising around the globe would "play a vital role in saving other nations from succumbing to the police-state system and thereby save American and the American way of life." Like general American advertising techniques, the brochure urged advertiser and business to use the "double-barrel" technique, combining "product advertising" with "campaign themes," a technique that had proven "more effective than straight institutional advertisements."[33]

The council claimed that the Cold War needed to be fought on the "economic front," which involved "the industrial reconstruction of Europe and the development of commerce among all free countries of the world." They insisted that the Cold War also had "the propaganda front," which advertising could help combat. American advertising could help by "refuting the untruthful propaganda of other countries." With the help of business, advertising could do "a positive job of acquainting the peoples of the world with the facts about the United States." In Europe, it could help explain "the real reason for America's economic aid to Europe." Around the globe, advertising could help by "selling our conception of democracy as the path to peace and prosperity."[34]

The brochure pointed to the success of the War Advertising Council during World War II to prove that "Advertising can sell freedom," because "in wartime—Advertising proved itself to be a new and powerful weapon, helping to mobilize our people behind vital home front programs." The brochure claimed that "World War II could never have been won without the know-how, the drive and the facilities of American industry." It insisted that "the people at home would not have been organized in support of vital home front projects without the Billion Dollars of advertising space and time placed behind war campaigns." The council explained to businesses that since World War II, American advertising helped the government "solve non-controversial national problems and make democracy work better." It perpetuated the idea that advertising could convince anyone of anything, "if the copy is right—if it says what will best promote understanding—American industry will help win the world-wide war of ideas, and thus serve both its own and our country's vital interests." The other front was "the propaganda front," which entailed "selling our conception of democracy as the path to peace and prosperity." The Advertising Council fully acknowledged that what it was producing represented propaganda, while domestic campaigns like the Freedom Train and the "Miracle of America" it called persuasion. Members referred to these campaigns as part of the country being "constantly alert to protect our individual liberties and our free economic system." They called the campaigns advertising's contribution to "fighting dangerous anti-American forces at home."[35]

Council members equated communism with fascism and warned American businesses that it was "active in every part of the world today and endangers world markets everywhere." They feared what would happen in Europe politically and economically "as one American businessman, intimately familiar with the situation in Europe, said recently: This is our last chance to save our way of life. The chips are down, and we had better realize it." The overarching message to business was that the United States protects "our own liberties by helping them protect theirs." Connecting the global to the local, the brochure stated that in order to "save America and the American way of life," American businesses needed to advertise their products around the globe as part of the "world-wide struggle against the spread of totalitarianism."[36]

The first objective was "to remove misconceptions" by telling "the important facts about the United States," such as "our way of life" and "our foreign policy to peoples around the world." The other primary objective was "to make clear the reasons for American economic aid in 'Marshall Plan' countries." The brochure contained a list of propaganda statements being spread by the Soviet Union. According to the council, the Soviets insisted that "The venal American press, radio and motion pictures support dollar diplomacy" and that "American newspapers and movies are instruments of capitalism, imperialism, and expansionism." To the Soviets, bribery, blackmail, and the threat of the atomic bomb" were the ways that the United States manifested "true democracy." As well, the Soviets insisted that "tens of millions of dollars have been allocated to the FBI for the investigation of the loyalty of employees, a purge carried out at the bidding of the Special

Conference Committee of the National Association of Manufacturers." This accusation also meant that the Soviets viewed the country as "persecuting true democrats and progressives."[37]

Some of the primary misconceptions the council described about the United States were related to ideas about social class. It claimed that around the globe, people believed that "in the United States, a few rich families live extravagantly while most people live in poverty" and that "a few men-or a few families-or Big Business-have monopolies on our production and distribution." These ideas resulted in the mistaken notion that in the United States "Big Business runs the country with the aid of Congress." The Soviets, the council argued, claimed that "the grim specter of mass unemployment, of poverty and famine hangs suspended over the workers of the United States." The council claimed that in some countries only a "minority" realized that in the United States that "there are no rigid class lines."[38]

To counter these myths, the council recommended stating that "a few live extravagantly as in most countries, but poverty is less in America than almost anywhere in the world" and "most Americans live comfortably and are neither very poor nor very rich." Business in America they explained was "Big Business" in that it was owned by "thousands of small investors" and did not represent "monopolies as that word is understood in many countries." They insisted that wealth in the United States results from "mass production methods," just as they stressed in their domestic "Miracle of America" campaign. They claimed that the lack of rigid class lines could be demonstrated by the American education system where "the children of workers, merchants, business men and scientists all go to the same school together."[39]

According to the Advertising Council, the Marshall Plan had been "called a smoke screen for economic imperialism" and "a means of subjecting Europe economically and politically, and converting it into a military and strategic base, an economic and political block against the Soviet Union." To counteract this idea the brochure suggested that advertising copy stress that the United States sought to help "the economic recovery of many countries" in order "to raise the standards of living of all peoples." The United States wanted "to promote peace," "to enable free nations to protect their independence," and "to enable individuals to protect their liberty."[40]

The Advertising Council also devoted part of the brochure to explaining the purpose of the Department of State's United States Information Service and justifying the Advertising Council working in such a capacity. The council explained the mission of the United States Information Service of the Department of State. They said that the federal organization conducted "a broad program of international information and education in an effort to spread the truth about us to other peoples of the world." They used "radio, the press, motion pictures, libraries, cultural institutions and the international exchange of students, professors and specialists to foster understanding of the United States among the peoples of other countries." Another one of the major purposes of the United States Information Service was to engage businesses in overseas information.[41]

The Advertising Council's mission was to enhance the government's official programs through private initiative, which would not be held to the same scrutiny as the U.S. federal government. According to the council, the U.S. government did not believe that government operations alone could win the Cold War and felt it would require "the day-in, day-out relationships of private citizens and private organizations and industries with the people of other countries." It suggested that it was questionable whether industry should work so closely with the American government to promote specific ideas. The council warned that "the world-wide fight for freedom can be lost—and defeat would bring an end to our political and economic system. The battle, therefore, amply justifies the active cooperation and help of American industry."[42]

According to the council, overseas advertising could help American foreign policy objectives in two ways. Foremost, it could "devote some of its product copy to removing misconceptions and telling some of the important facts about the United States, our way of life, or our foreign policy." It could also dispel rumors in Economic Cooperation Administration (ECA) countries that aid given by the United States represented "economic imperialism." The brochure described a way to make every advertisement in a foreign market more than an advertisement for a product—by making every ad an ad for America.

The Advertising Council and the federal government viewed each and every product and advertisement as an advertisement for the entire American system. American businesses represented the country around the world. The council claimed that "American industries doing business overseas advertising cannot avoid being on the 'information' front. The copy—even the product copy—influences other peoples' attitudes toward the United States." Like most advertising material at the time, the council brochure claimed that if done correctly, advertising could help win the Cold War. The brochure also clearly stated that one of the nation's goals was to expand American business and America's business system into other countries: "industry's support of this campaign will help to hold present markets, develop new markets, and create goodwill for participating concerns in every country still free from Communist control."[43]

According to the brochure, economic aid without a message would be "ineffective . . . if foreign people do not understand our true motives in giving it." These missions in many ways paralleled the messages of the Freedom Train, the American Economic System, and the Brand Names Foundation. Like the messages put forth with the Freedom Train and the American Economic System brochures, the council brochure linked personal liberty with mass production, claiming that "it is the existence of individual liberty in the United States that makes possible increased production. (Individual liberty permits competition, competition fosters ingenuity, ingenuity results in more production.)" It suggested that businesses use this theme of personal liberty to persuade "liberals and socialists." It urged business to use "copy recalling the proud history of the struggle for liberty in each country," claiming that it would "touch liberals and socialists especially."[44]

The brochure warned businesses not to use certain ideas and phrases in their advertisements, so as not to offend or alienate potential supporters of the United States and potential consumers of American brand-name goods. For instance, "advertisements proclaiming the greatness of America, its wealth, its generosity—'brag' advertising-are more undesirable. The richness of America is distasteful to many." It insisted that the phrase "individual liberty," not "individual freedom," be used. It claimed, "The word 'democracy' means one thing to us, and a single-party dictatorship to those influenced by Communism." In light of the criticism leveled at the United States regarding the close relationship between business and government, it urged advertisers to "avoid any statement which Communists could twist into 'proof' that the United States Government is a tool of American business or that business is used as an instrument of government." In order to do this, it suggested using "specific examples using named workers" rather than generalized statements and to "stress the relative independence of American business from government direction, control, or stimulus." It also recommended avoiding "themes which, by emphasis on free enterprise in the American system, may give the impression that we seek to impose our system on the rest of the world."[45]

According to the council, it was important to "influence three elements in each country." These groups were "those who are leftist but not Communist," "those who are somewhat left of center," and "those who, in their economic thinking, are poised midway between the right and the left." It saw these groups as holding "the balance of power" and that "where they go determines which way their nations go." Those central groups were of premiere importance because "those whose democratic convictions are firm and whose economic status would disappear with Communism," did not need to be persuaded. "Disciplined Communist Party members" could not be converted, and it urged businesses not to "waste verbal ammunitions." The Ad Council encouraged businesses to downplay economics because "our 'prospects' have differing ideas about economics, and we need the support of all of them."

The best approach in its view was to not "attempt to sell free enterprise as an inseparable component of freedom and democracy."[46]

It recommended that "the general theme and copy suggestions for this campaign, in addition to their use in newspapers, magazines and radio advertising, can be adapted for use in the following: pamphlets, leaflets, house organs, outdoor posters, window cards, counter cards, motion pictures, letters from workers, publicity and speeches, employee contacts, exchange of persons." It urged businesses to encourage their workers to write friends and relatives in foreign countries, and to incorporate "some of the copy suggestions of this campaign for inclusion in their correspondence." It also urged companies to hold "special indoctrination projects for employees in overseas offices," and to use "publicity and speeches" in overseas markets. In other words, any information put out there in foreign markets should incorporate this campaign. For instance, "publicity releases to the overseas press and speeches by foreign office heads—whatever their prime purposes may be—can frequently contain factual matter which will forward the purposes of this campaign."

In spite of the Advertising Council's efforts, American business did not immediately begin practicing what the council recommended. The council and the Department of State continued to encourage American business to be an active participant in overseas information. They claimed that they found business participation "disappointing." They reported that "most of American industry was not yet stimulated to take an active part in the American propaganda effort."[47] By 1950, the council's brochure had not changed the advertising of many of the American businesses operating overseas. The tactic of offering suggestions, rather than preparing full copy as with domestic campaigns, had proven ineffective.

Advertising Council vice president Allan M. Wilson released statements to the press asserting that the guide produced by the council had not succeeded in encouraging advertising overseas. *The New York Times* reported in 1950 that the "Advertising Council Program to Combat Lying Propaganda Held to have been Slowing." The article described the creation of advertising packets in the United States where "volunteer 'task-force' advertising agencies . . . usually donate their services for council sponsored campaigns," whereas the overseas campaign involved "no actual ads, merely a detailed outline of information for advertising messages, recommendations on major misconceptions, cautions against boastful statements, and warnings against those easily twisted by Soviet propagandists." The council held out as a model a "series of ads" prepared by the International General Electric Company that "told the story of the American way by showing how typical GE workers lived."

However, the guide was determined to not be enough so E.I du Pont de Nemours & Co. prepared new ads. In addition, the Export Advertising Association "offered voluntarily to prepare sample ads based on the council's program." According to Wilson, " 'we hear constantly of the dangers to this country.' " Dangers, he believed that were "likely to result from the widespread propaganda against us by the Communists." He urged business and government to work together, claiming that "business leaders aware of the dangers see the need for action. Government officials, particularly those in the State Department want to see something done on a large scale.' "

In spite of the ambivalence from many American businesses about using their foreign advertising as part of the Cold War information campaign, the Advertising Council made progress in creating an international brand for the country, symbolized by red, white, and blue, and stars and stripes. In doing so, it permanently blurred the lines between advertising, information, and propaganda. Early public diplomacy initiatives, such as the Fulbright Program, the VOA, and the Smith-Mundt Act, while subject to revision over the decades, lasted into the twenty-first century. With the Korean War, the Advertising Council's international role expanded. To mark the council's tenth year, Theodore Repplier, president of the council, wrote a brief statement about how "the information job keeps broadening." He said that because of "the world-wide anti-American Soviet propaganda mill, this country had an international information problem which scarcely existed ten years ago." He claimed that "the past year was one in which the Council faced the fact that the mass information job had broadened."

The council continued to fight "the bitter international propaganda war" by serving on government committees, continuing CARE until 1957, supporting the Crusade for Freedom, and organizing a series of Round Table discussions. The council helped countries in Europe form "European Advertising Councils." The 1951 council meeting in Washington focused on "the international situation and its relation to our domestic affairs."[49] With even Advertising Council members not yet expanding their businesses overseas, encouraging businesses at home remained as important as attracting markets overseas.

CHAPTER 5

Saving the World through Religious Revival

As the 1940s came to an end, religious worship emerged as a free enterprise tenet and the network grew to include churches and synagogues; religious institutions and practitioners embraced persuasive information as a means to increase religious participation. While publicly the council supported religion in general, several major council members supported evangelical Christianity and helped it gain political legitimacy in the Cold War ideological battles. Many council members were concerned about communist restrictions on religion and wanted to connect capitalism to religion, opening the door for free enterprise supporters to promote religion in several ways. Publicly, they developed the Religion in American Life (RIAL) campaigns.[1] Like most Advertising Council campaigns, RIAL tried to be as inclusive as possible so that no potential markets would be alienated; however, many of the Protestant endorsers considered free enterprise to be "God's system" and framed foreign policy as a religious mission to spread the American system.[2] While the council campaigns promoted Protestantism, Catholicism, and Judaism, behind the scenes, council members, such as Hearst Publishing and Henry Luce of Time-Life, Inc., promoted Protestantism by advancing the career preacher Billy Graham, whose national and international campaigns helped blend evangelicalism with the American brand.[3]

RIAL went on to become one of the council's longest running campaigns, and the council took credit for increasing national church and synagogue attendance in the 1950s and 1960s.[4] Described in the press as an "experimental program to stimulate church attendance and greater spirituality among Americans by means of a national advertising campaign," the first campaign was considered so successful that it became an annual campaign into the 1990s.[5] Founded in 1949, with an annual budget of 200,000 dollars, RIAL was designed for the purpose of " 'selling' religion through mass media." The organizers credited themselves with helping inspire the "religious boom" during the 1950s.[6] The RIAL campaign originated with a campaign done by the United Church Canvass. This organization began in the 1930s with the intent of using advertisements to increase church attendance. Originally a predominately Protestant organization, by 1942 it included churches and synagogues.

Using advertisements created by the J. Walter Thompson Company, community participation in the United Church Campaigns went from 150 communities in 1942 to 1,200 in 1948. By 1947, the Federal Council of Churches, the Synagogue Council of America, Church World Services, and 17 other religious organizations had joined forces in the RIAL campaign. Described in *The New York Times* as "a national interfaith movement," the Ad Council's RIAL campaign began in the fall of 1949. The chairman of the campaign was Charles E. Wilson, council member, and president of General Electric. The campaign ran from November 1 through Thanksgiving in newspapers and across radio networks, urging people to attend churches and synagogues. Wilson engaged Truman in the campaign by sending him a telegram stressing the importance of Americans participating in religious worship.[7] The 1949 campaign included the United Church Canvass, the Federal Council of Churches, the Synagogue Council of America, and "18 other religious groups including Catholic Churches." The J. Walter Thompson Company took the lead on RIAL.[8] Religion in American Life was run by a committee of laymen belonging to the Protestant, Roman Catholic, and Jewish faiths. It was considered a "drive by American businessmen to promote larger congregations in church and synagogues."[9]

God's System

Several prominent backers of advertising- and brand-based free enterprise had extensive Protestant religious backgrounds and viewed free enterprise capitalism in religious terms. They believed as did some of the country's early Puritan ministers, such as John Winthrop and John Cotton, when they described their mission in the "new world," that they were establishing a "City Upon a Hill," an example of an ideal religious society that others would look to for inspiration and guidance. They believed that capitalism was also part of that divine model and referred to free enterprise as "God's system."[10] The spreading of this system represented a continuation of the view that the United States represented a shining example of what God wanted a society to be.[11] Advertising Council architect James Webb Young worked for the Freedman's Aid Society of the Methodist Church, which operated 20 schools for African Americans in the south. He began his career as a book salesman, selling Bibles and books for "Methodist ministers and Sunday-school teachers," before he came to work for J. Walter Thompson's Cincinnati, Ohio, office. Stanley Resor had also been a Bible salesman while in college.[12] When William Procter chose the name Ivory for his soap, his inspiration came from a biblical passage. *Time-Life* creator, Henry Luce, grew up as the son of Protestant missionaries in China.[13] His declaration of the American Century represented a modern version of the "City Upon the Hill" concept. In 1951, he published *Life's Picture History of Western Man*, which described itself as a "spiritual biography of Western Man" and depicted the United States as a part of a long tradition of Christian civilization.[14]

Religion in American Life

In November 1949, the Advertising Council launched the first annual RIAL campaign, programmed, organized, and run solely by the J. Walter Thompson Co. and coordinated by Robert W. Boggs of the Union Carbide and Carbon Corporation. Charles E. Wilson, president of General Electric, was chairman of the campaign and General Foods, Hearst, Procter & Gamble, NBC, ABC, *Time*, Eastman Kodak, General Motors, and Ford were among the companies represented on the council during the late 1940s. The campaign theme designed by J. Walter Thompson was "Find yourself through faith—come to church this week." Advertisers, outdoor advertisers, broadcasters, and publishers contributed an estimated 3 million dollars worth of time and ad space, a rate of 1 million a week, which made the campaign the most supported of all the Advertising Council's "first-time" sponsorships.[15] The council's annual report, "How Business Helps Solve Public Problems," referred to the campaign as "a nation-wide program designed to re-emphasize in the minds of all Americans the full significance of religion in our daily lives and the importance of religious institutions." In order to emphasize "the spiritual values in American Life," the Outdoor Advertising Agency contributed 5,200, 24 sheet posters, newspapers ran upwards of 3,000 advertisements. In addition, it claimed that 1,800 newspapers across the nation ran "news items or editorials on the subject of religion during the month of the drive." Like council campaigns over the years, it created community activities for the month of the campaign. It claimed that during the 1949 campaign 2,000 communities participated. The council claimed that across the nation church attendance increased during the month.

President Truman endorsed and promoted the first RIAL campaign with a speech delivered at the White House and broadcasted over the radio. The speech that kicked off the campaign was broadcast on the last Sunday of October over most of the major radio stations on ABC, CBS, and NBC.[16] The text of his speech was printed in newspapers across the nation. Truman stated that the United States had been "a deeply religious nation from its earliest beginning." This foundation, he claimed, allowed the United States to grow "from a small country in the wilderness to a position of great strength and great responsibility among the family of nations." He expressed concern that Americans took religion "too much for granted." He emphasized a need for Americans to have "active faith" so that Americans can "strive to fulfill our destiny in the world." Charles Wilson was quoted in *The New York Times* as saying that the RIAL campaign ended on Thanksgiving Day to help Americans recognize the need for "faith in God" to cope with conflict around the globe. In support of the campaign, Bing Crosby broadcast from Hollywood on the importance of religious faith and training.[17] Mayor O'Dwyer of New York City officially proclaimed November "Religion in American Life" month and urged New Yorkers to "bear witness to their gratitude in God and to make their faith manifest anew in their churches and synagogues." Governors in 29 states either issued proclamations in support of the first RIAL campaign or mentioned church attendance in their Thanksgiving Day statements.[18] The 1949 RIAL campaign proved to be such a success that in January 1950 the Ad Council announced plans for a 1950 campaign. Charles E. Wilson, president of General Electric, was reappointed head of the campaign. Wilson claimed that the campaign had improved labor relations, announcing to the press that "even relations between labor and management are better in this atmosphere." He insisted that "disunity between labor and management will never be settled except at the spiritual level and through education and understanding." The 1950 campaign sought to create a religious revival throughout the nation and included the participation of 3,000 communities and 21 national religious organizations. Wilson asserted that "the people of America are seeking a renewal of the spiritual life as a solution to many of the problems which plague us and the world today." The RIAL campaign announced that the objectives for the 1950 campaign were "to emphasize the importance of all religious institutions as the foundation of American life and to urge all Americans to attend and support the church or synagogue of their individual choice." Truman endorsed the 1950 campaign also, issuing a statement that "these are times that demand the vision and fortitude of men of faith such as never before in the history of the world." Truman also stressed that "the religious strength of our nation is the heart of America's greatness." The 1950 campaign received over 4 million dollars worth of donated advertising and advertising space. Wilson received credit for increasing religious participation and remained head of the campaign in 1951, in spite of taking on the role as director of defense mobilization during the Korean War.[19] The RIAL campaign expanded onto television and became a staple of 1950s culture.[20]

In 1950–51 Charles E. Wilson, at the time director of the Office of Defense Mobilization where he had organized American businesses during the war, led the RIAL program. The council claimed that since the campaign began "reports from community after community reveal that church attendance was stepped-up from 10% to as high as 25%." The council claimed that for the year 1950–1951, over 48,000 billboards carried council messages for campaigns such as the U.S. Defense Bonds, American Economic System, American Red Cross, and Religion in American Life. Over 5,000 were RIAL billboards.[21] For the 1951 campaign, Wilson maintained his role as the head of Religion in American Life while remaining on as director of the Office of Defense Mobilization.[22] For the year Wilson claimed that "we must support our spiritual values without which the others would have little validity in the present crisis."

Companion projects also emerged. For instance, the American Bible Society coordinated its annual campaign the "Bible Reading Project" with the 1951 RIAL campaign. The annual Bible campaign had grown since the early 1940s from a national campaign for the armed services to include Bible readers in 38 countries. In promotion of Bible reading, the campaign had given away over 13 million bookmarks. In 1951, American Bible Society made an official announcement that its campaign would be "in step" with the RIAL campaign. During the Advertising Council's tenth anniversary year, RIAL received support from "twenty-one national and local religious groups." The campaign focused on "the importance of religion in family and community life." The campaign reportedly received more than 4 million dollars worth of donated radio, television, newspaper, and billboard advertisements. The council claimed that 3,278 "cities and towns tied in their local efforts with the national program." Over 300 "network radio and television messages" created an "estimated circulation of 126 millions radio and television home impressions."[23]

During the 1952–53 council year, RIAL received the endorsement of President Elect Eisenhower, who delivered a "Thanksgiving Day message carried by major radio and TV networks." In addition to the 300 messages "contributed" through the Radio and Television Allocation Plans, the "Jam Handy organization again produced two TV film shorts for RIAL which were included in the kit sent to 111 TV stations and the four major networks." In 1952, the United Synagogue campaign connected its annual campaign with the RIAL campaign.[24] In 1952, the RIAL campaign continued to take credit for increased attendance at religious services across the nation. Citing the importance of advertising, it also took credit for an increase in the size of Protestant, Roman Catholic, and Jewish congregations. Reportedly, American church attendance increased to 88,500,000, representing an increase of 9 percent since 1940 and 11 percent since 1930. The slogan for the 1952 campaign was "Show Them the Way . . . This Week" and public service ads ran in newspapers, magazines, public transportation and on billboards and television. In 1952, the RIAL campaign, like other Ad Council affiliated campaigns, issued awards to communities across the country for strengthening religion in their communities as a way of encouraging broader participation in such campaigns.[25] That year James Webb Young presided over an Advertising Council Round Table discussion among Harvard, Columbia, and Princeton University professors regarding religion. Held on April 14, 1952, at the Waldorf Astoria in New York City, the council called the session "The Moral and Religious Basis of American Society." The group concluded that the United States had a "religious foundation" and called for the further imbedding of religion into the Ad Council's brand for the United States.[26]

Christian Free Enterprisers

RIAL was not the only means of persuasive information that the council and its affiliates used for the promotion of religion to combat communism and advance free enterprise.[27] In the same year that the RIAL campaign started, Advertising Council members Hearst Publishing and Time Life Inc. began promoting the little known preacher Billy Graham. He went on to convert millions around the globe and meet with every American president into the twenty-first century.[28] Graham, like the council, promoted the free enterprise system and effectively used mass advertising and mass media at home and abroad to increase his audience and the number of converts. In his sermons, he told Americans that patriotism meant worshipping God, going to church, paying taxes, and participating in the free enterprise system.[29]

In 1949, evangelical preacher Billy Graham held a series of revival meetings in Los Angeles, known as the Los Angeles Crusade. Graham set up tents in a parking lot in order to hold a three week crusade. This effort attracted the attention of newspaper publisher William Randolph Hearst, who sent out a memo to his publishing staff to "puff Graham." The *LA Examiner* and *Herald Express* ran headlines and put Graham's crusade on the front page and soon other papers did as well.[30] This coverage brought more people to the revival meetings and the Los Angeles Crusade ended up lasting nine weeks.[31] The tent held 6,280 and as of November 14, 1949, 250,000 people had attended. Henry Luce made Graham a national name by running an article in *Time* on Graham's crusade in November 1949 while the LA event was still going on. *Time* referred to the Los Angeles Crusade as "the largest revival tent in history." The article quoted Graham as saying "we are standing on the verge of a great national revival." *Time* magazine even mentioned that William Randolph Hearst increased Graham's audience in Los Angeles by issuing his "puff Graham" memo. A week later, *Life* ran photographs of the Los Angeles Crusade.[32]

By running a series of articles, *Time* chronicled Graham throughout 1950 as he conducted revivals across the United States. The article titles, such as "Heaven, Hell & Judgment Day," "Revival," and "Evangelism," took on religious tones and promoted more revivals. The magazine reported both the numbers who attended Graham events and the number of people who came forward to make "decisions for Christ." *Time* discussed a wave of revivals happening throughout the country, mentioning that in the beginning of November 1950, three cities of the East coast hosted "big revivals." Luce's *Life* featured Graham's campaign in the South. That year, Graham began conducting campaigns in football stadiums, drawing large crowds—36,000 at the University of South Carolina football stadium, where 7,000 people made "decisions for Christ." In Ponce de Leon Ballpark, Graham attracted over 20,000. A six week revival in Portland, Oregon, attracted 632,000 with 8,000 converts.[33]

According to *The New York Times,* 150,000 attended Graham's tour of New England in the spring of 1950. In Boston, where an estimated 50,000 attended, Graham called upon Truman to declare a national day of prayer. Graham spoke at Boston Common, the same location where the historic preacher George Whitefield spoke in 1740. Whitefield, the Methodist preacher, brought Methodism to the American colonies, often called the First Great Awakening. Not only did Graham choose this historic location, he quoted Whitefield, asking the crowd "Shall God Reign in New England?"[34] In 1950, Advertising Council member *Reader's Digest* published an article written by Graham about "Why Don't Churches Practice Brotherhood?" In 1950, Graham also began his long-standing tradition of meeting with American presidents. Meeting with Truman in response to the outbreak of the Korean War, Truman and Graham prayed together in Truman's office for "divine guidance for the nation and its Chief Executive." Graham also urged Truman to declare a day of national prayer, which *Time* noted Truman declined to do.[35]

In 1951, *Time* magazine noted Graham's enthusiasm over his perception of an increase in religious activity across the United States. *Time* quoted Graham as stating that there were "more Christians in Congress than in many years." In 1951, Graham expanded his use of mass media from radio and television to film. He made a movie, *Mr. Texas,* which he called "the first Christian Western." The same year Luce also shined the national spotlight on Protestant minister Oral Roberts, featuring him in *Life* and calling him Billy Graham's "rival."[36]

In 1952, *Time* magazine called Graham "the hottest Protestant soul-saver since the late Billy Sunday." The magazine noted that Graham produced "his own TV and radio shows (cost: $20,000 a week)" and that he was "president and featured player of his own motion-picture company." It also emphasized that Graham held "month-long crusades in cities from coast-to-coast." Billy Graham crusaded in Washington, D.C., during the 1952 election. A change in legislation allowed him to preach from the steps of the Capitol building. He delivered two sermons broadcast across the nation by ABC radio, and spoke to public audiences on the steps of the Capitol and private audiences at the Pentagon.[37] Graham set up in Washington for five weeks of revival meetings, attracting crowds of 5,000 to 6,000 a night at the National Guard Armory.[38] After nine weeks in Washington, D.C., a reported 500,000 saw Graham and 6,244 converted. Graham reported to *Time* that while he was disappointed that Truman did not attend, he planned to eventually meet with every presidential candidate.[39]

Religious Campaigns and the Eisenhower Years

While Graham had met President Truman, he developed an advisory relationship with President Eisenhower. Once elected, Eisenhower continued to support the importance of religion in Cold War struggles and the RIAL campaign. He established a relationship with Billy Graham, eventually coming to rely on Graham to help with the country's turbulence over Civil Rights issues. In the fall of 1953 when Graham met with Eisenhower, he claimed that Eisenhower "agreed with him that the United States was 'experiencing the greatest religious renaissance in our history.'" According to *Time* magazine, Graham told Eisenhower that "the people look upon the President 'as a great spiritual leader more than a political leader.'"[40]

As the Eisenhower administration took charge, Charles Wilson called for a reassessment of how advertising could build the role of religion in American communities and among Americans.[41] He reiterated the importance of religion in resolving labor disputes and called for "'the injection of religious and spiritual considerations' in management and labor relationships as 'one of the greatest needs' in this country." President Eisenhower kicked off the 1953 campaign, the fifth, with radio and television broadcasts. He went on the RIAL radio show in 1953 and made the keynote speech for the campaign, claiming that the United States had undergone a "religious revival."[42] Stating that "by strengthening religious institutions, the Committee on Religion in American Life is helping to keep America good. Thus it helps each of us keep America great," he furthered the notion of brand America as a religious nation. In 1953, when Procter & Gamble set a new pattern for inserting council public service advertising into prerecorded television shows, RIAL messages were among the campaigns incorporated.[43]

Eisenhower continued to endorse and promote religion as a weapon in the Cold War speaking at a national conference organized by the Foundation for Religious Action in Social and Civil Order, an organization whose membership included Henry Ford 2d, Henry Luce, and Charles E. Wilson of GE, called "The Spiritual Foundations of Our Democracy." Other speakers at the event were Dr. Robert L. Johnson, formerly of the United States Information Agency, and Thomas Murray of the Atomic Energy Commission.[44] In 1955, the J. Walter Thompson agency's packet of prepared advertising material went out to 7,500 newspapers across the country. The campaign emphasized instilling religious values in one's children. Speaking on behalf of the American legion's "Back to God" campaign, Eisenhower declared that the founding fathers recognized "God as the authority of individual rights."[45]

By the end of the 1950s, the RIAL campaign took credit for helping increase religious participation over the 1950s. The Ad Council claimed credit for increasing American church attendance and the RIAL board estimated that a million more Americans attended worship services on a regular basis in part because of the RIAL campaign. The tenth annual campaign, in 1958, used the slogan "Find the Strength for Your Life . . . Worship Together This Week." Advertising, coordinated by the Ad Council, went out on "billboards, car cards, television, and radio and in newspapers and magazines." Mayors from hundreds of towns and cities, and governors from "most states" issued proclamations in support of the RIAL campaign.[46]

For the 1959 campaign, 8 million dollars worth of advertising and advertising space were donated, which included 7,000 billboards, 8,000 three-sheet posters, and 84,000 "car cards in buses, street cars, subway and commuter trains." At the Advertising Council awards luncheon in 1959, the council issued a series of awards to participants in the RIAL campaign, including J. Walter Thompson, the American Express Company, International Business Machine Corporation, and Union Carbide.[47] By 1960, the council claimed to have helped increase church and synagogue attendance by 35 percent over 1950. However, it insisted that the RIAL campaign continued because 60 million Americans still did not have a religious affiliation.

The RIAL campaign helped religious institutions become a part of the persuasive information apparatus and allowed for yet another means for delivering a message. For instance, during the 1960 elections, the American Heritage Foundation and the Religion in American Life, Inc., took politics to religious institutions. As a part of their drive to encourage Americans to vote in the elections, they asked religious leaders to issue statements encouraging participation in the upcoming elections.[48] The Sunday before elections, religious leaders urged eligible voters to vote, calling voting "a moral obligation."[49]

American Christianity Overseas

In 1952 Graham began spreading his crusade around the globe. While not an official spokesman of the United States, his messages spread the association of evangelical Christianity with the United States. His first trips did not draw the crowds that attended in later years but they did help his team establish a strategy for marketing future appearances. Graham traveled to London, where he did not draw large crowds, and he also visited the troops in Korea, met with Chiang Kai-shek in Formosa, and traveled to Hong Kong. The five nights he spent in Korea, preaching primarily to Koreans for three nights, and for two nights to American GI's, showed more promise with over 1,000 people allegedly converted during that time.[50]

In 1954, Graham made another attempt to save souls in Europe, embarking on a three month "Crusade for Britain" and touring Western Europe. *Time* magazine and *The New York Times* gave Graham extensive coverage throughout his time in England. They noted that British church membership was only between 5 and 15 percent of the population compared with 59 percent in the United States. The events were held at Harringay Arena. Unlike his previous trip to England, before his arrival, his promotional team placed advertising throughout London. The advertising campaign included 600 bus posters, 150 billboards, 3,000 units of "smaller outdoor advertising," and 1,500 "tube-station posters." Graham's team also handed out 20,000 stickers and organized 1,000 volunteers. The volunteers were to work in shifts of 200 for the 11,000 seat Harringay Arena. Graham's team also trained 2,700 "counselors" to take talk to the people that made "decisions for Christ." The training of these counselors to deal with people who had converted was generally a part of getting an area ready before Graham arrived.[51] Within weeks, *Time* referred to the country as "Billy's Britain." It reported that Graham filled Harringay every night and converted 3,687 people in two weeks.[52] According to *The New York Times,* Graham became one of London's "top attractions." For one event, 40,000 children were bussed to see Graham with television/film star Roy Rogers and his horse trigger.[53]

The Graham crusade hit the 1,000,000 mark in May 1954. By the end of Graham's crusade in Britain, he attracted crowds so large that he rented out sports stadiums. *Time* reported that "34,586 Decisions" had been made. According to *Time*, during the last two nights of the campaign 67,000 saw

Graham at London's White City Stadium and 120,000 at Wembley Stadium, reportedly "more than the 1948 Olympics."[54] The estimated total of those who attended in Britain was 1,750,000.[55] *Life* featured Graham receiving a blessing from the Archbishop of Canterbury. Toward the end of the British crusade, Graham met with Winston Churchill.[56] From London, Graham went on to Sweden, Germany, Denmark, Finland, Holland, and France.[57]

Upon returning from his trip, Graham said that he had preached to 2 million people at 300 rallies. He asserted that Britain and Europe were experiencing a "spiritual reawakening," which he saw as essential for preventing a "third world war." He claimed that the closer he got to the Iron Curtain in Finland and Sweden, where he argued there was less of a fear of the Russians, there was greater "spiritual hunger." When he met with President Eisenhower, he told the president that Western Europe was undergoing "a religious awakening that was bound to have tremendous social, political and economic consequences." Graham also publicly claimed that around the world a growing interest in religion existed, including in Russia.[58]

On October 25, 1954, *Time* featured Graham on the cover. In the article titled "The New Evangelist," *Time* referred to Graham as "the best-known, most talked-about Christian leader in the world today, barring the Pope." It reported that between 1949 and 1954, Graham "preached personally to 12 million people and brought 200,000 of them to various stages of Christian commitment." In the article Graham's public relations manager described how Billy Graham had become a brand. Comparing Graham to a Cadillac, he said "when you see an advertisement for a Cadillac, it just says Cadillac and shows you a picture. Billy is like a Cadillac. We don't have to explain."[59] In 1955, Graham filled Madison Square Garden in New York. He told the audience of 22,000 that both Sir Winston Churchill and President Eisenhower believed that only religious revival would save the world, particularly since Americans, Graham said, feared the hydrogen bomb.[60]

In the spring of 1955 Graham went to Scotland for a six week crusade.[61] He also conducted crusades in London's Wembley Stadium. For the first time, a member of the British royal family, the Duchess of Kent, aunt of Queen Elizabeth II, attended one of Graham's services at Wembley Stadium. Unlike his earlier crusade in Britain, *The New York Times* reported that Graham was no longer considered controversial in Britain.[62] In one week in London, 420,000 attended Graham's events, and 20,000 made "decisions for Christ." The British Broadcasting Company broadcasted Graham nationwide. Between his six weeks in Scotland and his week in London, 3,139,365 attended Graham's crusade. Graham also had the opportunity to preach for Queen Elizabeth II and her husband.[63] From Britain, Graham went on to France to conduct his first "Crusade for Christ" there, where he said that he would be careful not to offend Catholics. The five day crusade was attended by 42,883, and 2,254 made "decisions for Christ." *The New York Times* called it "the largest revival meeting in the history of French evangelism." From France, Graham went on to Switzerland, addressing 60,000 people in two Zurich football stadiums, and from there to Germany, preaching to 40,000.[64]

In 1956, Graham went to India, the Philippines, Taiwan, and Japan. In India, he preached to over 100,000.[65] In Manila, 25,000 filled a stadium in spite of a statement issued by the Archbishop of Manila. In Taiwan, Mme. Chiang Kai-shek, wife of the Chinese Nationalist president, joined Graham on the stage and joined in the singing of hymns. He spent seven days in Japan, where he spoke of the growth of Christianity in Asia.[66]

Though Graham's campaigns had far more influence regarding religion overseas than any of the council's activities, the council did try briefly to involve itself in religious activities overseas. Wilson urged the council to expand the RIAL campaign overseas. He claimed that Radio Free Europe, the CIA run counterpart to VOA, received many letters from listeners behind the Iron Curtain asking for an increase in religious programming.[67] In 1956, the Advertising Council finally followed through on Wilson's call to create a religious campaign overseas, launching the "Religious Overseas Aid."[68] The campaign only lasted several years, but it demonstrated the council's ongoing commitment to associate the American brand with religion.

Religion remained a part of the American brand and Cold War policy.[69] Publicly, the Advertising Council projected an image of religious inclusiveness and tolerance, while privately many members promoted Protestant ideas and linked Protestantism with free enterprise capitalism. The country retained the idea that it represented "the City Upon the Hill" with a religious duty to lead the world into the twenty-first century. Billy Graham went on to convert millions around the globe to Christianity and to meet with and give spiritual advice to every American president into the twenty-first century. And while the council's overseas religious campaigns proved short lived, the domestic RIAL campaign continued into the 1990s.[70]

CHAPTER 6

"The Crusade for Freedom"

With the 1950s, came further development in the American Cold War overseas broadcasting, information, and cultural diplomacy programs, and continued support from advertisers and brand-name manufacturers. The Ad Council and affiliates from publishing organizations such as *Reader's Digest* and *Time-Life* became involved in covert psychological operations working with the CIA to develop covert broadcasts and public campaigns. These operations brought American propaganda to Eastern Europe and enhanced the appearance of a consensus in the United States regarding the Cold War. They helped develop Radio Free Europe/Radio Liberty, the official sponsor the Free Europe Committee, the public fund-raising campaign "The Crusade for Freedom" and the balloon and leaflet campaign, "Winds of Freedom." While eventually, these activities would become more formalized with the United States Information Agency (USIA) and be officially called public diplomacy at the time the council's participation helped maintain a cover. Years later, it would be revealed that these operations were actually CIA programs whose funding through 1972 came primarily from Congress. Once revealed, the programs became an official part of the American international information programs and a part of the Broadcasting Board of Governors (BBG). In the twenty-first century, the programs were considered one of the reasons that the United States won the Cold War, but in 1950, they were offered up as the private alternative to the government run radio station Voice of America.[1]

Planning

In 1946, General Lucius Clay began discussing with the State Department the possibilities of creating alternatives to the VOA. His goal gained legitimacy with the 1947 National Security Council directive NSC 4-A, which called for the director of the CIA to conduct psychological warfare using surrogate radio stations. The goal was to create radio stations that would not be restricted in the same way as the official government broadcaster, VOA. Since VOA was the official U.S. radio station broadcasting overseas, the content faced government oversight and creating covert stations could avoid such restrictions.[2] Those involved presented Radio Free Europe as a private alternative to the government run broadcasting and information services. Even though the VOA had been operating since World War II and had been expanding since the Smith-Mundt Act of 1948, dropping leaflets from balloons and broadcasting for "waging psychological warfare" was still considered "experimental."[3]

The "Crusade for Freedom" announced the campaign in a press release on April 26, 1950. This announcement marked the ending of the confidential planning of the project in which Allen Dulles, then General Eisenhower, General Lucius Clay, C.D. Jackson, Henry Luce of *Time-Life* and Dewitt Wallace of *Readers Digest* had been among the participants.[4] George Kennan participated in recruiting members for the committee and many of the directors over the years had worked during World War II in covert operations, intelligence gathering or psychological operations.[5]

By 1950, the Advertising Council had proven that advertising represented a vital resource for the U.S. government. As the advertising trade publication *Advertising Age* noted, due to the council's noteworthy "public service advertising," the profession of advertising had become a "characteristically American equipment for the success in war and in peace, and its function and values have been recorded clearly in the history of the United States during the past nine years."[6] Thus, the use of advertising to raise money from Americans to build radio towers and send balloons carrying leaflets and newsletters to foreign countries went largely unchallenged. It also went unchallenged that an influential *Time-Life* editor, C. D. Jackson, and important American generals, Lucius D. Clay and Dwight D. Eisenhower, worked with advertisers to build an organization that gathered information and generated "propaganda." In addition to being the editor of *Fortune* magazine, and a confidant of Henry Luce, C.D. Jackson also became a "psychological operations specialist" during World War II and organized the Advertising Council's World Trade Campaign. General Lucius D. Clay served as part of the administration of western Germany and helped orchestrate the Berlin airlift in 1948–1949.[7] General Eisenhower launched the first Crusade for Freedom in September 1950, at the same time that the Advertising Council ads for the Marshall Plan started appearing in Britain.[8]

The Official Sponsor

The official story about the organization said that the National Committee for a Free Europe (NCFE) formed in June 1949 when a group of private citizens organized to help "exiled leaders from the prisoner countries of Central Europe" and used their stories to inspire "peoples behind the Iron Curtain." In order to reach the people of Eastern Europe, the NCFE intended to create its own broadcasting facilities to provide a private alternative to the government run VOA.[9] In February 1950, the NCFE began developing "the Crusade." In their press release, the NCFE claimed to be taking up the call put forth by President Truman and Secretary of State Acheson to the American Society of Newspaper Editors that private citizens needed to "join the government in the battle for men's minds" with "a stepped-up Campaign for Truth." President Truman quickly endorsed the goals of the National Committee for a Free Europe and thanked the committee sending them a letter May 1, 1950 to thank them for responding to the call he put out on April 20 when he "emphasized the important role of private groups and organizations in this great endeavor."[10]

Publicly, the Advertising Council started the "Crusade for Freedom" to raise money for Radio Free Europe (RFE) and eventually, Radio Free Asia and the Free Europe Press.[11] Officially, the National Committee for a Free Europe (NCFE) sponsored Radio Free Europe and the balloon operations into Eastern Europe and General Lucius D. Clay orchestrated the fundraising campaign with the Advertising Council.[12] NCFE organized formally in 1949 with "two aims" to create "propaganda services to oppressed peoples," and to develop "a huge intelligence and information service." They considered Radio Free Europe "a tough slugging weapon of propaganda," and the goal of the propaganda to prevent "the integration of the Iron Curtain countries into the Soviet empire."[13]

Broadcasts

While the fund raising part of the campaign did not start until September 1950, the first broadcast of Radio Free Europe occurred on July 4, 1950. The CIA's Special Procedures Group provided transmitters.[14] Initially, one station broadcast programming to "Bulgaria, Czechoslovakia, Hungary, Poland, Romania and Albania." The mission of the broadcasts was fighting "the Big Lies of Communism with the Truth" and convincing listeners that there was a global struggle pitting "world freedom versus world tyranny," with the hope that the programming might encourage nonviolent uprising[15] Though the

CIA actually provided the transmitters, the crusade claimed to have raised enough money from 1950 to 1952 to help Radio Free Europe go from one "low-powered transmitter" to "thirteen hard-hitting freedom stations in West Germany and Portugal." In addition to the expansion of RFE, the Crusade funded Radio Free Asia broadcasts in three languages and launched "millions of balloon-borne leaflets bearing messages of freedom."[16] The money raised by the crusade represented only a fraction of the total cost of the broadcast network, but the CIA involvement and government funding of the network remained covert until the 1970s.[17]

Radio Free Europe and Radio Free Asia served as both broadcasting networks and intelligence gathering services. They considered the broadcasting to be "propaganda services to oppressed peoples." They hoped to create "animosity" between Russia and the Eastern European countries receiving broadcasting. For instance, sports programming would try to exploit rivalries between eastern countries.[18] Radio Free Europe programming included "newscast analysis and commentary," as well as "drama, music, interviews, exposes, quiz, religious, youth, literary, labor, farm and satirical programs." The broadcasts also included "political and military comments," and "descriptions of life in the West."[19] Eventually, RFE even broadcast a 15 minute soap opera into Czechoslovakia six days a week. Initially, Radio Free Europe produced the broadcasts in New York and shipped them overseas. By 1952, they had enough money to build production facilities in Munich with 22 studio and six control rooms. Over the years, producers had to balance the desire to sell the "American Way of Life" to foreign nations with the fact that repeatedly market research, "intelligence" gathering, showed Eastern European audiences were not receptive to broadcasting that overtly promoted the United States.[20]

As per the original NCFE aims, the Radio Free Europe stations and offices in Europe also served as intelligence gathering organization.[21] While their primary focus was on the reception of the Radio Free Europe broadcasts and printed material delivered by balloons, they also provided general intelligence gathering on life behind the iron curtain. One concern was how the stations compared to VOA broadcasts.[22] Reports claimed that most households listened to RFE, VOA or Britain's BBC, but the Soviets more severely jammed VOA and BBC.[23] Other types of intelligence gathering included contacting "refugees" or "escapees" from Eastern European countries.[24] They made every effort to determine how many households had radios, particularly in Bulgaria, Czechoslovakia, Hungary, Poland, and Romania. They made every effort to intercept broadcasts from Eastern European radio stations in order to assess public opinion and determine anti-American propaganda. They compared user ratings to that of BBC.[25] They attempted to determine the amount of access people had to western films. By 1954, they also intercepted television programs from Czechoslovakia and Poland. During sporting and cultural events in which people from eastern bloc countries traveled to western countries, RFE employees made every effort to meet them in coffee shops or stores to conduct informal interviews.[26] A "Media and Opinion Research" unit existed, as well as a "Free Europe Press Research and Analysis Department." Within the United States, intelligence gathering included dropping leaflets on eight towns in the state of Washington and testing the effectiveness of the leaflets on influencing public opinion.[27]

"Winds of Freedom"

For years, they augmented radio broadcasts with millions of leaflets dropped from balloons. Between 1951 and 1956 upwards of 350,000 balloons were launched over Eastern Europe dropping over 300 million leaflets and other printed matter. By the time "Winds of Freedom" became a public campaign, the use of leaflets was nothing new to the United States. Millions were distributed during World War I and World War II. Cold War balloon leaflet drops began in the late 1940s. The first balloons dropped leaflets over Czechoslovakia in May 1949.[28] For the balloon operations they used gas filled balloons carrying leaflets and "envelopes" that held more leaflets and dry ice.[29] A large scale diagram called the "Printed Word Delivery by Balloon" showed the balloons floating at altitudes of 23,000 to 40,000 feet depending on the weight of the leaflets. The diagram made it clear that the balloons would not interfere with air traffic occurring at approximately 7,000 feet. The balloons were launched near the "iron curtain border" and quickly reached their cruising altitude. After floating a 160 miles, approximately five and half hours, enough dry ice would sublimate to cause the leaflets to begin falling. Around 150 miles, the "empty balloon" landed "with leaflets in envelope," all of the leaflets from the bundle ideally scattered up to 200 miles from the "launching site."[30] Naturally, the exact path of the balloons could never be predicted due to wind and other weather patterns. Thus, missions would require meteorological predictions so that printed material of the correct language would reach a country.[31]

In 1951, Frank Altschul wrote C.D. Jackson recommending that the coordination of balloon leaflet drops with Radio Free Europe would help as a trial run for future balloons and broadcasts into China and North Korea. Radio Free Europe staff recommended that some of the balloons drop "holiday" packages of "desired drugs addressed to hospitals." At other times, brand-name manufacturers contributed to packages; for instance, Procter & Gamble once sent Camay and Ivory soap.[32] By 1952, the balloon operations became "Winds of Freedom" responding to Soviet transmitters that jammed U.S. broadcasting that they claimed were located "in the Middle East and Mediterranean areas," and also broadcast Radio Moscow. As organizers prepared for the balloon delivery "Operation Easter Bunny," C.D. Jackson sent out a letter marked "strictly confidential" to project participants. In it, he lobbied for the creation of "a monthly Magazine of the Air." He recommended that balloons be used "as a medium on a regular schedule and not as an occasional freak." He argued that "radio words" were too "ephemeral and printed material would be passed from hand to hand." In order to achieve "maximum impact," material distributed by balloons and radio programming should be coordinated. For instance, the magazine could "be a transcript and/or digest of the best that has been put out over RFE." This idea eventually became the "Free Europe Press" delivered into the Eastern bloc countries by balloon.[33] By the time General Eisenhower became President Eisenhower, the balloon part of the project had dropped millions of leaflets. The leaflets contained messages such as the "Ten Demands" made by the "Czechoslovak People's Opposition." The demands included "more money, less talk," "workers must not be chained," and "goods for the people, not for the Soviets." Leaflets scattered over the 1955, Romanian youth festival showed the Soviets stealing a chicken and pig from a crying Romanian "peasant."[34]

The name Radio Free Europe changed to RFE/RL, due to the creation of Radio Liberty. The equivalent of Radio Free Europe, Radio Liberty broadcast into the USSR. Formed in 1951, it modeled itself after the National Committee for a Free Europe. On January 18, 1951, the American Committee for Liberation from Bolshevism incorporated. It quickly changed its name to the American Committee for the Liberation of the Peoples of Russia, and a former editor from *Reader's Digest* became the first president. The station did not begin broadcasting until March 1953. However, when broadcasts began, the station broadcast in Russian as well as "Adygei, Armenian, Avar, Azerbaijani, Chechen, Georgian, Ingush, Karachai-Balkar, Kazakh, Kyrgyz, Ossetian, Tajik, Turkmen, and Uzbek."[35]

The Crusade for Freedom

When the Crusade for Freedom sought incorporation in late October 1950, it stated its mission as raising money for the NCFE in order "to assist in education and alerting public opinion in the United States to the perils in which freedom and democracy have been brought by aggressive Communism and totalitarianism in all its forms." With the help of the Advertising Council, the Crusade would "employ all such practical public relations and promotional measures as are necessary to the marshalling of this public support, moral and financial." That year, the National Committee for a Free Europe changed its name to the Free Europe Committee, Inc. (FEC) and adopted as its logo the Freedom Bell ringed with the words inscribed on the bell "that this world under God shall have a new birth of freedom." While on a much smaller scale, the council patterned the Crusade for Freedom after the Freedom Train, creating community events coordinated with advertising campaigns and newspaper articles, a pledge to sign and a tour of a Freedom Bell. Unlike other council campaigns such as "Miracle of America" or "Religion in American Life," the crusade remained foremost a fund-raising campaign. The crusade encouraged the average American to counteract "false Communist propaganda" by donating money to pay for radio stations that broadcast into Eastern Europe and over the years, East Asia. That way, private citizens could tell the world that Americans wanted to extend "friendship and freedom for all peoples."[36] In addition to radio broadcasts, the campaign also included leaflets dropped from balloons over Eastern Europe, a program that eventually became known as the Europe Free Press.

Americans were encouraged to give donations and sign a Freedom Scroll that pledged them to a "Declaration of Freedom." For the Crusade for Freedom, the Advertising Council organized a campaign in a similar manner to how the Freedom Train was run for the American Heritage Foundation. According to the council's annual report, "American Business in the Country's Service," millions of people signed the scrolls "in a nationwide Roll Call for Democracy." The signatures and scrolls were presented at the ceremonies in Germany dedicating the Freedom Bell on United Nations Day, October 24, 1950. The bell did not have as extensive a tour as the freedom train. As with most campaigns, the council created advertising mats, radio messages and eventually television. The council claimed that newspapers across the nation ordered 11,900 mats. Corporate house magazines ran editorials in addition to advertisements. 37,167 car cards appeared on public transportation and 2,854 outdoor billboards and posters dotted the nation.[37]

The Freedom Bell Tour

On June 25, 1950, the same day that North Korean troops crossed the border into South Korea, the British company Gillette & Johnston began work on the ten-ton, twelve-foot tall Freedom Bell engraved with the statement "that this world, under God, shall have a new birth of Freedom. Finished in August of 1950, the Freedom Bell arrived in the United States to begin its tour on September 6. Over 20 cities hosted events for the Bell.[38]" General Eisenhower kicked off the first Crusade for Freedom with a speech covered by the nation's four major radio broadcasters on Labor Day, delivered in Denver, Colorado.

Eisenhower opened the speech by stating that "Americans are dying in Korea tonight." He said that they were "dying for ideals," but communist papers would report that they were dying to protect "American imperialism." Even though the American government had established the VOA to challenge "evil broadcasts," communist broadcasts continued to "overpower" and "outflank" VOA; therefore, Eisenhower said "we need powerful radio stations abroad, operated without Government restrictions." Eisenhower called on the nation to donate enough money through the Crusade for Freedom to make the one Radio Free Europe station into a network.[39]

The bell made its U.S. debut in New York City where Frederick Osburn, who had been "the chief of the Army's information and education program" during World War II, served as the chairman. The bell was paraded up lower Broadway mounted on a truck with a billboard that read "Help Lift the Iron Curtain Everywhere—the Crusade for Freedom" to ceremonies at City Hall. With General Lucius D. Clay by his side Acting Mayor Impellitteri tolled the bell for the first time on American soil. Then it traveled to Pittsburg by truck. Eventually, it was loaded on to a railroad flat car to cross the Rockies en route to San Francisco.[40] September 11, it was in California where it then turned back to head east. Leaving St. Louis, Missouri, as the bell toured the state, crusade organizers reported such a demand for Freedom Scrolls that more had to be rushed to the state.[41] Bell ended the western portion of its tour in Kansas City. By September 22, it had arrived in Texas. In Texas, it was displayed in El Paso and Houston. Returning east, it made a stop in Birmingham, Alabama. At the same time, a replica of the Freedom Bell toured cities and towns that the real one could not make it to.[42] In California, "film-industry leaders" on "every major studio lot" held "mass meetings" for the Crusade for Freedom. Thousands of Hollywood employees signed the Freedom Scrolls and donated to the Crusade for Freedom. These speeches left a strong impression on Screen Actors guild (SAG) President Ronald Reagan who quickly sent a telegram to General Lucius Clay pledging the support of SAG's membership "in the battle for men's minds" and who went to campaign for the Crusade for Freedom.[43]

Before the Freedom Bell left for Europe, the Crusade for Freedom urged religious leaders to discuss the "religious aspects" of the crusade and "the moral value of freedom" on Freedom Sunday. General Lucius D. Clay claimed that he "has appealed to 80,200 ministers, priests and rabbis for support in bringing to success a six-week campaign for millions of signatures on freedom Scrolls." New York hosted one last parade on October 8 where 3,000 marchers accompanied the bell down Eighth Avenue.[44] The Freedom Bell left New York for Berlin on October 10, the same day the Crusade for Freedom launched a 1,000 balloons from the Empire State Building. Each balloon carried a Freedom Scroll and a "contribution envelope." The Crusade asked that individuals who found the balloons also contact the crusade headquarters to let them know where the balloons landed.[45] Installation of the Freedom Bell at the Schoenberg Town Hall began in Berlin on October 22, 1950 and the Freedom Bell was dedicated on October 24, 1950, United Nations Day marking the fifth "birthday."[46]

The Ad Campaign

The Crusade for Freedom included ads that featured Eleanor Roosevelt, General Dwight D. Eisenhower, or Cardinal Spellman. A fourth advertisement in the series had the Freedom Scroll pledge to be signed by Americans and "taken to Berlin." The advertisements included "a coupon for making contributions to expand Radio Free Europe sponsored by the National Committee for a Free Europe."[47] Slogans for the campaign included: "Join the Crusade for Freedom and Back your Country's Cause!" "If Communism Triumphs, Democracy will Die," "The Big Truth is the best answer to the Big Lie of Communism," "I Believe," and "Help Lift the Iron Curtain everywhere."[48] Like the Freedom Pledge that accompanied the Freedom Train campaign, according to the Advertising Council, millions of Americans signed the Freedom Scroll. When they signed, they were asked to give a donation. The scroll contained the "Declaration of Freedom" which read as follows:

> Declaration of Freedom—I believe in the sacredness and dignity
>   of the individual.
> I believe that all men derive the right to freedom
>   equally from God.
> I pledge to resist aggression and tyranny wherever
>   they appear on earth.
> I am proud to enlist in the Crusade for Freedom.
> I am proud to help make the Freedom Bell possible,
> to be a signer of this Declaration of Freedom,
> to have my name included as a permanent part
>   of the Freedom Shrine in Berlin,
> and to join with the millions of men and women throughout
>   the world who hold the cause of freedom sacred.[49]

Like other campaigns conducted by the Advertising Council and its affiliates the events cultivated and presented a unified national culture. It came completely packaged with advertising mats, radio announcements, prewritten articles and editorials, as well as recommendations for how to organize local events. As the bell crossed the nation and local newspapers reported on the tour, the articles contained similar text.

Community Activities

Local groups were considered an integral part of the campaign strategy. The council sent out advertising mats, instructions, and displays to assist local groups in organization events. Women's clubs and organizations played an active role. The women's groups that participated in the 1950 crusade included the General Federation of Women's Clubs National Council of Catholic Women, American Association of University Women, American Home Economics Association, the National Women's Democratic Club, National Association of Colored Women, Future Homemakers of America, the National Council of Negro Women, and the Daughters of the American Revolution.[50]

Freedom Motorcade

The Advertising Council reported that the 1950 crusade helped Radio Free Europe build more facilities in West Germany and a station in Portugal, placing the total at 13 transmitters. The money also allowed Radio Free Asia to "start broadcasts to China in three languages."[51] The 1951 crusade launched August 28 in Detroit by General Motors included "World Freedom Day" and the ringing of bells throughout the world in time with the ringing of the "World Freedom Bell" in Berlin. CBS and ABC helped prepare "documentary" radio programs.[52] In conjunction with the Advertising Council, General Motor's Chevrolet launched a nationwide campaign with a "Crusade Motorcade in every state." Since the goal for the 1951 crusade was to raise three and a half million for Radio Free Europe and Radio Free Asia and to enroll 35 million more Americans, Chevrolet sent out letters to thousands of Chevrolet dealers and wholesalers encouraging them to participate in the crusade from September 3 through October 15. General Motors provided new Chevrolet station wagons for the crusade's motorcades. The Ford Motor Company also donated cars for the motorcades.[53]

In the cities that hosted the motorcade, the crusade dramatized the balloon messages that accompanied Radio Free Europe. Local festivities included the release of balloons delivering "Winds of Freedom" messages. In their internal company publication, Chevrolet explained that "Operation -Winds of Freedom" included "two types of hydrogen filled four-and-and-one-half-foot balloons." The larger type floated at 30,000 feet and carried a large load. When it "burst," it scattered leaflets over a large area. Smaller pillow balloons lost their buoyancy slowly and floated to the ground with the publications. Across the nation in conjunction with the motorcades, the crusade launched "Winds of Freedom" balloons.[54]

Every Chevrolet dealer in the country received a complete "crusade promotional kit." It included instructions on how to organize the crusade, such as "appoint a man in charge" and "advise all or your personnel," and a "window poster, a coin collector and enrollment blanks." Slogans for the year included "all of us can help keep a free America in a free world" and "freedom is everybody's business." The Advertising Council helped prepare newspaper advertisements and "radio spots." Press packets for the campaign included pictures of individuals holding pillow balloons with Wolnosc, the Polish word for freedom written on them. To help coordinate the campaign on a national level, the Crusade for Freedom established a headquarters in every state.[55]

Across the Nation

By 1952, the Crusade for Freedom had field offices in Arizona, Michigan, Minnesota, Tennessee, and Washington State. They also had a network of banks across the country that accepted donations. The same year the Advertising Council elected Procter & Gamble executive Howard J. Morgens to be Chairman of the council's board.[56] The council claimed that they had received positive feedback from 85 countries, and that universities in England, France, and Spain requested the "Miracle of America." James Webb Young worked with not only the Religion in American Life Campaign, the Crusade for Freedom consulted with J. Walter Thompson and director of the Ford Foundation. They claimed to have raised over 4 million dollars.[57]

Between April 1951 and February 1952, they recorded $1,930,134.57 in donations. Henry Ford II helped with the year's crusade.[58] Slogans for the year took on more religious overtones, such as "give us this day . . . our daily truth" and "a plea to all Americans of all faiths." The council also used the popularity of UFO's in American popular culture for the year's campaign. One series of ads included the slogan, "This 'Flying Saucer' carries Truth," with a picture of a balloon with the word Svoboda, Czech for freedom, printed on it. The 1952 United Nations Day campaign included a "leader's guide" for preparing UN Day activities and parties, "two 20-second television spots," and "thousands of copies of a special toast to the United Nations." The overarching goal of the campaign was for people to host parties on UN Day in which people got together and purchased CARE packages.[59]

For the 1953–54 council cycle, the American Heritage Foundation that organized the Freedom Train took over the Crusade for Freedom. It represents an example of how the Advertising Council handled the transition from the Democratic executive to a Republican executive branch. General Eisenhower had allowed himself to be featured in advertisements for the crusade and served as a trustee for the American Heritage Foundation. At the moment when the American Heritage Foundation took over the crusade, the mission read as follows:

> The Crusade for Freedom is the domestic information agency and principal fund raiser for the National Committee for a Free Europe, Inc., which through Radio Free Europe and other facilities utilizes the public funds raised by the Crusade to conduct programs of hope, aid, encouragement and information to and on behalf of the captive countries of Eastern Europe.[60]

By this point, Radio Free Europe claimed to have 21 transmitters with a listening audience of 70 million in Albania, Bulgaria, Czechoslovakia, Hungary, Poland, and Romania. In October, 1953, the Crusade for Freedom hosted a conference in Washington, D.C.. The event included First Lady Eisenhower hosting participants at the White House and a "closed session" at the Pentagon.[61]

United Nations

Other international causes at included public service messages about the United Nations and war time advertising during the Korean War. In spite of many conservative Republicans voicing opposition to the United Nation, the Advertising Council provided bipartisan support of the UN. In 1949 and 1950 the J. Walter Thompson Company managed the United Nations Day campaign on behalf of the Advertising Council. In April 1949, John Foster Dulles gave a speech to the Brand Names Foundation at a Waldorf-Astoria luncheon regarding the branding of the United Nations. He asked that professional advertising and brand-name advocates support the United Nations by helping to rebrand it. He insisted that the United Nations suffered from being "the victim of free advertising by well-meaning, but over-enthusiastic and inexperienced friends."[62] Under the management of Samuel C. Gale of General Mills, Inc., the United Nations campaign began in 1949 based on a formal request from the National Citizens' Committee for United Nations Day. In their report "How Business Helps Solve Public Problems," the Advertising Council claimed the campaign focused on celebrating the United Nations "fourth birthday" and reached 95 percent of American households with a radio "Birthday Message." They said that foreign language newspapers "cooperated generously" as a result of a special letter by the "Interracial Press" and that the "dedication of the UN cornerstone" reached the council's largest radio and television audience.[63]

For United Nations Day 1950, Alan M. Wilson of the Advertising Council, coordinated the J. Walter Thompson Company who created the advertising for the campaign. The National Association of Radio and Television Broadcasters mailed out radio advertising kits and retail stores featured UN day displays. The slogan for the year was "our best hope for peace with freedom."[64] The event was broadcast around the world. General Lucius D. Clay, reportedly with a "choke" in his voice, spoke in the dedication. The Crusade made a nine-minute documentary film called "The Bell" that featured General Clay and Henry Fonda.[65] For United Nations Day, a campaign also handled by the Advertising Council, the crusade asked Americans to ring a bell at three minutes past noon, to be timed with the first ringing of the Freedom Bell in Berlin, and to pray for world peace. For this "spiritual airlift," schools, churches, ships, trolleys, fire and police stations rang their bells in unison as the Freedom Bell rang in Berlin's Rathaus tower. After the bell's ringing in Germany, ceremonies broadcast by the VOA and Radio Free Europe included millions of Freedom Scroll signatures being given to Germany officials.[66]

With the Korean War, the Advertising Council launched war time campaigns. On June 26, 1950, President Truman stated that "willful disregard of the obligations to keep the peace cannot be tolerated by nations that support the United Nations Charter." On September 1, 1950, Truman addressed the nation. Again, he invoked the idea of World War II. He stated that "if the rule of law is not upheld, we can look forward only to the horror of another war and ultimate chaos." If the United States did not do anything about North Korea's invasion, Truman argued that "it would be an open invitation to new acts of aggression elsewhere."[67] With the United States committed to placing Korea's internal conflict into the larger global conflict of the Cold War, the Advertising Council's long-standing Savings Bond Campaign returned to being a Defense Bonds campaign as it had during War World II. In response to the military situation in Korea, by December 1950, the Advertising Council urged the country to "re-arm fast." They changed their general campaign slogan "the better we produce, the better we live" to "the better we produce, the stronger we grow." McCann-Erickson prepared advertisements that discussed the dangers of "communist puppets."[68]

Information Services

From 1948 to 1952, the budget for the State Departments' information activities increased from $20 million to $115 million. By 1951, the country had information activities directed at 93 countries, broadcast the VOA in 45 languages and published upwards of 60 million "booklets and leaflets."[69] By the winter of 1956, the Free Europe Press claimed that since the balloon operations into Eastern Europe began, "more than 400,000 balloons" had dropped "over 250 million leaflets" over Czechoslovakia, Hungary and Poland. By autumn, the numbers had increased to nearly 300 million. The leaflets were usually "small newspapers published bi-weekly." Occasionally, they included supplements such as "President Eisenhower's Christmas message to the captive peoples."[70]

In spite of intelligence gathering and market research efforts, conclusive evidence regarding how the broadcasts and balloon drops affected public opinion seemed to elude the participants. As evidence of Radio Free Europe's success, they turned to anecdotal evidence and Soviet reaction. The Crusade for Freedom claimed that they had "correspondents" across Europe who reported that the "satellite peoples" listened to RFE. They also claimed that escapees reported that people listened to RFE, which helped create resistance. In addition, they claimed to receive letters from behind the Iron Curtain. Another determinant of success was that Soviet papers such as Moscow's *Pravda* printed "attacks" on the balloon campaigns.[71] They also referred to the Soviet transmitters that jammed Radio Free Europe and Radio Liberty and broadcast their counterpart, Radio Moscow, as evidence of RFE/RL's success.[72]

With the help of the Advertising Council, the Crusade for Freedom raised money for Radio Free Europe, Radio Liberty and Radio Asia from 1950 through 1960. It coordinated the United Nations Day advertising and campaigns for the United Nations into the late 1970s.[73] With the election of Eisenhower, the American Heritage Foundation joined the crusade's leadership, and the urgency in the crusade increased. The "freedom kit" for the 1953 crusade said the year's campaign needed to raise 10 million to "help stop World War III."[74] In 1953, Radio Liberty started broadcasting into the Soviet Union, and Radio Free Europe and Radio Free Asia continued to expand during the Eisenhower administration. The information gathering capacity also expanded under Eisenhower.

The Advertising Council's work with Crusade for Freedom and Radio Free Europe marked the success of the council at connecting advertisers to the U.S. national security apparatus and further spreading the free enterprise mission. The council had become a part of the CIA's network for using broadcasting, culture, and information as part of psychological operations overseas. Domestic fund raising for Radio Free Europe created the illusion that this was an organization developed by private citizens for the peoples of other nations. It also furthered the image of the American brand by using popular American music to promote American culture, a technique that remained part of American foreign policy. The Advertising Council continued their fund-raising campaigns through 1970, changing the campaign name to "Radio Free Europe Fund" and again in 1963 when it became simply

"Radio Free Europe" the name used through 1970.[75] In the twenty-first century, the Freedom Bell still chimed daily, and Radio Free Asia, Radio Free Europe, and Radio Liberty remained part of the United State's information services.[76] In 1998, the Foreign Affairs Reform and Restructuring Act made the organizations, along with the VOA and others, a part of the Broadcasting Board of Governors (BBG). In October of 1999, the BBG officially became the "independent federal agency" that was responsible for "all U.S. government and government sponsored, non-military, international broadcasting." In the twenty-first century, in addition to Radio Free Europe, Radio Liberty, and Radio Free Asia, the BBG operated the VOA, Alhurra, Radio Sawa, and Radio and TV Martí.[77]

CHAPTER 7

One Nation, One World with Television

A t the same time that free enterprise advocates ran "public service" campaigns and organized advertisers and businesses to help the U.S. government, many of them worked to develop commercial television within the United States and around the globe. Television proved to be an ideal free enterprise, persuasive information media allowing brand manufacturers to develop an even more intimate relationship with viewers. Campaigns such as the Freedom Train and the Crusade for Freedom were designed to create a sense of national community and national unity and national commercial television would streamline this process. It also allowed free enterprise advocates to develop another popular medium into a commercial one based on advertising. Like radio, television gave the American people free entertainment, news and sports, in exchange for bringing advertising into their lives, a deal Americans did not mind. Television brought to maturity James Webb Young's vision of American politics incorporating advertising and free enterprise principles, and provided an even more efficient vehicle for public information campaigns.

Television fit the free enterprise agenda by creating no distinction between "the selling and programming functions." Some tension existed about using television programming to elevate American culture instead of purely for financial gain, but appealing to mass markets and consumer interests won out. American television was designed to be inoffensive so that Americans would eagerly welcome it into their homes. The programming was designed to persuade people to buy brand-name goods. Like radio, clients could call upon advertising agencies to exercise a "degree of editorial control," and advertising agencies were held responsible "for the character of the production." The American public did not protest this arrangement of using advertising to provide free television to the American public. While television developed in the United States, polls showed that Americans would accept commercials and sponsored programming in exchange for free television ideal for institutionalizing free enterprise and its invisible hand.[1]

The major contributors to the development of commercial television, the companies that built the televisions, the broadcasting stations that expanded their business from radio to television, and the brand-name manufacturers that used television to advertise their goods had worked together previously in persuasive information programs. Broadcasters Columbia Broadcasting System (CBS) and National Broadcasting Company (NBC) served on the War Advertising Council. In 1943, NBC had to sell off one of its networks. The end result was the establishment of the American Broadcasting Company (ABC).[2] Once established, the American Broadcasting Company also had representatives that served on the council. By the Advertising Council's seventh year, the presidents of ABC, CBS, and NBC had all served on the council's Board of Directors.[3] Council advertising agencies Young & Rubicam and McCann-Erickson quickly brought their clients to television. Procter & Gamble, one of radio's biggest advertisers and soap opera pioneer, quickly expanded their radio broadcasting into television programming. J. Walter Thompson entered television more gradually than its counterparts, but when it did, it quickly became one of the top television agencies. J. Walter Thompson's clients such as Kodak, Ford Motors, and Kraft dominated early television programming. Other Advertising Council members and free enterprise supporters who made good use of early television included *Time-Life, Inc.*, General Electric, General Motors, Standard Brands, and Standard Oil of New Jersey and A.C. Nielsen provided television ratings.[4]

Television Advertising

In 1930, Advertising Council pioneer, the J. Walter Thompson Company boasted that it had broadcast "the world's first television advertising program." Broadcast in Chicago on behalf of Libby, McNeil & Libby, it reached 48 locations around Chicago. One local television dealer reportedly had 5,000 people visit his store during the broadcast.[5] They claimed to have been pioneers in radio advertising helping their clients create commercial entertainment for radio. For instance, they produced a two-hour commercial radio program they created for Kraft Miracle Whip in 1933. In 1946, they produced one of the first televised events of a new product for Ford Motors.[6] In the late 1930s, England, the United States, France, Russia, Japan, and Germany experimented with television broadcasts, and advertisers endorsed the creation of commercial television supported by advertising revenue. In the 1930s, NBC created television demonstrations at Rockefeller Center in New York City. NBC had an advantage in the early years of television as a subsidiary of the Radio Corporation of America (RCA) who manufactured radios and then television, allowing NBC easy access to new technology. CBS started television broadcasts in 1931-32 in New York City to an estimated 7,500 television receivers in the area.[7]

In 1936, NBC hosted a demonstration of television for advertisers. Most of the companies represented at the preview, "General Foods, Philip Morris, Sealtest, General Motors, Bristol Myers, Young & Rubicam, Batten, Barten, Durstine & Osborne, J. Walter Thompson," later served on the War Advertising and Advertising Council. By 1938, the J. Walter Thompson Company included television rights in its contracts.[8] That same year, the J. Walter Thompson Company worked with the General Electric Company in Schenectady, New York to conduct local broadcasting experiments. In 1940, J. Walter Thompson produced a "full variety show" for Shell. However, J. Walter Thompson did not invest as rapidly in television as other major agencies, such as Young & Rubicam and McCann-Erickson. By the late 1940s, J. Walter Thompson clients Ford Motor Co., Kraft, RCA Victor, and Elgin Watch Co. all participated in local television markets.[9] Other early television advertisers included Procter & Gamble, General Foods, General Mills and Chevrolet. In 1946, J. Walter Thompson helped their client Standard Brands present "The Hour Glass," one of the early "regular, weekly, hour-long sponsored television" programs. That same year they helped Ford Motors sponsor a rodeo and horse show, and then a dog show in 1947. They also sponsored a broadcast of Ringling's Barnum & Bailey Circus. J. Walter Thompson helped RCA advertise televisions, making it the first company to advertise "via their own product," and helped Kraft produce the *Kraft Television Theater* one of the earliest hour-long weekly dramas. The same year they made the first commercial television telecast from Los Angeles. In 1948, the J. Walter Thompson Company had six clients with television programming. NBC made the announcement that it would be opening Radio City in New York. They started building facilities in Hollywood in 1945 and in 1952 they opened their Burbank studios.[10]

By the fall of 1948, some American cities had regular evening programming. From 1949 through 1954, the number of American television markets increased from 48 to 243. The expenditures on television advertising increased from over 57 million to over 800 million, as the number of homes with televisions increased from 1.5 percent to 71 percent as of May 1951.[11] By the early 1950s, J. Walter Thompson Company clients dominated the airwaves, having as much as "five sponsored network shows in one evening." Television remained primarily in urban areas until the early 1950s due to an almost four year freeze by the Federal Communication Commission (FCC) over licensing. In the early 1950s, NBC and CBS expanded their markets, and refined programming and sponsorship strategies. Initially, programming had one brand- name sponsor, and the early 1950s proved to be a period of negation between the television networks and the advertisers, until a system of multiple sponsors for a show evolved. The creation of television entertainment and the programming choices were patterned after radio, initially, with one sponsor. As television matured, competition between networks and the approach of Sylvester Weaver at NBC created a system of paid advertising spots versus sole sponsorship. Children's television offered two major advantages to advertisers. By the late 1940s, advertisers assumed brand loyalty could be created in childhood and children's shows proved to be inexpensive to produce.[12]

By 1950, even though television had not become national, almost 8 million American homes had televisions, almost double the year before. A.C. Nielsen, the market research organization that dominated television analysis, estimated that television reached more American homes than *Life*. One hundred and seven stations in 65 cities brought television within the reach of 65 percent of the American population. Houses in the pioneering suburban Long Island planned community Levittown came with built in televisions beginning in 1950.[13] By 1952, the American Telephone and Telegraph Company had connected the east coast and the west coast with coaxial cable. The first transcontinental broadcast occurred when President Truman spoke at the Japanese Peace Conference in 1951.[14]

Throughout the 1950s, the volume of commercial advertising time grew. Advertising agencies, such as the J. Walter Thompson Company, increased their research into television markets and programming. In the mid-1950s, JWT invested heavily in television.[15] It built its own production facilities "equivalent to a network program department." In 1957, the department staffed 200 people in offices in New York, Chicago and Los Angeles. They established a "local live TV group," that analyzed local television shows across the country to determine their suitability for sponsorship by JWT clients. In 1955, the J. Walter Thompson Company opened the J. Walter Thompson Company Television Workshop, its production studio and their longtime client Kodak client Kodak had three television series.[16][17] Within several years the workshop produced commercials in color and J. Walter Thompson took credit for being the "first color-taped commercial" included in a live television program.[18]

Why TV Should be Free

From the beginning of television, it could have developed as a subscription service, but major participants pushed for advertising based commercial television. The major television networks resisted FCC recommendations that subscription television be allowed to develop.[19] In 1956, the major networks entered statements to the Senate Interstate and Foreign Commerce Committee against pay television. Again in 1958 hearings before a House of Representative Committee on Interstate & Foreign Commerce, major executives from NBC, CBS and ABC all took a strong stand against pay television. Robert Sarnoff from NBC expressed concern over whether the public would still receive free television. He insisted pay-TV and free television could not coexist, and pay-TV would create a situation where Americans had to choose "to pay or not to see." He warned Congress that "pay-TV can succeed only by cannibalizing free TV." He warned that if television no longer remained a commercial enterprise "our economy will lose one of its great driving forces." He argued that the money spent on television advertising, $1.3 billion in 1957, created and maintained "a mass market, resulting in lower cost to the consuming public." Business in the United States, he insisted, relied "on mass-circulation TV as a primary instrument for selling goods and services." He urged the Committee to "officially request the FCC to withhold action on the pending pay-TV tests until the Congress has resolved the public policy issue."

Leonard H. Goldenson, President of American Broadcasting-Paramount Theatres, Inc., told the committee that pay TV would not add to what free television offers. He insisted that by having "the programming bill paid by the advertiser" offered opportunity for greater growth and broader audiences than pay TV controlled by a "limited segment of the public." Frank Stanton from Columbia Broadcasting System, Inc. suggested that it would be unfair to the 42 million American families who watched on average five hours of television per day. These people he argued had invested $22 billion based on the idea that television would be accessible free of charge.[20]

The Council Campaigns on TV

The Advertising Council first made use of television in the late 1940s. The council committed to using television in 1950. They designed a "Television Allocation Plan" similar to the radio allocation plan. Howard J. Morgens, Vice President of Procter & Gamble chaired the council's Radio and Television Committee that developed the plan. In the early 1940s, the Procter & Gamble Company represented radio's most major advertiser.[21] Morgens played an important role in prompting Procter & Gamble and other brand-name companies to guide the development of television toward "advertiser-supplied entertainment programming and sponsorship." Inaugurated August 14, 1950, by March 1951, "50 advertisers with more than 60 programs were enrolled" in council's television plan.[22] All four networks at the time, ABC, CBS, DuMont and NBC, as well as the 50 agencies advertising on the networks, offered cooperation with the council's plan.

The council claimed that during the first four months of the television plan "more than 200 network TV messages were telecast." For the year's seven major and 17 total campaigns, the council estimated "television home impressions" as 267,506,000. A "home impression" represented "one message heard or seen once in one home."[23] By 1952, the council expanded its television program when it "introduced a new monthly Mobilization—Public Interest Information Guide giving all radio and TV stations complete information on current public service campaigns." The wide spread use of the guide lead to "more than one billion television home impressions," and the cooperation of over "100 national advertisers and the four national networks." In 1953, the Advertising Council urged television advertisers to use pretaped televised public service messages. It said that radio and live television had been including Advertising Council public services messages, but filmed programming had not yet been as inclusive. The council said that Procter & Gamble had "pioneered" the use of filmed Advertising Council messages by including them in the "Red Skelton Show," the "Fireside Theater," and "The Doctor." The council made an appeal to brand-name manufacturers sponsoring television shows and offered them Advertising Council produced "free film spots, flip cards, balops and slides."[24] Throughout the 1950s, the Advertising Council increasingly added the use of television to their campaigns. Between 1952 and 1956, the delivery of council messages via television increased 200 percent.

Public Service Television Programming

In addition to advertising campaigns, television provided the opportunity create public service television shows. In March of 1953, the Advertising Council worked with ABC, CBS, and NBC to broadcast the March 17 "atomic explosion" in Yucca Flat, Nevada. The council claimed the broadcast had been requested by the government. The atomic test was to determine "the effect of the blast on frame structures and vehicles." The purpose of broadcasting the test was "to alert citizens to the need for civilian defense activities."[25] The use of television advertising also brought The Crusade for Freedom into American home, making over 350 million home impressions in one year and bringing the CIA and American information services directly into American living rooms television to solicit monetary donations from the American public diplomacy.[26]

Television also allowed for quick action to be taken when the council and affiliates in the private and public sectors identified an issue. For instance, in response to recession, the council launched the "Future of America Program." They produced the "emergency" campaign because "a psychological business recession seemed likely and there were numerous rumors of worse to come." Like the "Miracle of America" campaign, the council created a booklet called "The Future of America" to educate the American public. To support the campaign on January 2, 1955, ABC, CBS, DuMont and NBC all aired "a half-hour campaign film produced by the Council and based on the campaign booklet." Paul Hoffman, former administrator of the Marshall Plan and current chairman of the Studebaker-Packard Corporation, narrated the show.[27]

Ad Council Television Shows

By the mid-1950s, the Advertising Council had offices in New York City, Washington D.C., Chicago, San Francisco, and Hollywood, giving the council easy access to the major media hubs, and all the major campaigns, such as the Crusade for Freedom, Religion in American Life, "Better Schools," Red Cross, ran on television. In the mid-1950s, the National Association of Radio and Television Broadcasters annual convention included a "special Public Service Exhibit." The council claimed that over 40 "government agencies and private organizations, whose cause receive radio-TV support through the Council, set up individual displays showing how broadcaster and the Council serve the public interest."[28]

Segregation and Sports

One of the major unresolved dilemma's for television broadcasters and programmers was how to include African American audiences without offending racist white audiences. Entertainment programming that included African Americans generated more complaints of stereotypes than audience. Some of the variety shows maintained the World War II precedent of including African American performers, as had been urged by the federal government, in order to appeal to African American audiences. Early shows on CBS and DuMont in New York included African American performers. But most attempts In 1950, the ABC comedy *Beulah* starred Ethel Waters as the maid. The show was canceled in 1953. In 1951, the popular radio *Amos 'n' Andy* became a television show and ran for two seasons, however the NAACP objected to the racial stereotypes. Wanting to expand markets, New York based television productions did not want to offend potential audiences in the Jim Crow segregated cities of the South and television broadcaster focused televised sports as a means of attracting African American audiences.[29]

From television's early days, sports proved to be one of the "most popular" types of television program.[30] During World War II, RCA donated televisions and NBC donated programming to the U.S. Army and Navy run hospitals in the New York City area. Among these early experimental networks, they broadcast sports event from Madison Square Garden. In 1946, the J. Walter Thompson Company had "the biggest sports package on television." Their client Ford Motor Company sponsored pro-football and collegiate football, as well as sports events from Madison Square Gardens. Sports which were popular radio programming translated well to television. The first television commercial for Bulova clocks in 1941 happened during a Brooklyn Dodgers versus a Philadelphia Phillies game. The commercial pictured a clock and the map of the United States, and a voiceover stated "America runs on Bulova time."[31]

In 1946, J. Walter Thompson helped Ford broadcast professional tennis matches. In 1947, JWT arranged for the Ford Motor sponsorship of Brooklyn Dodgers and Chicago Cubs games and the World Series. By the end of the 1940s, bars with televisions which ran live sporting events proved popular. Henry Luce and *Time* sponsored the televised broadcasts of the 1948 Olympics. The J. Walter Thompson Company took credit for being the first to broadcast a President throwing out the opening pitch, when they televised Truman throwing out the opening pitch at the World Series.[32]

The hiring of Jackie Robinson, in 1947, by the Brooklyn Dodgers and the integration of baseball allowed televised sports to show an integration not found across the United States. Branch Rickey who made the decision to hire Robinson for the Dodgers discussed Myrdal's book with friends as discussion of integrating baseball occurred during the World War II. In February of 1944, in a speech before the Brooklyn Rotary Club Rickey gave a speech that described a plan for the gradual integration of baseball. It finally matured when he hired Jackie Robinson who debuted for the Brooklyn Dodgers on April 18, 1946. Jackie Robinson signed a contract with NBC.[33] In 1950, Robinson missed part of his third and forth seasons to play himself in the movie *The Jackie Robinson Story*, a fictionalized movie about his life. For international viewers, the film provided a very visual image to disassociate the United States as a whole from racist elements within American society. Thousands of white fans cheering for an African American player offered an image other than the one Myrdal painted in *The American Dilemma*. Throughout the 1950s, major league baseball teams across United States integrated.[34]

Television News

In 1952, surveys showed that the American public still preferred to get their news from newspapers and radio rather than television. Ratings for news and political programming remained low. Networks had broadcast the hearings for the Marshall Plan, United Nations sessions, and the House Un-American Committee hearings of Alger Hiss. One of the most popular early government coverage was the Senate Special Committee to Investigate Organized Crime in 1951 lead by Senator Kefauver. In 1954, the McCarthy hearings before Congress did not receive good ratings, particularly as compared to Kefauver's organized crime hearings, and televising congressional hearings fell out of fashion.[35]

Politics and Television

For advertisers who believed they should be directly involved with politics, everything came together for the 1952 presidential election. In addition to television advertising campaigns during the election, for the first time advertisers sponsored the conventions. While Henry Luce's *Time* magazine sponsored the 1948 national conventions, but the television viewing audience was not yet truly national.[36] Westinghouse sponsored the Republican convention on CBS and Philco sponsored the Democrat convention on NBC. Stations broadcast the conventions in Chicago, and the conventions received good ratings and many in the industry felt election campaign increased television viewing.

In January 1952, NBC and ABC said they would sell advertising time to candidates and their representatives. By March the Republicans bought time and ran Eisenhower commercials, but none were bought for Democrats.[37] During the election cycle the Eisenhower campaign made pioneering use of television advertising. The campaign helped the Republican Party in general organize their campaign strategy for broadcasting and political campaigns. Meetings began in 1951 and eventually Eisenhower used longtime Advertising Council agency Young & Rubicam to produce his campaign. Young & Rubicam made television a major part of his advertising campaign and made upwards of 40 television commercials. As often occurred with news or public information programming, the candidate's speeches did not get good ratings. With ratings as low as ten to 15 percent, television commercials could make more television home impressions.[38]

In addition to television commercials created by advertising council affiliates, the Council cosponsored the American Heritage Foundation campaign "Get Out and Vote," a bipartisan campaign to encourage Americans to vote. Sponsored by the American Heritage Foundation, it represented the first campaign done by Democrats and Republicans together to increase voter turnout. Since the foundation had worked with the council to produce the Freedom Train, they had expressed concern over voter turnout. The 1948 presidential election in which only 51 percent of eligible voters voted, versus 75–90 percent across Europe, 71 percent in Japan, and 72 percent in Israel caused more concern. They described Americans' voting habits as "our horrible habit of not voting." For the voting campaign, the council worked with "leading psychologists and public opinion consultants." Their findings resulted in a strategy that would avoid criticism or negativity about previous low voter turnout. To reframe it, they created a campaign that would "stress that people everywhere are tremendously interested in this election." They chose campaign phrases such as "don't be left out" and "see you at the polls." Winthrop Aldrich and Thomas D'Brophy who worked on the Freedom Train worked on the campaign.[39]

The combined council and foundation campaign published information about voting in 25 languages and distributed information to "nationality organizations," and "foreign-language newspapers." In conjunction with their campaign the Common Council for American Unity worked with the American Heritage Foundation to publish the booklet "Voter's ABC" that described the nation's "literacy test, the poll taxes, registration, absentee balloting, and what to do once inside the voting booth." For the first time in history, they claimed product packaging would be devoted "to a public service campaign urging all citizens to register and vote."[40] The Kellogg Company put the faces of both major candidates on Corn Flakes boxes with the slogan "vote as you please—remember to vote." The back of the boxes had information regarding "voting regulations" entitled "facts your family should know about voting." The side panels had "voting statistics and instructions on the proper display of the American flag."[41] The foundation took credit for halting the trend of voter apathy in the United States. They said they had "reversed" a "20 or more years of increasing citizen lethargy and indifference." In a press release after the election, they took credit for "the largest voter turnout in American history" claiming that 11,727,549 more people voted in 1952, an increase of 23 percent.[42]

Ronald Reagan

Television also laid the seeds for President Ronald Reagan's political career and his commitment to the use of persuasive information in the Cold War. In 1954, Reagan signed a contract with General Electric to host the *General Electric Theater*. In addition to hosting the show and starring in some of the episodes, the contract obligated Reagan to 16 weeks of touring the country to speak to GE employees. Within four years, Reagan visited 130 factories and spoke to nearly 200,000 G.E. workers. General Electric also built Reagan "The House of the Future" featuring state the art GE appliances, televisions and lighting and other advanced household technology. One of Reagan's topics was the Cold War which included raising money for the Crusade for Freedom.[43]

Global Television

From the beginning, American companies wanted to put American style television around the globe. In December 1945, the J. Walter Thompson issued an internal, confidential report regarding the expansion of business around the globe.[44] The J. Walter Thompson engaged in the "foreign distribution and production" of television beginning around 1951.[45] JWT had anticipated and hoped to have commercial television operating in Britain by 1952. Since they had offices in Britain beginning in 1899, the agency hoped to be able to replicate successes in the United States as they usually did with British markets. The office in London had long served markets in both the British Empire and Europe.[46] However, commercial television did not begin in Britain until 1955. The British Broadcasting Corporation which had been public broadcasting in England since radio in the 1920s had complete control over British radio and then television. By the late 1920s, commercial radio had been broadcast into England from Europe by Radio Luxembourg, Radio Normandy, and the International Broadcasting Company in 1933. The fact that British audiences tuned into these networks and did not object to the use of advertising over them was used as evidence that Britain should have commercial broadcasting. The topic remained under debate through the early 1950s. On July 30, 1954, a bill created the Independent Television Authority that in turn put on first commercial "on air 14 months later" September 22, 1955.[47]

Television's early pioneers also dreamed of building "global television." In the late 1940s, former consultant to VOA, Henry Holthusen and engineer William Halstead met with Karl Mundt and others to outline a plan for global television. Since the United States and the United Kingdom were among the few countries with television, the first goal needed to be convincing other countries to install a similar television network as in the United States. Senator Mundt gave a speech to Congress that the press picked up on. In 1952, Japanese publisher Masutaro Shoriki invited Halstead and Holthusen to present in Japan. The following year, Halstead's company supervised the launching of station JOAX. Beginning in the early 1950s, the J. Walter Thompson Company worked with Latin American countries to expand their television networks and production facilities. Several Advertising Council members worked to make sure that countries around the world established television as commercial broadcasting systems similar to the United States.

In Latin America, television networks were primarily commercial, with little public broadcast.[48]

By 1953, 16 countries had television service and seven had it in development. Japan began commercial television broadcasts in 1953 and within a few years programming executives from Radio Tokyo-TV reached out to the J. Walter Thompson Company to help with television commercials. By 1956, 44 countries had consistent television programming and 196 stations. American distributor Screen Gems had offices in Canada, the United Kingdom and Latin America, and by the late 1950s they had shows such as "Rin Tin Tin" running in 21 countries. Shows were supported by a mix of local sponsors and major American companies, and Advertising Council members, such as Procter & Gamble, Colgate, Delmonte, General Electric, Goodyear, Max Factor, Bristol-Myers, and Westinghouse. In Mexico City, J. Walter Thompson helped sophisticated television production facilities.[49]

By 1956, J. Walter Thompson clients sponsored American shows around the world. Kellogg sponsored "Lassie" in Mexico, and Kraft sponsored "I Love Lucy" in Germany.[50] In Latin America, J. Walter Thompson client Standard Brands sponsored televised bowling. Ford Motor's *Ford Theatre* aired in Puerto Rico.[51] They claimed that their first televised commercial in Latin America was for Squibb, and by mid-1950, they claimed to advertise in Latin America for "Lever Brothers, Pond's, Eastman Kodak, Kellogg, Mobil Oil, Carnation, Scott's Emulsion, Standard Brands, R.T. French, Scott Paper, Eno, Mentholatum, and Ford Motor."[52] In Australia, J. Walter Thompson helped with the first year of Australian television. By 1957, their clients Kraft, Kellogg's, Coca-Cola, Chesebrough-Pond's, Whitehall Pharmaceutical Company, and Lever Brothers advertised on Australian television.[53] NBC's Sylvester Weaver supported global television and the use of it to counter the threat of the Soviets. ABC, NBC and CBS gave technical support to Latin American broadcasters. NBC worked with J. Walter Thompson and Kraft to bring the *Kraft Television Theatre* to Mexico. In the early 1960s, NBC helped establish the first television station south of the Sahara in Africa in Nigeria.[54]

Commercial television did not develop in Europe as quickly as it did in South America. In 1955, Britain finally allowed commercial television and in 1956 Australia got its network up and running. Europeans could watch Britain's commercial broadcasts, but did choose a combination of public and private broadcasting networks. By the late 1950s, council agencies Young & Rubicam, J. Walter Thompson and McCann-Erickson had substantial billings from around the globe. American agencies conducted market research around the globe, in countries such as Pakistan, Mexico and Japan. By 1957, 375 television stations were in operation in countries other than the United States, and 24 countries had commercials on television. While the dream of a global television network did not fully materialize, commercial television markets upon which American advertisers could advertise goods for American brand-name manufacturers emerged around the globe. By 1958, there were 566 foreign television stations and 404 of them were strictly commercial television. American television shows were dubbed into Chinese, Finnish, Flemish, French, Italian, Japanese, and Tagalog and subtitled in Thai and Arabic, and more than 100 shows ran in 43 countries. By the late 1950s, the American ratings company and longstanding Advertising Council participant A.C. Nielsen, established an office in Japan. American shows, such as "Lassie," "I Love Lucy," "Father Knows Best" and "Highway Patrol" aired in Japan at the time.[55]

State Sponsored Television

The State Department funded several educational exchanges that involved building television networks in other countries. When the Eisenhower administration streamlined overseas information with the creation of the United States Information Agency (USIA) in 1953, which took over the VOA, the agency served as a research body for foreign television broadcasting. During this period, CIA director Allen Dulles routinely hosted parties that brought together CIA officers and CBS executives. The United State Information Agency helped countries develop radio and television infrastructures, while at the same time monitoring broadcasters, newspapers and news agencies around the globe.[56]

In 1958, USIA claimed of the 70 million television sets in the world, the United States had 44 million, Canada a little over two and a half million and remaining countries had 23 million. Of that, they claimed three and half million sets were in communist countries.[57] The Voice of American began exploring the use of television in 1952 and throughout the 1950s, the American military developed the Armed Forces Radio and Television Service (AFRTS) to provide television to American service personnel and their families around the globe. By 1959, Armed Forces Television operated 37 stations on six noncommercial television circuits in Central America, North Africa, the Middle East, Western Europe, East Asia, Greenland, Iceland, Philippines, Okinawa, Guantanamo Bay, South Korea, Germany, Cuba, Puerto Rico, Guam, and Alaska. Networks donated television shows. In the areas where the stations operated, local audiences could also intercept the broadcasts.[58]

The Three "Hows" of Television

In 1955, with a strategy for how television would operate fairly well in place, the Television Bureau of Advertising, a nonprofit organization devoted to promoting television broadcasting to advertisers, published a promotional booklet called *The Three "Hows" of Television*. In over 50 pages, the Television Bureau of Advertising sought to bring on board any advertisers still shying away from investing in television. They claimed that since 1950, television advertising had "multiplied 14 times over the past five years." The Institute for the Research in Mass Motivations, Inc. conducted research in supermarkets across the United States that the Television Bureau of Advertising claimed as important evidence for televisions' success. Based on a survey of American housewives, television had proven to be far more effective than magazines, newspapers, and radio. For nationally advertised products, they argued that as much as half of all dollars spent at the grocery store could be credited to television advertising. They argued this figure was five times what radio advertising could generate, and three and a half times that of newspapers. Indicative of the prevailing attitudes among major advertising agencies, they described the importance of television to the American economy. The Television Bureau of Advertising quoted a speech from President Eisenhower, given before the National Association of Radio and Television Broadcasters. Reportedly, President Eisenhower praised radio and television to the group. He called print media cold in comparison with "the television or with the radio, you put an appealing voice or an engaging personality in the living room of the home, where there are impressionable peoples from the ages of understanding on up."[59]

They called it the "newest and most emphatic motivation force in the economy of our nation" and "the most massive motivating force." As of 1955, the Television Bureau claimed that the "average television family spends more time watching TV than with any other activity except working or sleeping." Based on A.C. Nielsen ratings for 1955, the "average television home" had the television on for 5 hours and 28 minutes a day, or 38 hours a week. Television, they argued, "moves people as nothing else has" and "moves goods as nothing else has." With the level of "motivation," television could provide, it helped "circulate more money, more swiftly, and more productively than any other device yet perfected by men's minds." They claimed that 15,000 people a day were still purchasing televisions. Television for the first time "in the history of the world" could bring together "80 million people at one time to witness a single spectacle." Television represented the only way to consistently "command the attention of individual programs of 30 to 40 million persons, who so enthusiastically hail their favorite entertainers as friends and heroes." At the same time, it could "sell more goods to more customers more efficiently than any other vehicle of mass communications."

Utilizing the fears of recession brought on by the 1953–54 economic downturn, they urged advertisers to expand their use of television or risk inhibiting the expanding economy. In less than ten years, television had "become one of the major energizers of our expanding economy." They warned that "unless customers continue to absorb today's super and growing volume of industrial output, economic retrenchment is inevitable." Television represented the way to stimulate the "dynamic drive to keep our economic flywheel turning at the pace to preserve today's prosperity." Television above all other sources of advertising, represented "the most effective, omnipresent catalyst in existence for bringing products and prospects together," because it could convert "productivity into prosperity." The best audience for brand-name manufacturers and the advertising agencies working on their behalf were "big families with young housewives." The "three hows of television," were the ways to make the most out of television advertising dollars. The three questions that advertisers should ask about television commercials were "how many prospects," "how much does it cost," and "how effective" have advertising time at those times in those markets been.[60]

By the mid 1950s, American television had permanently developed into a commercial media. Commercial television, with entertainment and information produced to facilitate advertising emerged as a permanent part of American culture, survived even the transition to pay television.[61] In exchange for free television programming television audiences watched commercials, and broadcasters, advertisers and brand-name manufacturers had determined what types of programming attracted the audiences most likely to be persuaded by their commercials. In addition to precedents being set in programming and financing, the system of market research and television ratings done by the A.C. Nielsen Company also came together during the 1950s. By mid century, the top 40 advertising agencies placed $964 million worth of radio and television advertising, and advertisers expected billings over the next five years to reach upwards of $2 billion. The J. Walter Thompson Company predicted that by 1957 over 71 percent of American households would own television and 85 percent of the national market would be saturated. However, they anticipated that the television market would continue to expand as color television came to dominate the market.[62] Television made free enterprise capitalism an even more intimate part of American culture. It surpassed film and radio in terms of how Americans spent their entertainment time Television enhanced the ability of the Advertising Council, and hence the American government, to create persuasive information campaigns, and television also provided businesses a way to further expand their business overseas and promote the free enterprise system.

CHAPTER 8

"The Conscience of America" and "The Arsenal of Persuasion"*

During the 1950s, what had been a piecemeal and loosely organized series of public information campaigns became an American institution. With the election of Eisenhower, the use of the Advertising Council by the White House survived the transfer of the executive branch from the Democrats to the Republicans, and the use of persuasive information, as J. Walter Thompson Company executive James Webb Young described at Hot Springs in 1941, was now part of the American economic and political structure. Public relations and advertising on behalf of a country or government entities within the country became a standard part of American politics. With the Eisenhower administration openly embracing the use of advertising for domestic and foreign politics, supporters of free enterprise capitalism implemented their strategies of advertising and brand management across the political landscape. Advertising Council members continued expanding their businesses around the globe, and with

* The phrase arsenal of persuasion comes from a 2009 panel discussion about the Smith-Mundt Act, "Rebuilding the Arsenal of Persuasion," ARMSTRONG STRATEGIC INSIGHTS GROUP, January 13, 2008; http://mountainrunner.us/symposium/panels. html; last accessed August 3, 2009. In 1954 Richard Deems director of Ad Council and VP and General Advertising Manager, Hearst Magazine, Inc. in speech celebrating Advertising Council day in Los Angeles said "The Council has been called the conscience of advertising. Today, it might almost be called the conscience of America." He mentioned Hearst's long time affiliation with the Ad Council and said "improvements in our American way of life which would not have happened had not American advertising developed a massive and effective system for delivering persuasive messages to our citizens about what needs to be done." Richard Deems, Speech, August 17, 1954, box 10, Advertising Council General 1954, Files of Special Assistant Relating to the Office of Coordinator of Government Public Service Advertising, James M. Lambie Jr., Staff Files, EL.

each year more American companies joined them. President Eisenhower pursued policies that fit with the council's free enterprise agenda and incorporated advertising and public relations at all levels of American policy. He openly included the council when he revamped the national security strategy to make overseas information a more important part of foreign policy. Eisenhower called the council "one of our greatest agencies for the preservation of free government."[1] He allowed the council to continue their tradition of off-the- record White House conferences and on-the record Round Tables and he called on the Advertising Council to help the administration with new council campaigns, such as the People's Capitalism program, the Atoms for Peace campaign, and People-to-People. For his secretary of defense, Eisenhower chose representatives from long-standing council corporations, brand-name manufacturers General Motors and Procter & Gamble.

As president, Eisenhower embraced the use of advertising by the federal government. He called for "a broader use of the public service advertising mechanism provided by the Advertising Council." He claimed, "we must undertake the task of laying before the people of the world the facts of today's life."[2] To council president T.S. Repplier, President Eisenhower referred to the council "one of the most important agencies in the country." In 1953, White House officials described the council as "a private organization" that "enables the nation to call on the talents of advertising people without creating another government bureau staffed by such people." They claimed that when the government needed "voluntary action by American citizens," the Advertising Council was the agency that provided "the advertising which stimulates that action." Membership in the council remained similar to that during the years of the Truman administration and included "leading advertisers (i.e. businessmen), publishers of magazines and newspapers, radio and television executives, and advertising agency officials." President Truman's Advertising Council liaison Charles W. Jackson helped with the council and suggested to Eisenhower's' staff "that the President might wish to ask the Council member to consider donating even greater amounts of advertising in the future."[3]

President Eisenhower quickly hired *Time-Life's* C.D. Jackson who had been vital in developing Radio Free Europe and the Crusade for Freedom for advice on psychological operations and Congress began hearings to revamp the United State's international information system. C.D. Jackson promoted the use of the Advertising Council's methodology and network to members of Eisenhower's administration. Jackson called American business "the catalyst agency" which had allowed the "country to furnish the most at the least material and moral cost." He promoted the idea of American businesses also helping the world, because "that accomplishment can be extended to the whole world on a partnership basis, not just partnership between nations but partnership within the U.S., the nation from whom intellectual, spiritual and material initiative must flow."[4] He told Secretary of Commerce Sinclair Weeks that "you know that despite their rather hucksterish title, they are a real force for good in the nation, and can be of tremendous values in interpreting this Administration to the nation."[5] James M. Lambie, special assistant in the White House Office from 1953–61, worked primarily as the coordinator of programs between the government and the Advertising Council. Early in the administration, Lambie wrote to Eisenhower regarding the positive feedback he had received from the council. He claimed that the council felt that "you are the first President in their memory who seems to understand what the conference and The Advertising Council is all about!"[6]

In 1953, the tasks listed for Lambie's charge included "functions heretofore performed by the White House in connection with Government Information Campaigns," including working with the Advertising Council. They set priorities for the Advertising Council's services and helped the Advertising Council "in obtaining many millions of dollars worth of free advertising space and time for government information campaigns." They acted as a "channel for all requests for Advertising Council assistance from all government agencies." They coordinated meetings "between government agencies and Advertising Council volunteers" and helped with contracts and approval of campaign material. They also helped coordinate the Advertising Council's annual White House meeting.[7]

Religion in American Life

As president, Eisenhower continued to support the Religion in American Life (RIAL) campaign and attributed much of the increase in religious worship to it.[8] Eisenhower launched the fifth RIAL campaign with a speech broadcast on all the major radio networks and aired on television November 1, 1953. The campaign phrase for the year was "Light Their Life with Faith, Bring Them to Worship This Week," and Bing Crosby, Samuel Goldwyn, Jackie Robinson and Norman Rockwell also participated in the campaign.[9] During the Eisenhower years, the council expanded their work onn religious campaigns to a worldwide campaign called Religious Overseas Aid. The campaign included the usual range of newspaper, radio, television, and advertising on public transportation and in in-house company magazines. The ads urged Americans to donate clothing, food and medicine. The religious groups involved included Church World Services-National Council of Churches, the Catholic Relief Services-National Welfare Conference and the Synagogue Council of America.[10]

Smokey the Bear

In 1952, the Advertising Council received Congressional trademark protection for the Smokey the Bear logo. The campaign done in conjunction with the U.S. Forrest Service to prevent forest fires had become popular enough that Congress passed an act imposing a $250 fine or up to six months in prison for use of the logo without permission of the council. After having imitators attempt to create products using the Smokey the Bear symbol, the council sought congressional protection. Once granted, it launched a campaign in the fall of 1953 that featured a variety of retail products. They sought to make Smokey the Bear as recognizable and endeared by children as Mickey Mouse and Hopalong Cassidy. Song publisher Hill & Range published a Smokey the Bear song. The merchandise created included bags, belts, fabrics, and scarves. President Eisenhower accepted "the first Smokey doll for his grandchildren."[11]

Under Attack

In 1953, the Advertising Council faced its most aggressive attack in the House of Representatives. In spite of protests during the Freedom Train that came from left wing antiwar groups the only major objective to the Advertising Council came from conservative Republicans. The conflict reflected tension within the party between the liberal, pro-Eisenhower Republicans and more conservative party members.[12] Republican representative Carroll Reece of Tennessee spoke out against the Advertising Council and the Ford Foundation. Calling the Council's "Miracle of America" brochure a "socialistic document," he claimed that it promoted a "British labor-socialist-party platform." He also attacked the Ford Foundation for granting $15 million to the Fund for the Republic for the investigation of civil rights in the United States. He called the actions communistic and encouraged other members of Congress to speak out against the organizations.

In response to his outcry, the House majority leader, Rep. Joseph Martin, Republican of California, granted Reece $50,000 of the $75,000 he requested for investigating "tax-exempt foundations." Reece organized a committee to investigate. At the same time, Rep. Bob Wilson also a Republican from California defended the Advertising Council. He expressed concern that the council would be attacked and described it as "a non-profit organization devoted to selling to America and the world the continuing importance of the free-enterprise system."[13]

USIA

In 1953, Henry Ford II became the chairman of the American Heritage Foundation replacing Winthrop Aldrich, who left to become the American ambassador to Great Britain. The foundation took over the Crusade for Freedom. It did not take over advertising for the campaign, which remained in the hands of the Advertising Council. At the time, the Crusade for Freedom was also the entity "organized in 1950 to raise funds for the National Committee for a Free Europe and the Committee for a Free Asia."[14] At the time, the foundation described itself as a "non-partisan, non-political educational organization" which was designed "to develop a greater awareness and a keener appreciation of the advantages we have in this country," and "to persuade all Americans that only by active participation in the affairs of our nation can we safeguard our freedoms."[15]

President Eisenhower called his reorganization of national security policy the "New Look," and it included the use of advertising and public relations on behalf of the federal government and the military.[16] In 1953, recommendations to President Eisenhower by Arthur Goodfriend, done at the urging of C.D. Jackson, advised Eisenhower to use "a philosophy of propaganda that speaks to people in terms of their own personal daily life, rather than hi-sounding phrases." They suggested that the propaganda would be most effective if "only a small part of America's overseas effort should be visible," and the rest remained "out of sight." They also suggested extensive research into other nations because "victory may depend on whether America will be the first nation in history to find out what others want."[17]

In the spring of 1953, on the heels of the death of Joseph Stalin, the Senate Subcommittee on Overseas Information Programs of the Committee on Foreign Relations held hearings regarding the "Overseas Information Programs of the United States."[18] President Eisenhower appointed William H. Jackson, to chair the President's Committee on International Information Activities. The hearings were designed to restructure the overseas information programs and resulted in the basis of the new United States Information Administration.[19] Testimony at the hearings explored the presentation of messages about America overseas and stressed the need for more sophisticated overseas information campaigns. The hearings included discussions about the motion picture industry, advertisements, books, libraries, and information centers. Generally, officials felt that the American film industry did a good job self censoring and creating movies that contributed favorably to American Cold War interests. During the hearings, the chairman of the committee, Senator Bourke B. Hickenlooper, expressed concern that American films "created the idea that everyone in America was rich." He argued that these films had contributed to "deep-seated jealousy and resentment against the United States."[20] Throughout the testimony, they analyzed the means to delivery information in various countries. For communist countries, radio represented the only media for reaching audiences and the VOA was being redesigned so that it would only be broadcast in languages and inside the Iron Curtain of "approved countries." In Western Europe, considered "highly developed," they recommended that information programs operate through "indigenous channels of communication." For the Middle East, they instituted a library program.[21]

Theodore Repplier, president of the Advertising Council, gave a statement before the subcommittee on March 31. In addition to being the long-standing president of the council, he was also "a member of the advisory committee of the International Press Service," a unit in the International Information Administration. Couching his testimony with the claim that he was not an overseas information "expert" and primarily understood "overseas propaganda" as it related to the "press and publication section," he discussed studying "how advertising might be used to help the overseas American information job." Repplier recommended that "defensive material" would be most effective if it followed principles used by advertising, in particular "transmitting one idea at a time." He advised that "our word and picture propaganda" should be divided into three groups "one segment for offense, one segment for defense, and the third, and probably the largest, segment a flexible one varied in each locality to meet local problems." Edward L. Bernays, public relations expert, often considered the founder of public relations, called American overseas information services at the time "inefficient, feeble, and inadequate." Bernays testified that overseas information programs alone could not "win the hearts and minds." They were connected to national foreign "policy and processes." He insisted that "psychological warfare should be an instrument of national policy, but is not a substitute for other strengths or national policies" and that the United States had been failing at "mass persuasion."[22]

Boris Shishkin, the Director of Research, from the American Federation of Labor, and Council participant, testified that an official "Government imprint" on any form of information media whether "a radio broadcast, a printed pamphlet, or a mimeographed release" decreased the impact. He insisted that the most effective information came "presented by private organization and particularly by bona fide trade-union organizations." He argued that the Mutual Security Agency's "labor information program" alone had not been sufficient in depicting labor unions overseas and that the State Department ran "hot" and "cold." He expressed concern that the United States Information Service (USIS) booklet "Sinews of America" failed to mention unions or organized labor. Shishkin stressed the ideological nature of the conflict between the Soviet Union and the United States. He said that it was not a conflict "between two geographic units," but was conflict between "freedom and self-government."[23]

Long time Advertising Council participant, Mr. Gallup, of the Gallup poll testified about how to research the effectiveness of propaganda. He said that "new research techniques" allowed for them to determine whether it was "possible today to find out just what propaganda ideas of the enemy are being accepted in any country." Gallup insisted that information programs need to be continually researched, evaluated and revised. He said, "Christ and his disciples were among the best propagandists of the world, and the only reason that some 600 million persons on this globe today embrace the Christian religion is through the continuing and highly skilled propaganda efforts of the church."[24] In the end, after much debate and recommendations made in both Congressional hearings and the Jackson Committee for psychological warfare, the United States Information Administration (USIA) was established on August 1, 1953 as a subordinate of the Department of State. However, the director of USIA would be subject to only the oversight of the National Security Council (NSC). President Eisenhower had requested $96 million for USIA, but Congress only approved $75 million.[25]

At the time, the United States already had 200 information centers in over 60 countries. The overseas library program had upwards of 2,000,000 books and the International Information Administration of the Department of State claimed that in 1952 36,000,000 people around the world used the library services. In July 4, 1953, Egypt launched the Voice of the Arabs radio broadcasts. The equipment for the radio station came from the Central Intelligence Agency who equipped "the Egyptian government with the region's most powerful broadcasting equipment."[26] In October 1953, the "Advisory Committee on Voluntary Foreign Aid, Foreign Operations Administration" sent a confidential report with advice and recommendations to the White House to be used by the White House and the Advertising Council. They recommended the expansion of programs in Korea, which at the time included the Advertising Council's long-standing CARE campaign that had been extended from Europe to Asia. They recommended that CARE and other programs be expanded into India, the Middle East and Pakistan.[27] President of the Advertising Council, Repplier weighed in when tensions rose between Congress and USIA supporters over budget appropriations for overseas information. Appropriations of 75 million in 1954 were considered to be restrictive and in danger that "our propaganda will be badly hurt in important areas like Guatemala, Southeast Asia, Indo-China and India."[28] Repplier warned that the lack of funding would further contribute to the problem of not being able to find enough qualified personal to staff USIA facilities around the globe.[29]

Atoms for Peace

The Eisenhower administration also mounted a global public relations campaign regarding atomic energy. Still facing a negative image as a result of the American atomic bombings of Hiroshima and Nagasaki Japan, the Eisenhower Administration faced the image of the mushroom cloud representing Cold War fears.[30] The Advertising Council had included members of the country's atomic energy industry at its annual White House conferences.[31] At the 1950 annual conference, the prevailing attitude regarding Atomic Energy assumed that the "new phenomenon" would eventually "affect practically every phase of life, business and industry as well as military strategy."[32] During the Council's 1952–1953 year, they helped sponsor the Yucca flat atomic bomb test broadcast on radio and television.[33] In December of 1953, Eisenhower gave a speech before the United Nations calling for atomic energy to be shared. He suggested that both the United States and the Soviet Union contribute material to an International Atomic Energy Agency. The program developed from "Operation Candor," radio and television statements given by Eisenhower's and administration officials regarding the Cold War. It included the radio series *The Age of Peril.* After Eisenhower's speech to the United Nations, USIA launched a campaign on the programs, getting foreign newspapers to reprint the speech and creating a pamphlet with the speech in 17 languages. The United States Information Services set up book displays of books on atomic energy. USIA created a traveling Atoms for Peace exhibit that included a film produced by long time council member General Electric called *A Is For Atom.* ABC, CBS and NBC as well as many major newspapers covered the opening of the exhibit. *Life* ran a long pictorial.[34]

What is America?

In 1954, Arthur Goodfriend published the book, *What is America?* based on the Advertising Council's American Round Table Forum from 1952–53. USIA distributed the book to nations through its overseas information programs. The Round Table included the participation of "forty-one specialists in American art, business, communications, education, letters, religion and science." Included in the list were James Webb Young, and Paul Hoffman of

ECA. The book described Young as a "consultant on communications to the Mutual Security Administration and the Ford Foundation." Council president Ted Repplier called the book "of outmost importance in our moral and psychological fight against communism." *Life* contributed pictures. The Ford Foundation and other organizations donated $100,000.[35]

Civil Rights

During the Eisenhower administration civil rights disparities for African Americans took on a very public place in the national media. During his second term President Eisenhower created national actions that made for better Civil Rights information overseas. A 1952 report analyzing American civil rights problems and U.S. Information programs reported that the country's civil rights record hurt the nation's image overseas. It recommended that to create effective information overseas the situation within the country needed to improve. The Truman Administration started the process of repairing the country's international image regarding Civil Rights with the desegregation of the military.[36] During the Eisenhower administration, the council faced criticism in Congress; among the issues was their support of Civil Rights issues.

Many free enterprise supporters and members of the Advertising Council had advocated at least creating the appearance of positive American race relations. When the Freedom train toured, the American Heritage Foundation insisted that viewings in the South be integrated. In 1951, the Advertising Council assisted the United Negro College Fund in raising $1.4 million.[37] In the early 1950s, non violent protests emerged as a means to resist Jim Crow segregation in the south. The U.S. Information Agency created a pamphlet called "The Negro in American Life," and tried to send conservative African Americans abroad to counter Du Bois and Robeson who toured and criticized American policies. In 1954, the Supreme Court ruling on Brown v. Board of Education of Topeka determined that public schools could not be segregated. On December 1, 1955, Rosa Parks was arrested for refusing to move to the back of the bus in Montgomery, Alabama, and several days later on December 5, the Montgomery Bus Boycott started as African American residents refused to ride the bus. The protests went on for a year and received national news coverage and put Reverend Martin Luther King in the public spotlight. King framed the Montgomery bus boycott as part of an international movement.[38]

Eisenhower, aware that problems in the United States regarding the treatment of African Americans created problems for the country in fighting the Cold War and expanding American businesses overseas, pushed civil rights legislation in his 1956 State of the Union address. The Civil Rights of 1957 allowed for the creation of a Civil Rights Division in the Department of Justice and a Civil Rights Commission. In the fall of 1957, when he put the Arkansas National Guard under federal control in order to send troops into Little Rock, Arkansas, and force the governor of Arkansas, Orville Faubus, to remove the National Guard from blocking African American students from desegregating Little Rock's Central High School, Eisenhower very much had the international situation on his mind. In his speech on September 24, 1957 about the incident, he presented the international problems to the public. International coverage of the situation in Little Rock began as early as September and followed the story closely often noting the harm it did to the United States' image around the world. The coverage included newspapers and filmed news footage. Before the incident in Little Rock, USIA distributed a pamphlet on school desegregation called *The Louisville Story*. In response to the Little Rock incident, USIA and USIS presented segregation and racial hatred as regional issues among an isolated part of the United States and not the national standard for behavior. The end of colonial rule in Asia, the Middle East and then Africa as the 1950s progressed increased the need for a positive image for the United States regarding race relations. Anticolonial and nationalist movements brought to the forefront white European rule over nonwhite majority populations.[39]

Advertising around the Globe

Increasingly throughout the 1950s, American businesses expanded into foreign markets and a positive public image around the world made that expansion easier. Their foreign sales and marketing activity represented a type of overseas information. By the Eisenhower Administration, the countries of Western Europe had recovered and were now manufacturing goods that could compete with American goods. This recovery meant competition around the globe for American companies. American Advertising members such as Procter & Gamble, General Motors, Kodak, Coca-Cola, General Foods, Pan Am Airlines, B.F Goodrich, Kraft, RCA, Reader's Digest, and agencies such as J. Walter Thompson focused on expanding their global markets. J. Walter Thompson maintained their presence in South American markets while trying to expand into the Middle East, Asia, and continue expanding into Western Europe.[40] They worked in South America to continue the growth of television patterned after American commercial television, and television continued to spread throughout the region.[41] Already established in India, they also attempted to branch out into the Middle East and East Asia.[42] Procter & Gamble created its first South American subsidiary in Venezuela in

1950. In 1954, they established a plant in France establishing their presence in Western Europe.[43]

As American companies expanded their business overseas, they also promoted America's free enterprise culture and social values. For instance, long time Advertising Council member, McCall's worked with Bancroft textile to use the Miss America pageant system for marketing. Bancroft's expansion into foreign markets and their use of Miss America as a promotional tool provides one example of how "private initiative" manifested itself in foreign markets during the early Cold War.[44] Founded in 1831, Bancroft Textile expanded over the course of the nineteenth century and early twentieth century. After World War II, Bancroft shifted its focus to the promotion of synthetic fabric treatments marketed under the names "Everglaze" and "BanLon." As petrochemical products, these glazes signified the rise of oil-based products after World War II.[45] To promote Everglaze and the company, Bancroft sponsored the Miss America pageant from the mid-1940s through the late 1960s. One of the original "outstanding leaders in industry" that sponsored the "Miss America Scholarship Fund," Bancroft helped finance the pageant and provided money toward the scholarships awarded to pageant winners.[46] In return, Miss America served as a promotional tool for Bancroft products. Bancroft directly connected the quality of its products with the image of Miss America and capitalized on this image in its domestic and international campaigns.

As part of her contractual obligations for winning the competition, Miss America modeled for print ads and toured on behalf of Bancroft. In the United States, Bancroft held a licensee agreement with a textile firm called Everfast that billed its product as "truly American cotton."[47] In conjunction with McCall's patterns, the company launched a joint marketing campaign geared toward middle-class women. The campaign consisted primarily of a national tour of fashion shows held in stores throughout America. In the mid-1950s, Bancroft organized an elaborate promotional package that included press releases, sample print ads, invitations, and scripts for the show's announcer. Miss America modeled clothes made with Everglaze-treated Everfast fabric. Each fashion modeled by Miss America had a corresponding McCall's pattern number announced during the show. Thus, middle-class women could make affordable replicas of high fashion using Everglaze treated fabrics.[48]

With Miss America, Bancroft sought to project the image of the ideal middle-class white woman. Bancroft promoted the Miss America pageant as a "very serious" scholarship competition, not a beauty pageant. Bancroft described Miss America as the pinnacle of "intelligence, poise and good breeding."[49] Bancroft used these same marketing images when selling their products overseas. In January 1954, Miss America 1954, Evelyn Ay, embarked on a European tour "accompanied by Mrs. Lola Martin, Assistant Director of the 'Everglaze' marketing Division."[50] Visiting England, France and Germany, Ay modeled in Everglaze Fashion shows, was "feted at the 'Night of Fashion Ball' " and went "backstage in the haute couture houses."[51] Based on the success of the European tour, Bancroft brought Miss America 1955 to South America in the fall of 1954. The tour consisted of appearances, not fashion shows as in the United States and Europe. Bancroft executives viewed this as an exceptionally successful promotional campaign. Business increased in the countries Miss America toured.[52] Bancroft also sponsored several pageants in South American countries. In 1954, the company launched "Miss Everglaze Argentine 1955." The company sponsored the competition in conjunction with one of its Argentinean licensees, Emore. The advertisement for the competition stated, "Emore searching for Miss Argentina 1955. You can be a movie actress." The winner received a film role, "a silver cup, a radio-gramophone and 35 metres of Everglaze fabrics."[53] Bancroft felt the competition helped increase sales in South America and sought to sponsor further local pageants. According to Bancroft executives, a substantial number of South Americans connected with the image of women projected by Bancroft.

As Bancroft licensed textile firms across South America, they attempted to expand into the Middle East. In 1952, Bancroft started exploring the possibility for establishing patents. A year later, Bancroft attorneys started the patent process in Egypt, Iraq, Syria, Lebanon, Ethiopia, "Tripoli," Iran, "Arabia," Greece and Turkey.[54] While Bancroft executives perceived Israel as a developed, "very small market," they viewed veiled Moslem women as a significant obstacle to Bancroft's ability to penetrate Middle Eastern markets. Miss America never toured the near or Middle East on behalf of Bancroft.[55] Bancroft did not attempt to sponsor any beauty pageants in the region. However, Bancroft did sponsor a scholarship program in Turkey. The scholarship program contained no beauty element. Bancroft used this program as one of their few promotional campaigns in the region. The program functioned as a scholarship, student exchange program. Establishing the program involved the Turkish Ambassador and the State Department.[56]

The Council around the Globe

At the same time that American businesses expanded overseas, the council's network attempted to set up organizations similar to the Advertising Council in other countries. The Advertising Council claimed that the "Council idea goes Global" as France, Belgium, Philippines did the UN Day campaign and "vote messages." The council also claimed that Canada, England, Denmark, Holland, Mexico and Switzerland were interested in implementing something similar to the council.[57] In 1955, President Eisenhower used the Advertising Council's annual White House Conference to ask advertising and business executives to support his plan for expanding foreign trade. He told them that a "free trade program" would help stop Communist expansion. He also told them businesses had not been appealing to markets in Africa, Southern Asia or the Middle East.[58]

President Eisenhower, like members of the Advertising Council, believed American free enterprise capitalism could help unify the world. A 1955 marketing presentation called "If We, as a People," prepared by a joint Association of National advertisers (ANA) and the Association of American Advertising Agencies (AAAA) Committee describes how they believed the new free enterprise system benefited the country and would benefit the world. They described both "America's capacity to produce" and "America's capacity to consume" as "almost unlimited." They claimed that "human wants are really insatiable" and that "in America this is especially true." This capacity among Americans created "almost unlimited possibilities for expansion." They called for businesses to make better use of advanced marketing techniques to cultivate "new markets" and "new customers." Advertising working together with "the other forces in marketing . . . had helped to bring a national way of living to the entire U.S." The incorporation of advertising into the American economy turned "luxuries into conveniences and conveniences into necessities" and allowed for "a penetration of the market known to no other economy." The use of advertising had proven to be "the greatest accelerating force" in the economy and "by constantly stimulating new wants . . . advertising has widened markets and raised the standards of living generally."[59] These same principles could be applied around the globe.

The Crusade for Freedom and Radio Free Europe thrived during the Eisenhower administration, remaining in close contact with the White House.[60] In January 1955, the Crusade for Freedom's self promotion newsletter, "The Crusader, News of the Crusade for Freedom," promoted their value describing themselves as a crusade "that lives up to the traditions of ancient Crusades in the finest sense."[61] In the aftermath of the Hungarian uprising of 1956, however, Radio Free Europe took criticism for allegedly lifting the expectations of the Hungarians beyond what the United States could actually deliver. The 1957 Crusade for Freedom urged those participating that because of events in Hungary, the campaign for 1957 would be the "most vital" since the crusade began. As he came close to leaving office, Eisenhower called the Crusade for Freedom "the only way to frustrate this evil manipulation of human minds and emotions."[62] In spite of raising money from the public, by 1958 the Free Europe Committee, the organization that officially organized Radio Free Europe and the Free Europe Press, received most of its funding covertly from the federal government, and "more than two-thirds of the Committee's funds come from secret government monies." They also worked with the Congress for Cultural Freedom, an organization that promoted the cultural exchange of writers and artists. The Congress for Cultural Freedom received "millions of dollars available which appear on the surface to come from the Ford Foundation and other groups."[63]

People's Capitalism

One of Eisenhower's propaganda campaigns was the People's Capitalism campaign, based on the recommendations made by Advertising Council president Ted Repplier to USIA. Designed to help businesses expand into the markets in question, USIA eventually adopted all of Repplier's recommendations. In White House reports they described Repplier as someone who's "primary interest and experience has long been in the propaganda field." In the spring of 1955, the Advertising Council created a committee to advise the Department of Commerce on how to improve the impact of exhibits from the United States at trade shows in other nations.[64] In 1955, Paul Hoffman told attendees at an Advertising Council Public Policy Committee Luncheon that the United States only spent $80 million on "propaganda," as compared with the Soviet Union spending $1–2 billion. He insisted that in Asia the council and their supporters needed "to make these people understand what is important about America. The thing that is important about America is that here we have freedom." By that year's annual White House conference, the government was the "primary beneficiary of the Council's operations" and as such the government remained "interested in its continuance and strength."[65]

The call for further action resulted in Theodore Repplier spending six months traveling on an Eisenhower Exchange Fellowship, becoming "the first non-government American to study our information activities abroad." He studied Burma, Cambodia, China, England, Egypt, France, Greece, Hong Kong, India, Italy, Japan, Laos, Pakistan, Philippines, and Singapore, and Thailand.[66] Repplier found "serious ideological shortcomings in the U.S. information program" and recommended the term "People's Capitalism" to represent America's system of free enterprise capitalism. In spite of the criticism, he still believed that the country's information skills had improved. "Americans," he said, had "now learned to be propagandists."[67] He insisted it be used "to make clear that a new economic system has been born—a system which gives more benefits to more people than any yet devised." He argued that during his trip he found capitalism "synonymous with either colonial exploitation or restrictive practices." He felt the United

States needed an "inspirational concept" to counteract America's "serious propaganda handicap."[68] Hence he recommended the name People's Capitalism and helped the Advertising Council and USIA develop an exhibit called People's Capitalism. Repplier also wanted to ask the Ford Foundation for money to tour the exhibit within the United States. At a speech to the Advertising Council's Board of Directors, Repplier told the council's leaders that "we desperately need a crusade" and that "the idea war needs more firepower." Repplier also recommended that the United States spend more money across Asia for "quickly establishing superiority in the important new medium of television" and improving the "Chinese language program directed to the Chinese outside Red China."[69]

At the annual meeting of the Association of National Advertisers in November 1955, Repplier gave a speech called "The Whisper that Should Be a Shout." He told advertisers that the Cold War was "the world's largest advertising contest." He warned them that "the communists have both a huge advertising program and fanatical grass-roots salesman." They also had launched a "cultural offensive" of artists and performers and started using "exhibits and trade fairs" as propaganda. In addition to describing the People's Capitalism exhibit, he explained to advertisers the variety of American information work. He described Radio Free Europe and the balloon operations of Free Europe press, libraries that were in actuality United States Information Services (USIS) distribution centers for "films, press releases, books, pamphlets and magazines." In India USIS, put out a weekly paper called "The American Reporter." He said the best way to judge "the success of our propaganda" was to "watch the overseas elections."[70] Based on Repplier's recommendations, the council created the People's Capitalism exhibit on behalf of USIA. McCann-Erickson helped plan the exhibit.[71]

The Advertising Council also sponsored a round table at Yale University about people's capitalism to discuss how American capitalism differed from older forms of capitalism. They never mentioned the use of advertising, advertising controlled media, brand-name manufacturing, and expanding markets as the new American capitalism. Instead they said it created a world without "rigid class barriers." It created an "equality of opportunity," a more equitable distribution of wealth and an "equalitarian distribution of leisure." Portions of the round table were recorded and broadcast over the VOA. The discussion also resulted in a 64 page booklet on the same subject.[72] President Eisenhower thanked the council for enthusiastically and "imaginatively" responding to his "plea for constructive ideas and assistance in the ideological struggle."[73]

Eisenhower used the People's Capitalism exhibit as an example of how the United States should be promoting trade. At the council's 12th Annual Washington Conference, he urged the several hundred American businessmen in attendance to help him use trade over weapons manufacturing for foreign relations in Africa and the Middle East.[74] When Eisenhower initiated the creation of the People-to- People program in order to bring together the citizens of the United States and other nations on September 11, 1956. The Advertising Council helped the program. Repplier was asked by Eisenhower to head the "advertising committee of People-to-People program inaugurated by the President last September."[75]

Eisenhower also relied on the private sectors for the reorganization of the Defense Department. He appointed Charles Wilson of General Motors his first secretary of defense.[76] Then, in 1957, he integrated the principles of brand management with the American military when he nominated Procter & Gamble's former Camay salesman and brand management pioneer Neil McElroy.[77] Eisenhower had appointed him to his 1954 White House Conference on Education, and he became the chairman of the committee for 1955–56. While Congress expressed concerns about the potential of conflict due to his ownership of Procter & Gamble stock, his appointment as secretary of defense went largely uncontested.[78] McElroy served for two years as Secretary of Defense before returning to Procter & Gamble.[79] McElroy's service symbolized the rise of advertising to power and prestige in the United States.

Public Diplomacy

In 1959, when Eisenhower addressed the Advertising Council at the White House conference, it marked his seventh time addressing the council. His administration marked the full integration of advertising into the American "arsenal of persuasion" Upon leaving office, Eisenhower warned of the growth of the military-industrial complex but not the role of advertising in the complex.[80] In the United States, the Advertising Council now connected news and entertainment media, brand-name manufacturers, the federal government, and the military. Advertising affected every aspect of American society from race and class relations to gender relations. Information campaigns at home and abroad coordinated by advertisers represented standard operating procedure and the institutionalized practice of public diplomacy and the network coordinated by the Advertising Council for producing foreign and domestic persuasion campaigns remained into the twenty-first century.

Conclusion

Free enterprise capitalism, the use of persuasive information, and the Advertising Council survived in.o the twenty-first century. In the twenty-first century, their strategies went by the terms "nation branding" and "public diplomacy," and modern masters of the invisible hand orchestrated political campaigns and headed cable news networks. Organizations such as the Advertising Council had commonly been bipartisan, having emerged during the Democratic Roosevelt and Truman presidencies and become institutionalized during a Republican administration. With the transition to the administration of John F. Kennedy, advertising and advertising strategies became an official part of American public diplomacy. The ideas behind brand management enabled companies to develop into enormous multinational corporations. For instance, in 2008, the J. Walter Thompson Company remained America's largest advertising agency and was "the fourth-largest marketing communications network in the world," but it was just one of the several hundred companies owned by WPP, "a world leader in advertising and marketing services."[1]

In the first decade of the twenty-first century, free enterprise capitalism and the Ad Council's role in helping to orchestrate it remained institutions. Seven of the top ten spenders on advertising in 2007—Procter & Gamble Co., General Motors Corp., AT&T, Inc., Ford Motor Co., Johnson & Johnson, Time Inc., Kraft Foods Inc., as well as the Nielsen Company who did the analysis—had helped build the Advertising Council and had laid the foundation for public diplomacy in the 1940s and 1950s. Combined, these top ten advertisers spent over $12 billion on advertising in traditional media, television, cable, radio, magazines, and newspapers. At the same time, America's top 2,000 SuperBrands spent "$250 billion on media in the U.S each year."[2] In 2007, the Procter & Gamble Company alone spent over two and a half billion on advertising. In 2010, despite a recession in the United States and around the globe, the Procter & Gamble Company increased its advertising spending by another billion dollars, bringing the total close to $8.6 billion.[3]

In 2008, the Board of Directors for the Ad Council included representatives from major advertising agencies and broadcasters. Many of the companies had representatives on the council during the 1940s and 1950s, but the list also included more contemporary companies and organizations. Long-standing members such as Procter & Gamble, the New York Times, Johnson & Johnson, IBM, Coca-Cola, Nielsen, the Outdoor Advertising Association of America, CBS, NBC, the Hearst Corporation, and Exxon Mobil served with newer members such Google, Inc., Target, Best Buy, Turner Broadcasting System, Inc., Time Warner Inc., BET Networks, Discovery Communications, Clear Channel Radio, Fox Broadcasting Company, Facebook, Yahoo!, NASCAR, Wal-Mart Stores, the National Basketball Association, and the National Football League.[4]

Public Diplomacy

In 1948, President Truman signed the "first law endorsing public diplomacy," the U.S. Information and Educational Exchange Act of 1948. Often referred to as the Smith-Mundt Act, it established the foundation for overseas broadcasting, cultural, and information programs. It also banned the distribution of this material within the United States. Into the twenty-first century, the Smith-Mundt Act continued to prevent public diplomacy materials and U.S. international broadcasting programs from being disseminated within the United States.[5]

Nation branding and public diplomacy remained part of the United States' global strategy. The United States Information Agency (USIA) went through a brief name change between 1978 and 1982 but remained in charge of public diplomacy and overseas information until 1999, when it became the Broadcasting Board of Governors (BBG).[6] President Ronald Reagan, who campaigned on behalf of the Advertising Council for the Crusade for Freedom, invested heavily in public diplomacy. During his administration, USIA director Charles Wick created "the first live global satellite television network." While the administration of William Jefferson Clinton scaled back on the agencies of public diplomacy, the administration of President George W. Bush reinvested heavily in the use of public diplomacy for his war on terror.[7]

Sixty years after it formation as the War Advertising Council, the Ad Council openly, but discreetly, helped the Bush administration with public service campaigns. In addition to the campaigns responding to the September 11, 2001, attack on the World Trade Center, "I Am an American" and the "Campaign for Freedom," in support of the war on terror, the council helped the Department of Defense with "America Supports You." A modern version of a classic council campaign, it included a website; a heart with stars and stripes logo; magazine, newspaper, and radio advertisements; and a television special. Sponsored by the United Services Automobile Association and "its insurance, banking, investment and other companies," the special "American United in Support of Our Troops" included musical performances by Snoop Dogg, Janet Jackson, ZZ Top, Toby Keith, and Jessica Simpson. One of the ads showed the silhouette of a helicopter and several troops with the slogan "Your Firearm Is Not the Only Thing at Your Side."[8]

By an executive order in 2003, President G.W. Bush established the White House Office of Global Communications to streamline the projection of the American brand. The mission of the office was to "ensure consistency in messages that will promote the interests of the United States abroad."[9] That same year, Secretary of Defense Donald Rumsfeld approved an "Information Operations Roadmap" for public information regarding the U.S. War on Terrorism. In 2004, within a year of invading Iraq, the United States used Iraq as a base "to broadcast directly to the people of the Middle East over five time zones in 22 countries, from Morocco to Iraq to Yemen." The "24-hour-a-day Arabic language television network," Alhurra, "the free one," complemented the Broadcasting Board of Governors radio broadcasts in the region and provided an alternative to Al Jazeera, believed to be a threat to the United States for instilling in the "Arab world" a picture of the United States "distorted by institutional prejudices and sensationalism."[10]

Also, during the administration, American aid to other nations became "more fully integrated into the United States' National Security Strategy." In order to make those programs more effective, USAID adopted a new brand logo. First debuted in 2004–2005 with the United States "tsunami relief effort," the new logo included the logo for USAID, the "brand name" USAID, and the "brandmark" "from the American people."[11] The *New York Times* claimed that the tsunami relief campaign represented the Advertising Council's "fastest reaction to urgent need in its 63-year history." The council's campaign featured a bipartisan effort with "former Presidents George Bush and Bill Clinton" requesting "donations through the U.S.A. Freedom Corps."[12] USAID considered the branding used during the tsunami relief to be effective, claiming that "in 2004, favorable opinions of the U.S. were at record lows in many Muslim countries. But, in early 2005, favorability of the U.S. nearly doubled in Indonesia (from 37 percent to 66 percent) thanks to the massive delivery of—for the first time 'well branded'—U.S. foreign assistance."[13]

In January 2006, Secretary of State Condoleezza Rice announced that through "Transformational Diplomacy" the United States would "use America's diplomatic powers to help foreign citizens to better their own lives, to build their own nations, and to transform their own futures."[14] In order to "reduce poverty and facilitate free enterprise" around the globe, the 2009

Budget allotted "$2.225 billion for the Millennium Challenge Corporation (MCC)" to help foreign nations "improve agricultural productivity, modernize infrastructure, expand land ownership, improve health systems, and improve access to credit for small business and farmers."[15]

Rice also helped implement "Sesame Street diplomacy."[16] In 2004, Gary Knell, president and CEO of the television program *Sesame Street,* announced that "*Sesame Street* will continue to be an important vehicle for cultural diplomacy as it expands into India, Korea and many other countries in the years to come."[17] Two years later, Secretary of State Rice posed for pictures with Elmo, a puppet from *Sesame Street,* at a school in Jakarta while she announced that the United States would fund an "Indonesian Sesame Street." At the cost of eight million over four years, the show incorporated puppets that wore Islamic veils.[18]

During the early twenty-first century, public diplomacy and the use of branding to define a nation on the international stage became open strategies. In 2003, the first graduate program for public diplomacy opened at the USC Center on Public Diplomacy. The center presented the study of public diplomacy as a "new and expanding field" without a "single agreed upon definition"; it loosely defined it as "government-sponsored cultural, educational and informational programs, citizens' exchanges and broadcasts used to promote national interest of a country through understanding, informing and influencing foreign audiences." The idea of nation branding became a standard strategy for nations to compete on the global stage. In 2008, *Nation Branding: Concepts, Issues, Practice* by Keith Dinnie presented several case studies to describe how countries can brand their nation. The first formal public handbook for the practice described nation branding as "an exciting, complex and controversial phenomenon" and defined the practice as "the unique, multi-dimensional blend of elements that provide the nation with culturally grounded differentiation and relevance for all of its target audiences."[19] By analyzing the branding techniques of several nations, *Nation Branding* provides a step by step guide for conceptualizing and implementing a brand identity of a country. Dinnie concludes that nation branding would continue to expand both in practice and as an academic discipline.

Many considered a tarnished U.S. image around the world as jeopardizing America's free enterprise strategy. For instance, in 2002, author and journalist Naomi Klein criticized public diplomacy, claiming that using advertising and marketing techniques to sell "Brand USA" would ultimately fail.[20] Five year later, the American Management Association published an in-depth study by a former brand management and public relations executive, Dick Martin, that urged American businesses to employ "corporate diplomacy." In *Rebuilding*

Brand America: What We Must Do to Restore Our Reputation and Safeguard the Future of American Business Abroad, Martin analyzed the reasons for low public opinion of the United States around the globe in order to maintain the involvement of American businesses that developed during the Cold War.

Seeing the nation's image as having lost its "former glory," Martin called the twenty-first century the "Anti-American Century." He connected the American corporation with the foundation of the nation. He argues that many of the original 13 colonies were corporations and that by the early twentieth century American corporations provided the country with a new way of life, one that grew and flourished around the globe into the twenty-first century.[21] Martin described the Procter & Gamble method as the twenty-first-century model for the expansion of American business. In the past, Procter & Gamble shipped "pallets of packaged goods to foreign markets from Cincinnati." In the new century, the company handled "each new market as a green field to be planted and cultivated by a corps of local managers sensitive to the prevailing climate and the country's ways." Martin questioned the merits of eliminating USIA and the cultural programs, particularly those designed to promote higher culture, such as jazz, art, and dance. He expressed concern that the "giant tsunami" of American popular culture was "washing away everything in its path." He argued that since popular culture dominated the images associated with brand America, "the world tends to equate America with violence and pornography."[22] While he offered suggestions to improve the nation's image, the J. Walter Thompson Company studied ways to continue the expansion of American markets. In 2007, the Advertising Council pioneer conducted an extensive study called "A Religious Experience, Marketing to Muslims in America and Britain: JWT Accepts the Challenge." In step with U.S. policy to engage Muslim audiences, the goal was "to understand the wants and needs of one of the most alluring and untapped consumer groups today."[23]

Within the United States, private organizations and individuals helped with public diplomacy. Working for BBG, Norman Pattiz, whose company Westwood One produced news and information for many major American networks, played an instrumental role in creating Radio Sawa and Alhurra television, which went on to serve the 22 Middle Eastern countries.[24] In 2005, *The New York Times* reported that "at least 20 federal agencies, including the Defense Department and the Census Bureau, have made and distributed hundreds of television news segments in the past four years, records and interviews show." It described prepackaged news as "a well-established tool of public relations...that major corporations have long distributed to TV stations to pitch everything from headache remedies to auto insurance."[25] In 2008, *The New York Times* reported that the Pentagon, beginning "with the buildup to the Iraq war," hand selected TV analysts to "generate favorable news coverage." Many of the analysts had "ties to military contractors vested in the very war policies they are asked to assess on air."[26]

In 2008, BBG claimed that "every week, more than 155 million listeners, viewers, and internet users around the world turn-on, tune-in, and log-on to U.S. international broadcasting programs." These programs included the following American broadcasters: the VOA, Alhurra, Radio Sawa, Radio Free Europe/Radio Liberty (RFE/RL), Radio Free Asia (RFA), and Radio and TV Martí.[27] Their purpose was "marrying the mission to the market," so that the United States could "reach large audiences in complex, competitive media environments worldwide with straight news as well as perspectives on American culture and information on official U.S. government positions and policies."[28]

The 2009 Budget for the United States included "$699 million for the Broadcasting Board of Governors to provide accurate and objective news and information about the United States and the world to international audiences via television, radio, and the Internet with a continued focus on broadcasting throughout the Middle East and to people living under tyranny in North Korea, Burma, Iran and Cuba."[29] At the same time, the U.S. Department of Commerce spent over $2 billion on America's Digital Television Fund "to help consumers continue receiving free, over-the-air television when full-power television stations cease analog broadcasting after February 17, 2009, as authorized in the Digital Television Transition and Public Safety Act of 2005 (the Act)." The program included public service advertising, a website, and $40 coupons for digital television converter boxes, all designed to make sure that Americans would not go without television.[30]

Even the Advertising Council's involvement in religion survived into the twenty-first century. In 2008, the marketers of the *Left Behind* series advertised that they would give away a million copies of the computer game *Left Behind: Eternal Forces*. The computer game was based on the popular turn-of-the-century book series that chronicled "the end of the world in stories based on prophecies from the Bible's Book of Revelation." The computer game storyline occurred during the "tribulation years" after the occurrence of the Rapture, "the extraction of the believers in Christ from the Earth" when "millions disappear around the globe in one cataclysmic moment," leaving behind nonbelievers "to face the emerging antichrist." Many of the billboards in *Left Behind: Eternal Forces* city were for the Advertising Council.[31]

American advertisers achieved all that James Webb Young had envisioned for them. Since the 1940s, they worked successfully with businesses and government to persuade the people of the world to follow the United States and to adopt America's economic and political vision. Together with American government and industry, they forged extensive networks for creating and implementing persuasive information campaigns. The use of persuasive information developed into a standard part of American foreign policy and a central part of the American political system. The multiplatform, multimedia approach developed in the 1940s with campaigns like the Freedom Train informed and guided the development of television, cable, internet, and social media into persuasive information medium.

Notes

Introduction

1. War Advertising Council, "From War to Peace, The New Challenge to Business and Advertising," 1945, box 1, Advertising Council, Charles W. Jackson Files, SMOF, Truman Papers, Truman Library; James Webb Young, "Some Advertising Responsibilities in a Dynamic Society," speech delivered at Cornell University, March 11, 1949 (Cornell University Press, J. Walter Thompson Company, 1949), 11.

   Other works using the concept of Brand America include Simon Anholt and Jeremy Hildreth, *Brand America: The Mother of All Brands* (London: Cyan Books, 2004), and Dick Martin, *Rebuilding Brand America: What We Must Do to Restore Our Reputation and Safeguard the Future of American Business Abroad* (New York: American Management Association, 2007).

2. For a discussion of the history of advertising and consumerism in America see Lizabeth Cohen, *A Consumers' Republic: The Politics of Mass Consumption in Postwar America* (New York: Alfred A. Knopf, 2003); Richard Wrightman Fox and T.J. Jackson Lears, eds., *The Culture of Consumption: Critical Essays in American History, 1880–1980* (New York: Pantheon Books, 1983); Alfred DuPont Chandler, Jr.'s, *The Visible Hand: The Managerial Revolution in American Business* (Cambridge: Belknap Press of Harvard University Press, 1977); Roland Marchand, *Advertising the American Dream: Making Way for Modernity, 1920–1940* (Berkeley: University of California Press, 1985), 29–30; Roland Marchand, *Creating the Corporate Soul: The Rise of Public Relations and Corporate Imagery in American Big Business* (Berkeley: University of California Press, 1998), 316; Stuart Ewen, *PR! A Social History of Spin* (New York: Basic Books, 1996); T.J. Jackson Lears, *Fables of Abundance: A Cultural History of Advertising in America* (New York: Basic Books, 1994), 2, 201, 235. For a discussion of the role of the J. Walter Thompson Company and Cold War campaigns see Laura A. Belmonte, *Selling the American Way: U.S. Propaganda and the Cold War* (Philadelphia: University of Pennsylvania Press, 2008), 7, 9–11, 117; Victoria de Grazia, *Irresistible Empire: America's Advance through Twentieth-Century Europe* (Cambridge, Massachusetts: Belknap Press of Harvard University Press, 2005), 234–237, 548, 552–554; Reinhold Wagnleitner, translated by Diana M. Wolf,

Coca-Colonization and the Cold War: The Cultural Mission of the United States in Austria after the Second World War (Chapel Hill: University of North Carolina Press, 1994), xii, xiv, 2, 58, 64–65, 134, 157, 166, 201–221.

3. Keith Brasher and Carter Dougherty, "Economic Uncertainty Spreads," *New York Times*, October 11, 2008; Michael M. Greenbrae, "Retail Sales Slump by 1.2% as Economy Downshifts," *New York Times*, October 16, 2008; Louis Uchitelle, Andrew Martin, and Stephanie Rosenbloom, "Full of Doubts, U.S. Shoppers Cut Spending," *New York Times*, October 6, 2008.

4. Stuart Elliott, "Campaign for Tsunami Aid Assembled in What May Be Record Time," *New York Times*, January 7, 2005; quotes from the "Campaign for Freedom" commercials from Jane L. Levere, "The Media Business: Advertising; An Ad Council campaign sells freedom, but some call it propaganda," *New York Times*, July 2, 2002; Advertising Council campaigns can be found at http://explorefreedomusa.org/hear/index.html http://www.adcouncil.org/timeline.html.

5. Henry J. Hyde, chairman of the Committee on International Relations, "The Message is America: Rethinking U.S. Public Diplomacy," hearing before U.S. House of Representatives International Relations Committee, November 14, 2001 (Washington, D.C.: U.S. Government Printing Office, 2001), 1; definition of public diplomacy taken from the Charter of the United States Advisory Commission on Public Diplomacy, U.S. Department of State, Advisory Commission on Public Diplomacy, http://www.state.gov/r/adcompd/, April 2, 2008. For further definitions of public diplomacy see Nicholas John Cull, *The Cold War and the United States Information Agency: American Propaganda and Public Diplomacy, 1945–1989* (New York: Cambridge University Press, 2008), 486; Hans Tuch, *Communicating with the World: U.S. Public Diplomacy Overseas* (New York: St. Martin's Press, 1990), 3.

6. Robert L. Wehling, "The Message is America: Rethinking U.S. Public Diplomacy," hearing before U.S. House of Representatives International Relations Committee, November 14, 2001 (Washington, D.C.: U.S. Government Printing Office, 2001), 19.

7. Norman J. Pattiz (founder and chairman, Westwood One), "The Message is America: Rethinking U.S. Public Diplomacy," hearing before U.S. House of Representatives International Relations Committee, November 14, 2001 (Washington, D.C.: U.S. Government Printing Office, 2001), 8, 11. In January 2008, Pattiz was appointed "chairman of the board of both Los Alamos National Security LLC (LANS LLC) and Lawrence Livermore National Security LLC (LLNS LLC)"; see "Pattiz appointed chair of laboratory governing boards," January 17, 2008; http://www.universityofcalifornia.edu/news/article/17166, accessed May 7, 2008; "About the BBG," http://www.bbg.gov/bbg_aboutus.cfm, accessed May 6, 2008.

8. Pattiz, "The Message is America: Rethinking U.S. Public Diplomacy," 6, 8.

9. Regarding Norman Pattiz see http://people.forbes.com/profile/norman-j-pattiz/86314.

10. "The American Century," *Time*, June 9, 1941; *Life*, February 1941. See James L. Baughman, *Henry R. Luce and the Rise of the American News Media* (Boston: Twayne Publishers, 1987), 129–157; Robert E. Herztein, *Henry R. Luce, Time, and the American Crusade in Asia* (Cambridge: Cambridge University Press, 2005).

11. See Cull, 36, 39–41, 42, 95, 26, 315, and 494; see also John Lewis Gaddis, *Surprise, Security, and the American Experience* (Cambridge: Harvard University Press, 2004); Melvyn P. Leffler, *For the Soul of Mankind, The United States, the Soviet Union, and the Cold War* (New York: Hill and Wang, 2007); Alvin A. Snyder, *Warriors of Disinformation: How Charles Wick, the USIA, and Videotape Won the Cold War* (Arcade Publishing, 1995); William Appleman Williams, *The Tragedy of American Diplomacy* (New York: The World Publishing Company, 1959). For the stark absence of the Smith-Mundt Act in Cold War historiography see John Lewis Gaddis, *We Now Know: Rethinking Cold War History* (New York: Oxford University Press, 1997); Gaddis, *The Cold War: A New History* (New York: The Penguin Press, 2005).

12. Adam Smith, *An Inquiry into the Nature and Cause of the Wealth of Nations* (1776); reprinted in Smith, *Wealth of Nations* (New York: Prometheus Books, 1991).

13. Conference: The White House, September 17–18, 1946, box 4, Ad Council 50th Anniversary File, 1943–1993, Ad Council Archives.

14. This list represents only a small sampling of who the Advertising Council brought together in the 1940s and 1950s: Dr. Gallup, A.C. Nielsen, Eastman Kodak, Procter & Gamble, General Electric, General Motors Corporation, BF Goodrich Company, General Mills, Inc., Sylvania Electric Products, General Foods Corporation, the Ford Motor Company, Coca-Cola, the Kellogg Company, International Business Machines, J. Walter Thompson, Young & Rubicam, Inc., the Rockefeller Foundation, Carnegie Endowment for International Peace, Colgate-Palmolive-Peet Company, Bristol-Myers Company, Johnson & Johnson, Westinghouse Electric Corporation, American Telephone & Telegraph Company, RJ Reynolds Tobacco Company, Canada Dry Ginger Ale, Inc., E.I DuPont deNemours & Co., Inc., Hearst Magazines, Inc., the Washington Post, Time, Inc., Reader's Digest, NBC, ABC, CBS, and the Motion Picture Association.

Chapter 1

1. See Edward Bernays, *Propaganda*, edited by Mark Crispin Miller (Brooklyn, NY: Publishing, 2005).

2. Davis Dyer, Frederick Dalzell, Rowena Olegarion, *Rising Tide, Lessons for 165 Years of Brand Building at Procter & Gamble* (Boston, MA: Harvard Business School Press, 2004), 1, 5, 23–24; William James Carlton Diaries and Biography, 1862–1877, JWTCA, HCAMR; Jonathan Silva, "J. Walter Thompson Company and its Clients: Marketing a Relationship," *Business and Economic History*,

25, no. 1 (Fall 1996), 2–4; "Product Packaging at Eastman Kodak Company, Rochester, New York," July 1951, box F2–5, KHC.

3. Procter & Gamble Corporate Archives, *P & G Company History* (SourceOne Business Information Services, Global Business Services), nd. 6; Davis Dyer, Frederick Dalzell, Rowena Olegarion, *Rising Tide, Lessons for 165 Years of Brand Building at Procter & Gamble* (Boston, MA: Harvard Business School Press, 2004), 1, 5, 23–24.

4. "Transcript Proceedings of the Public Relations Executives' Clinic; held as a part of the 'Brand Names Day' program," April 18, 1947, 4, Waldorf Astoria Hotel, UWML; Oscar Schisgall, *Eyes on Tomorrow: The Evolution of Procter & Gamble* (Chicago: J.G. Ferguson Publishing Company, 1981).

5. Davis Dyer, Frederick Dalzell, Rowena Olegario, *Rising Tide: Lessons from 165 Years of Brand Building at Procter & Gamble* (Boston, MA: Harvard Business School Press, 2004), 1, 5, 23–24, 62; Procter & Gamble Corporate Archives, P & G Company History (SourceOne Business Information Services, Global Business Services).

6. "When Kodak Started to do Business Directly in Each Country," nd, "Kodak and The World Market," nd, 140, Overseas Development, KHC.

7. Howard Henderson, "The Kodak—Thompson Partnership," Notes on talk for the Kodak International Group from Rochester, February 26, 1958, 1–6, box F2–5, KHC.

8. Silva, "J. Walter Thompson Company and its Clients," 2–4; "Product Packaging at Eastman Kodak Company, Rochester, New York," July 1951, box F2–5, KHC.

9. Derveaux, Kodak-Pathé, "E & O.O. Managers Conference, Paris, 1952," "Section Ten—Advertising," Eastman Kodak Box E & O.O. Managers Conference, 1, Kodak Historical Collection; regarding the United States pursuing European markets see Victoria de Grazia, *Irresistible Empire: America's Advance through Twentieth-Century Europe* (Cambridge, MA: The Belknap Press of Harvard University Press, 2005).

10. Howard Henderson, "The Kodak—Thompson Partnership, Notes on talk for the Kodak International Group from Rochester, February 26, 1958," 1–6, box F2–5, KHC; Victoria de Grazia argued that Woodrow Wilson was a proponent of expansion, citing his attendance at the World Salesmanship Conference in 1916; see de Grazia; see also Amy Kaplan and Donald E. Pease, eds., *Cultures of United States Imperialism* (Durham, NC: Duke University Press, 1993); Lester D. Langley and Thomas Schoonover, *The Banana Men: American Mercenaries and Entrepreneurs in Central America, 1880–1930* (Lexington, KY: University Press of Kentucky, 1995); Thomas J. McCormick, *China Market: America's Quest for Informal Empire, 1893–1901* (Chicago: Quadrangle Books, 1967); Louis A. Perez Jr., *The War of 1898: The United States and Cuba in History and Historiography* (Chapel Hill, NC: The University of North Carolina, 1998); Emily S. Rosenberg, *Financial Missionaries to the World: The Politics and Culture of Dollar Diplomacy, 1900–1930* (Cambridge: Harvard University Press, 1999). For a complete list of dates that JWT began business in other countries, see http://library.duke.edu/digitalcollections/rbmscl/jwtinternationalads/inv/#bioghist.

11. "The J. Walter Thompson Company London, Some Significant Dates and A Brief History," nd, box 14, Offices London, Colin Dawkins Papers, JWTCA, HCAMR.

12. During an interview with the Columbia Oral History Project in 1963, Prescott Bush refers to Dupree and Resor as "two of his best friends." See Prescott Bush, The New York Times Oral History Program, Columbia University Oral history Collection, Eisenhower administration Project, No. 35—Prescott Bush (Sanford, NC: Microfilming Corporation of America), 1979, 24–26, 40.

13. Allen J. Scott, *On Hollywood: The Place, The Industry* (Princeton, NJ: Princeton University Press, 2005); Walter Resor to Howard Henderson, December 23, 1930, box 14, Offices Cincinnati, 1930, Colin Dawkins Papers, JWTCA, HCAMR; Dyer et al., *Rising Tide*, 51–52; Thomas Ellsworth, "Follow the Leader," JWT Newsletter," June 15, 1935, box 14, JWT Testimonial Advertising, Colin Dawkins Papers, JWTCA, HCAMR.

14. James Webb Young, Biographical Data," nd, box 2, Howard Henderson Papers, JWTCA, HCAMR; "Jim Young—Ad Man, Nomad," box 6, Colin Dawkins Papers, Officers and Staff, JWTCA, HCAMR.

15. "Cincinnati Office . . . . Cradle of J.W.T.," box 14, Offices Cincinnati, Colin Dawkins Papers, JWTCA, HCAMR; Stephen Fox, *The Mirror Makers: A History of American Advertising and Its Creators* (Urbana and Chicago: University of Illinois Press, 1997), 82–99; Howard Henderson, "The Kodak—Thompson Partnership, Notes on talk for the Kodak International Group from Rochester, February 26, 1958," KHC; Thomas Ellsworth, "Follow the Leader," JWT Newsletter," June 15, 1935, box 14, JWT Testimonial Advertising; "JWT: the fleet-footed tortoise," *Broadcasting*, November 23, 1964, 46–48, box 14, JWT TV-Radio Department, 1930–1964, Colin Dawkins Papers, JWTCA, HCAMR.

16. The University of Southern California Center on Public Diplomacy states that

> In some respects, the story of modern American public diplomacy began during World War I, when the U.S. government created the Committee on Public Information (the Creel Committee) which was designed to build public support for America's entry into that war, and to inform and influence foreign audiences about U.S. was efforts in support of democratic ends.

USC Center on Public Diplomacy, Center Overview, http://USCPublic Diplomacy.org, accessed April 2, 2008; see also "James Webb Young, Biographical Data," nd, box 2, Howard Henderson Papers; "James Webb Young," box 6, Colin Dawkins Papers, JWTCA, HCAMR.

17. For the history of the Creel Committee and a discussion of the fallout resulting from the Creel Committee after the war see Alan Axelrod, *Selling the Great War: The Making of American Propaganda* (New York: Palgrave Macmillan, 2009); Susan A. Brewer, *Why America Fights: Patriotism and War Propaganda from the Philippines to Iraq* (Oxford, New York: Oxford University Press, 2009); George Creel, *How We Advertised America* (New York: Harper & Brothers, 1920).

See also, C.H. Sandage, *The Promise of Advertising* (Homewood, IL: R.D. Irwin, 1961), 1, 4–5; Frank Fox, *Madison Avenue Goes to War: The Strange Military Career of American Advertising, 1941–45* (Provo, UT: Brigham Young University, 1975), 12–13, 47, 51; Stephen Fox, *The Mirror Makers: A History of American Advertising and Its Creators* (Urbana and Chicago: University of Illinois Press, 1984, 1997), 74–76, 87; "James Webb Young, Biographical Data," Howard Henderson Papers; "James Webb Young," Colin Dawkins Papers, JWTCA, HCAMR; Robert Jackall and Janice M Hirota, *Image Makers: Advertising, Public Relations, and the Ethos of Advocacy* (Chicago: University of Chicago Press, 2003), 13–14.

18. "When Kodak Started to do Business Directly in Each Country," nd; "Kodak and The World Market," nd, 140, Overseas Development, Kodak Historical Collection; The J. Walter Thompson Company London, Some Significant Dates and A Brief History," box 14, Offices London, Colin Dawkins Papers, JWTCA, HCAMR.

19. "The J. Walter Thompson Company London, Some Significant Dates and A Brief History," box 14, Offices London, Colin Dawkins Papers, JWTCA, HCAMR; "When Kodak Started to do Business Directly in Each Country," nd.; "Kodak and The World Market," nd, 140, Overseas Development, KHC.

20. "The J. Walter Thompson Company London, Some Significant Dates and A Brief History," box 14, Offices London, Colin Dawkins Papers, JWTCA, HCAMR; "When Kodak Started to do Business Directly in Each Country," nd.; "Kodak and The World Market," nd, 140, Overseas Development, KHC.

21. Dyer et al., *Rising Tide*; Frank Fox, *Madison Avenue Goes to War*, 12; Stephen Fox, *The Mirror Makers*, 79, 127, 139–149; Alfred Lief, *The Moon and Stars: The Story of Procter & Gamble and Its People* (Procter & Gamble Company, 1958); Procter & Gamble Corporate Archives, "P & G Company History" (SourceOne Business Information Services, Global Business Services), nd. 6; Alecia Swasy, *The Inside Story of Procter & Gamble* (New York: Times Books, Random House, 1993).

22. Douglas B. Craig, *Fireside Politics: Radio and Political Culture in the United States, 1920–1940* (Baltimore, MD: John Hopkins University Press, 2000), 19–58.

23. Dyer et al., *Rising Tide*, 63; Lief, *The Moon and Stars*, 24; Swasy, *The Inside Story of Procter & Gamble*, xiv.

24. Dyer et al., *Rising Tide*; Stephen Fox, *The Mirror Makers*, 151–153; Lief, *The Moon and Stars*; Procter & Gamble Corporate Archives, "P & G Company History," 6; Swasy, *The Inside Story of Procter & Gamble*.

25. Douglas B. Craig, *Fireside Politics: Radio and Political Culture in the United States, 1920–1940* (Baltimore, MD: John Hopkins University Press, 2000), 19–58.

26. "Ad Industry Also Benefits from Ad Council Campaigns," *Advertising Age*, April 18, 1955, 58, Advertising Age Clippings 1945–1959, Ad Council 50th Anniversary Files, 1943–1993, Advertising Council Archives, University of Illinois Archives, Urbana-Champaign; Stephen Fox, *The Mirror Makers*, 6,

118–127, 169; Inger L. Stole, *Advertising on Trial: Consumer Activism and Corporate Public Relations in the 1930s* (Urbana, IL: University of Illinois Press, 2006). See also Charles F. McGovern, *Sold American: Consumption and Citizenship, 1890–1945* (Chapel Hill, NC: The University of North Carolina Press, 2006), 1–3, 5, 14–16, 62, 89, 103, 124, 300, 302, 336, 363.

27. "JWT: the fleet-footed tortoise," *Broadcasting*, November 23, 1964, 46–48. Research Department to Miss Nelson, July 1, 1946, box 14, JWT TV-Radio Department, 1930 1964, Colin Dawkins Papers, JWTCA, HCAMR.

28. Procter & Gamble Corporate Archives, P & G Company History, (SourceOne Business Information Services, Global Business Services), nd, 7.

29. "The J. Walter Thompson Company London, Some Significant Dates and A Brief History," box 14, Offices London, Colin Dawkins Papers, JWTCA, HCAMR.

30. See Bernays, *Propaganda.*

31. Dyer et al., *Rising Tide*, 60–62; Frank Fox, *Madison Avenue Goes to War*, 51; Stephen Fox, *The Mirror Makers*, 52, 127, 139–149; "James Webb Young, Biographical Data," nd, box 2, File 1, Howard Henderson Papers; "James Webb Young," box 6, Colin Dawkins Papers, JWTCA, HCAMR; Procter & Gamble Corporate Archives, P & G Company History (Source One Business Information Services, Global Business Services), nd, 6.

32. "The Advertising Council Public Service Award," 1960, box 5, Speeches, Statements, Press Conferences, Neil McElroy Papers, 1948–62, Staff Files, Eisenhower Library; Dyer et al., *Rising Tide*, 60; Alfred Lief, *"It Floats" The Story of Procter & Gamble* (New York: Rinehart & Company, Inc., 1958), 155, 165, 172, 235, 242–243, 323–324; Lief, *The Moon and Stars*, 22–24; Alecia Swasy, *Soap Opera: The Inside Story of Procter & Gamble* (New York: Times Books, 1993), 10.

33. Dyer et al., *Rising Tide*, 60–64; Lief, *"It Floats" The Story of Procter & Gamble*, 166, 235, 242–243; Procter & Gamble Corporate Archives, "P & G Company History"; Schisgall, *Eyes on Tomorrow*, 105.

34. "Australia—J. Walter Thompson Co. (Aust.) Pty. Ltd.," December 2, 1965; "Clients of The J. Walter Thompson Company in the British Empire," June 1937, box 14, Office Australia 1930–31, 1937; J.A.P. Treasure, "The History of British Advertising Agencies, 1875–1939," lecture, Edinburgh University Commerce Graduates' Association Jubilee Lecture 1976 (Edinburgh: Scottish Academic Press); "The J. Walter Thompson Company London, Some Significant Dates and A Brief History," box 14, Office London; "J. Walter Thompson Company's," July 28, 1947, 2, box 14, TV-Radio Department; "J. Walter Thompson International," 1952; *J. Walter Thompson News*, June 1930, box 14, Offices London, Colin Dawkins Papers, JWTCA, HCAMR.

35. J. Walter Thompson Company Limited, London, "A Technique of Planning applied to influencing Opinion and Behaviour" (Printed by Waterlow & Sons Limited, London, 1948), 14, box 14, Offices London; "Frankfurt Office Advertises 117, Products, *J. Walter Thompson Company News*, February 28, 1964, box 14, Offices Frankfurt, Colin Dawkins Papers, JWTCA, HCAMR.

36. "When Kodak Started to do Business Directly in Each Country," nd.; "Kodak and The World Market," nd 140, Overseas development, KHC.

37. Other expansions included Puerto Rico 1947, Mexico 1948, Europe throughout the 1950s, and Saudi Arabia 1957, see The Procter & Gamble Company, "Worldwide Operations," "Facts about P & G, 2003–2004, Worldwide" (Cincinnati, OH: Procter & Gamble, 2003).

38. "The J. Walter Thompson Company London, Some Significant Dates and A Brief History," box 14, Offices London, Colin Dawkins Papers, JWTCA, HCAMR.

39. "James Webb Young, Biographical Data," nd, box 2, Howard Henderson Papers; "James Webb Young," box 6, Colin Dawkins Papers, JWTCA, HCAMR; Frank Fox, *Madison Avenue Goes to War*, 51; Stephen Fox, *The Mirror Makers*, 52; David M. Kennedy, *Freedom from Fear: The American People in Depression and War, 1929–1945* (New York: Oxford University Press, 2001); Paul A.C. Koistinen, *Arsenal of World War II: The Political Economy of American Warfare, 1940–1945* (Lawrence: University Press of Kansas, 2004).

40. "James Young Makes Plea for Free Enterprise," *Advertising Age*, September 29, 1941, box 6, Colin Dawkins Papers, JWTCA, HCAMR.

41. "On Midsouth's Busy Program," *New York Times*, April 12, 1942, D10; Display Ad 21, "When One Day Must Do the Work of Two," *New York Times*, April 15, 1942, 16.

42. William J. Enright, "Batt Bids As Men Get Into Defense," *New York Times*, November 15, 1941; G.D. Crain Jr., "Footnotes," *Advertising Age*, September 11, 1950, 40; Advertising Age Clippings 1945–1959, Ad Council 50th Anniversary Files, 1943–1993, ACA; Memo by Paul West, President, ANA, August 28, 1941, reprinted in Sandage, *The Promise of Advertising*, 18.

43. James W. Young, "What Advertising Learned From the War," Speech at the Annual Meeting, Central Council, American Association of Advertising Agencies December 11, 1945, box 2, Howard Henderson Papers, JWTCA, HCAMR.

44. William J. Enright, "Batt Bids As Men Get Into Defense," *New York Times*, November 15, 1941; Frank Fox, *Madison Avenue Goes to War*; Robert Griffith, "The Selling of America: The Advertising Council and American Politics, 1942–1960," *Business History Review*, 57, no. 3 (1983), 388–412; Jackall and Hirota, *Image Makers*, 40–47, 51–53, 58–59, 61–62, 249, 252–257, 259–261; Daniel L. Lykins, *From Total War to Total Diplomacy: The Advertising Council and the Construction of the Cold War Consensus* (Westport, CT: Praeger, 2003).

45. Charles W. Jackson, March 28, 1950, box 62, CD Jackson Papers 1931–67, Eisenhower Library; "The Advertising Council: in 10 years it has become the major public relations force for all business," *Tide*, October 10, 1952, box 1, Correspondence 1953, Files of Special Assistant Relating to the Office of Coordinator of Government Public Service Advertising, James M. Lambie Jr., Staff Files, EL; Sandage, *The Promise of Advertising*, 20–25, 36.

46. Sandage, *The Promise of Advertising*, 20, 25, 36.

47. Frank Fox, *Madison Avenue Goes to War*; Brewer, *Why America Fights*, 117–142; "Memorandum of the work of The War Advertising Council, 1942–1943," "Words That Work For Victory, The Second Year of the War Advertising Council, March 1, 1943–March 1, 1944," Advertising Council Annual Reports, ACA; "Minutes of Meeting of Advertising Council," January 22, 1942; "By-Laws of the Advertising Council, Inc.," Minutes Bylaws Objectives, Certificate of Incorporation, January-February 1942, Ad Council Minutes, 1942–89, ACA.

48. T.S. Repplier, "Business Gears Itself For Continuing Public Service," nd, 1–4, box 1 Ted Repplier Letters, Speeches, Reports, Articles, Obituary, 1944–45, 1955, 1966, Ad Council Fiftieth Anniversary File, ACA.

49. "Support of War Campaigns by Clients," box 14, Colin Dawkins Papers, JWTCA, HCAMR.

50. War Advertising Council, "From War to Peace, The New Challenge to Business and Advertising," 1945, 4–5, box 1, Charles W. Jackson Files, Staff Member and Office Files, Truman Papers, Truman Library; "J.W.T. Personnel in the Government or Volunteer Services," nd, box 14, Colin Dawkins Papers, JWTCA, HCAMR.

51. The Depictor, "Advertising Goes to War" (publisher), Edward Stern & Company, Inc., nd, box 2, WAC 1944–45, Advertising Council 50th Anniversary File, 1943–1993, ACA; War Advertising Council, "From War to Peace, The New Challenge to Business and Advertising," 1945, 4–5, box 1, Charles W. Jackson Files, SMOF, TPTL; "Words That Work For Victory, The Third Year of the War Advertising Council, March 1, 1944-March 1, 1945," Advertising Council Annual Reports, ACA; see also Brewer, *Why America Fights*, 117, 119

52. "Contribution: Sale of War Bonds"; "Project: Support O.W.I. Radio Allocation Plans," box 14, Colin Dawkins Papers, JWTCA, HCAMR; "Five Years of American Business's Public Service Advertising Through Radio, May 1, 1942–May 1, 1947," 1, box 1, Charles W. Jackson Files, SMOF, TPTL; "Memorandum on the work of The War Advertising Council, 1942–1943," 5, Advertising Council Annual Reports, ACA; "Newspaper Cooperation Plan," May 19, 1952, 7, box 4, Spencer R. Quick Files, SMOF, TPTL; War Advertising Council, "From War to Peace, The New Challenge to Business and Advertising," 1945, 4–5, box 1, Charles W. Jackson Files, SMOF, TPTL.

53. "Current Information Objectives and Proposed Programs," 1942, Minutes Bylaws Objectives, Certificate of Incorporation, January-February 1942, Ad Council Minutes, 1942–89, ACA.

54. "Ad Council Issues Report on 8th Year," *Advertising Age*, September 11, 1950, 22, Advertising Age Clippings 1945–1959, Ad Council 50th Anniversary Files, 1943–1993, ACA; "J.W.T. Personnel in the Government or Volunteer Services," nd, box 14, Colin Dawkins Papers, JWTCA, HCAMR; War Advertising Council, "From War to Peace, The New Challenge to Business and Advertising," 1945, 4–5, box 1, Charles W. Jackson Files, SMOF, TPTL; "Memorandum of the work of The War Advertising Council, 1942–1943"; "Words That Work

For Victory, The Second Year of the War Advertising Council, March 1, 1943–March 1, 1944," 4–7; "Words That Work For Victory, The Third Year of the War Advertising Council, March 1, 1944–March 1, 1945," Advertising Council Annual Reports, ACA.

55. "Coal Conservation Campaign"; "Contribution, Anti-Inflation Campaign"; "Contribution: Campaigns for Saving Tires, Rubber, and Gasoline"; "Contribution: National Health Campaign"; "Contribution, Support Cadet Nurse Recruiting"; "Paper Salvage Campaign"; "Project: Recruit Women for War Industry and Civilian Jobs as Well as the Armed Forces"; "Project: Sell War Bonds"; Cover Letter and War Ad Packet, J. Walter Thompson Company, 1944, box 14, Colin Dawkins Papers, JWTCA, HCAMR; "Memorandum on the work of the War Advertising Council, 1942–1943," 6–9, Advertising Council Annual Reports, ACA.

56. "Words That Work for Victory, the Third Year of the War Advertising Council, March 1, 1944–March 1," 1945, 8, 10–16, Advertising Council Annual Reports, ACA.

57. "James Webb Young, Biographical Data," nd, box 2, Howard Henderson Papers, JWTCA, HCAMR; "James Webb Young," box 6, Colin Dawkins Papers, JWTCA, HCAMR; Memorandum of the Conversation Between the President and T.S. Repplier, August 3, 1955; Theodore S. Repplier, Confidential Memorandum, box 23, People's Capitalism 1955; T.S. Repplier Biographical Sketch, July 25, 1956, box 25, Ad Council Repplier TS 1956; T.S. Repplier to the Board of Directors, December 1, 1954, box 15, U.S. Information Agency, Files of Special Assistant Relating to the Office of Coordinator of Government Public Service Advertising, James M. Lambie Jr., Staff Files, EL.

58. "Memorandum of the work of The War Advertising Council, 1942–1943"; "Words That Work For Victory, The Second Year of the War Advertising Council, March 1, 1943—March 1, 1944"; "Words That Work For Victory, The Third Year of the War Advertising Council, March 1, 1944—March 1, 1945," Advertising Council Annual Reports, ACA; War Advertising Council, "From War to Peace, The New Challenge to Business and Advertising," 1945, 4–5, box 1, Charles W. Jackson Files, SMOF, TPTL.

59. Dyer et al., *Rising Tide*, 64; Franklin D Roosevelt, Remarks to the Advertising War Council Conference, March 8, 1944, The American Presidency Project, http://www.presidency.ucsb.edu/, accessed October 21, 2008; "Project: Promote Goodwill for the United States in Latin America," nd, box 14, Colin Dawkins Papers, JWTCA, HCAMR.

60. "Kodak created, U.S. Government Adopts 'V-Mail' for communication with our men on distant fronts," 1944, box 14, Colin Dawkins Papers JWTCA, HCAMR.

61. D. McMaster, "The Philosophy of a Business," Cornell University, April 27, 1961, Box Speeches, 1961–1962; "Kodak People—Perley Smith Wilcox," 6, Binder 141; "Products and Uses," *Eastman Kodak Annual Report* 1943, 25, box—Kodak Annual Reports, 1934–1946; "War-Production Postscript,"

Eastman Kodak Annual Report 1946, 39, Box—Kodak Annual Reports, 1934–1946, KHC.

62. James W. Young, "What Advertising Learned From the War," Speech at the Annual Meeting, Central Council, American Association of Advertising Agencies December 11, 1945, box 2, Howard Henderson Papers, JWTCA, HCAMR; "Notes on Results Achieved By Home Front Campaigns," February 1947, box 4, Advertising Council 50th Anniversary File 1943–1993; T.S. Repplier, "Business Gears Itself For Continuing Public Service," nd, 1–4, box 1, Ted Repplier Letters, Speeches, Reports, Articles, Obituary, 1944–45, 1955, 1966, Advertising Council 50th Anniversary File 1943–1993; " 'Voice of Freedom,' News Feature for House Magazine Editors," Advertising Council, Historical File 1941–1997, ACA.

63. The Depictor, "Advertising Goes to War" (publisher), Edward Stern & Company, Inc., nd, box 2, WAC 1944–45; "Notes on Results Achieved By Home Front Campaigns," February 1947, box 4; "Public Service Ad Program Enters Its Sixth Year," *Advertising Age*, May 5, 1947, 36, box 1, Ad Council 50th Anniversary Files, 1943–1993, ACA.

64. "In The Wake of the War, the Fourth Year of the Advertising Council, March 1, 1945 to March 1, 1946," 7, Advertising Council Annual Reports; "Top Executives Discuss Foreign Policy Program," *Advertising Age*, November 3, 1947, 57, box 1, Ad Council 50th Anniversary Files, 1943–1993; "Notes on Results Achieved By Home Front Campaigns," February 1947, box 4, Advertising Council 50th Anniversary File, 1943–1993, ACA; see also Brewer who describes the Advertising Council as an organization devoted to "free enterprise" and "American international leadership," 144.

65. Harry Truman to A.E. Winger, chairman Magazine Advertising Committee, War Advertising Council, November 2, 1945, box 544, PPF, TPTL; "Media Programming Division," nd, 4, box 7, Charles W. Jackson Files, SMOF, TPTL.

66. Jackall and Hirota, *Image Makers*, 255; "War Ad Council Launches Peacetime Service Plan," *Advertising Age*, September 17, 1945, 1, box 1, Ad Council 50th Anniversary Files, 1943–1993, ACA; War Advertising Council, "From War to Peace, The New Challenge to Business and Advertising," 1945, 4–5, box 1, Charles W. Jackson Files, SMOF, TPTL.

67. "Industries Advertising Committee, the Advertising Council," August 10, 1950, box 1, Ad Council: Industry Advisory Committee File, 1950–1964; Report of Public Policy Committee Meeting, November 17, 1954, Reports for Public Policy Committee Meeting, 1954–1963; Public Policy Committee Meeting Reports and Minutes, 1954–1986; "In the Wake of the War, The Fourth Year of the Advertising Council, March 1, 1945 to March 1, 1946," 9–10, 12, Advertising Council Annual Reports, ACA.

68. "Business Steps Up Its Candle Power," 1948; "The White House Meeting for the Board of Directors and Committees of the Advertising Council," February 9, 1949; "The Sixth White House Meeting for the Board of Directors and Committees of the Advertising Council," February 15–16, 1950; "Briefing

on America," "Off the Record," January 15, 1951; "The Eighth White House Conference in cooperation with the Advertising Council," March 4–5, 1952; "The Ninth White House Conference in cooperation with the Advertising Council," March 23–24, 1953; "Cherry Blossom Time in Washington," "Confidential and off the record," March 31, 1953; "The Tenth White House Conference, the Advertising Council," January 11–12, 1954; "The Eleventh Washington Conference, the Advertising Council," March 22, 1955; "The Twelfth Washington Conference, the Advertising Council," April 3, 1956; "The Thirteenth Washington Conference, the Advertising Council," April 2, 1957; "The Fourteenth Washington Conference, the Advertising Council," May 6, 1958; "The Fifteenth Washington Conference, the Advertising Council," April 13 and 14, 1959, box 1, Washington Conference Programs, 1949–1960, Washington Conference File 1944–1959, ACA.

69. Conference: The White House, September 17–18, 1946, box 4, Ad Council 50th Anniversary File, 1943–1993; "In the Wake of the War, The Fourth Year of the Advertising Council, March 1, 1945 to March 1, 1946," 13, Advertising Council Annual Reports; "Memorandum on White House Meeting," December 15, 1949, box 1, Washington Conference Programs, 1949–1960, Washington Conference File, 1944–1959, ACA; "Top Executives Discuss Foreign Policy Program," *Advertising Age*, November 3, 1947, 57, box 1, Ad Council 50th Anniversary Files, 1943–1993, ACA; War Advertising Council, "From War to Peace, The New Challenge to Business and Advertising," 1945, 4–5, box 1, Charles W. Jackson Files, SMOF, TPTL.

70. "Certificate of Change of Purpose of the Advertising Council, Inc.," Ad Council Minutes, 1942–89, Minutes Bylaws Objectives, Certificate of Incorporation, January-February 1942; "In the Wake of the War, The Fourth Year of the Advertising Council, March 1, 1945 to March 1, 1946"; "What Helps People Helps Business, The Sixth Year of the Advertising Council, March 1947–March 1, 1948," 1, Advertising Council Annual Reports, ACA; James W. Young, "What Advertising Learned From the War," Speech at the Annual Meeting, Central Council, American Association of Advertising Agency, December 11, 1945, box 2, Howard Henderson Papers, JWTCA, HCAMR; "Trends to Brands Shown by Survey," *New York Times*, May 18, 1946, 26; War Advertising Council, "From War to Peace, The New Challenge to Business and Advertising," 1945, 4–5, box 1, Charles W. Jackson Files, SMOF, TPTL.

71. "Articles of Agreement of the International Bank for Reconstruction and Development, July 22, 1944," The Bretton Woods Agreements, Article I (i), Article II (ii), *A Decade of American Foreign Policy: Basic Documents, 1941–49* (Washington, D.C.: Government Printing Office, 1950); War Advertising Council, "From War to Peace, The New Challenge to Business and Advertising," 1945, box 1, Charles W. Jackson Files, SMOF, TPTL.

72. "Articles of Agreement of the International Bank for Reconstruction and Development, July 22, 1944," The Bretton Woods Agreements, Article IX (iii), *A Decade of American Foreign Policy: Basic Documents, 1941–49* (Washington, D.C.: Government Printing Office, 1950).

73. "In the Wake of the War, The Fourth Year of the Advertising Council, March 1, 1945 to March 1, 1946," 4–5, 14, Advertising Council Annual Reports, ACA; "Report on Major National Problems," the Advertising Council, February 12 and 13, no year, box 1, Charles W. Jackson Files, SMOF, TPTL.

74. Conference: The White House, September 17–18, 1946, 4, box 4, Ad Council 50th Anniversary File 1943–1993, ACA; Procter & Gamble Corporate Archives, "P & G Company History" (SourceOne Business Information Services, Global Business Services), nd, 6.

Chapter 2

1. The Advertising Council, "The Miracle of America: As Discovered by One American Family," 1949, 19, Historical Files 1941–1947, ACA; Susan A. Brewer, *Why America Fights: Patriotism and War Propaganda from the Philippines to Iraq* (Oxford; New York: Oxford University Press, 2009), 147; Nicholas John Cull, *The Cold War and the United States Information Agency: American Propaganda and Public Diplomacy, 1945–1989* (New York: Cambridge University Press, 2008), 44.

2. See Richard Fried, *The Russians are Coming! The Russians Are Coming! Pageantry and Patriotism in Cold War America* (New York: Oxford University Press, 1998); Michael Kammen, *Mystic Chords of Memory: The Transformation of Tradition in American Culture* (New York: Alfred Knopf, 1991), 573–581; Stuart J. Little, "The Freedom Train: Citizenship and Postwar Political Culture 1946–1949," *American Studies*, 34, no. 1 (Spring 1993);35–67; Wendy L. Wall, *Inventing the "American Way" : The Politics of Consensus from the New Deal to the Civil Rights Movement* (New York, Oxford: Oxford University Press, 2009).

3. William Coblenz to Colonel McInerny, September 9, 1946, Tom C. Clark Papers, Files of the Attorney General, Box 37, TPTL; "Our American Heritage Campaign," presented to the Public Advisory Committee, the Advertising Council, Inc., January 8, 1947, Truman Papers, Files of Charles W. Jackson, TPTL; "Statement by the Attorney General before the House of Representatives Committee on Expenditures in the Executive Departments concerning the Freedom Train," June 18, 1947, box 37, Tom C. Clark Papers, Files of the Attorney General, TPTL; see also Stuart Jon Little, *The Freedom Train and the Formation of National Political Culture, 1946–1949* (Masters Thesis, University of Kansas, 1989), 13.

4. Conference: The White House, September 17–18, 1946, 13, box 4, Ad Council 50th Anniversary File, 1943–1993, ACA; Harry Truman to Charles C. Mortimer, Jr., The Advertising Council, April 23, 1947, box 1705, PPF, WHCF, TPTL.

5. American Heritage Foundation, Inc., "Conference at the White House for the Purpose of Organizing The American Heritage Program, May 22, 1947," box 12, State Department of Overseas Information, Charles W. Jackson Files, SMOF, TPTL; "Meeting is Called on 'Freedom Train,' " *New York Times*, May 16, 1947, 11; "Why Is There a Freedom Train? How It Started," NYPL.

6. "The American Heritage Program for New York City," 1948; "Why Is There a Freedom Train? How It Started," 1948, a collection of pamphlets, clippings, postcards, et cetera, related to the Freedom Train, 1947–1948, New York Public Library; "What Helps People Helps Business," "The Sixth Year of the Advertising Council, March 1947–March 1, 1948,"Advertising Council Annual Reports, ACA.

7. American Heritage Foundation, Inc., "Conference at the White House for the Purpose of Organizing the American Heritage Program, May 22, 1947," box 12, State Department of Overseas Information, Charles W. Jackson Files, SMOF, TPTL; "The American Heritage Program for Your Community," 5, 11, NYPL; Conference: The White House, September 17–18, 1946, 10, box 4, Ad Council 50th Anniversary File, 1943–1993, ACA.

8. Advertising Council, Board of Directors, Committees, January 5, 1951, Advertising Council Rosters of Board Members, 1944–63, ACA; "The Freedom Train," interim Report of Thomas D'Arcy Brophy, president of the American Heritage Foundation, November 4, 1948, NYPL; also in Box 38, Papers of Tom C. Clark, Attorney General Files, SMOF, TPTL.

9. Paul G. Hoffman, administrator, Economic Cooperation Administration, 1948–50, Oral History Interview, New York, New York, October 25, 1964, by Dr. Philip C. Brooks, TPTL; "What Helps People Helps Business," "The Seventh Year of the Advertising Council, March 1948–March 1949," 15, ACA.

10. Advertising Council, Board of Directors, Committees, January 5, 1951, Advertising Council Rosters of Board Members, 1944–63, ACA; American Heritage Foundation, Inc., "Conference at the White House for the Purpose of Organizing the American Heritage Program, May 22, 1947," TPTL; "The American Heritage Program for Your Community," 28, NYPL; "The Freedom Train," interim Report of Thomas D'Arcy Brophy, president of the American Heritage Foundation, November 4, 1948, NYPL.

11. William H. Harley and John Dugan, *Your Heritage of Freedom—Suggestions for Teachers* (New York: McGraw-Hill Book Company, Inc., 1948), NYPL; "Why Is There a Freedom Train? How It Started," 1948, NYPL.

12. American Heritage Foundation, Inc., "Conference at the White House for the Purpose of Organizing the American Heritage Program, May 22, 1947," box 12, State Department of Overseas Information, Charles W. Jackson Files, SMOF, TPTL; "'What Helps People Helps Business,' The Sixth Year of the Advertising Council, March 1947–March 1948," 2, 13, ACA. Wall, *Inventing the 'American Way'*.

13. American Heritage Foundation, Inc., "Conference at the White House for the Purpose of Organizing the American Heritage Program, May 22, 1947," box 12, State Department of Overseas Information, Charles W. Jackson Files, SMOF, TPTL; "The American Heritage Program for Your Community," 5, 11, NYPL; Conference: The White House, September 17–18, 1946, 10, box 4, Ad Council 50th Anniversary File, 1943–1993, ACA; see also Wall, *Inventing the 'American Way,'* 180–181.

14. The American Heritage Foundation, *The Documents of the Freedom Train*, the American Heritage Foundation, box 37, Correspondence, Papers of Tom. C. Clark Attorney General Files, TPTL; American Heritage Foundation, Inc., "Conference at the White House for the Purpose of Organizing the American Heritage Program, May 22, 1947," box 12, State Department of Overseas Information, Charles W. Jackson Files, SMOF, TPTL; "Why Is There a Freedom Train? How It Started," 1948, NYPL.

15. "Precautions Taken for Freedom Train," *New York Times*, August 28, 1947, 25; "52 Roads Promise Freedom Train Aid," *New York Times*, August 17, 1947, 13; "Why They Throng to the Freedom Train," *New York Times*, January 25, 1948, 18.

16. The numbers vary slightly from 322 to 324 cities, from 3.5 million to 3.8 million attending the train. The estimate of 50 million participating in Rededication Week events that can be found in both the *New York Times* and Little is from a number provided by the American Heritage Foundation. Therefore, these figures could be overestimates to create more publicity. See Bill Coblenz to Attorney General, November 17, 1948, box 38, Papers of Tom C. Clark, Attorney General Files, SMOF, TPTL; Freedom Train Postcard, NYPL; "President Receives Freedom Signatures," *New York Times*, January 15, 1949, 19; "U.S. Tour Is Ended by Freedom Train," *New York Times*, January 9, 1949, 50; See Little, 38; For train route see http://www.lincoln-highway-museum.org/FT/FT02 Route-Index.html; and memorabilia collector, http://www.freedomtrain.org/.

17. The American Heritage Foundation, "The Freedom Pledge," Freedom Train Postcard, 1948, NYPL.

18. "The American Heritage Program for Your Community," 6–7, 13–15, 18–19, NYPL; "Freedom Is Everybody's Job: Highlights of the National Rededication Program of the American Heritage Foundation," 1948, NYPL; "Freedom Rallies to Publicize Train," *New York Times*, October 31, 1948, 39.

19. American Heritage Foundation, *Good Citizen, the Rights and Duties of an American*, An Official Freedom Train Publication, American Heritage Foundation, 1948, 61, NYPL; "Sermon Notes, Religious Foundations of Our American Heritage," prepared for the American Heritage Foundation by the *Reader's Digest* Program Services (Pleasantville, New York), nd, NYPL.

20. "Jews to Honor Freedom Sabbath," *New York Times*, June 28, 1948, 5; "Freedom Train Due in City Next Week," *New York Times*, December 24, 1948, 15.

21. "The American Heritage Program for Your Community," 20–21, NYPL; "The Freedom Train," interim Report of Thomas D'Arcy Brophy, president of the American Heritage Foundation, November 4, 1948, NYPL.

22. "Aids City Schools," *New York Times*, November 7, 1948, 72; William H. Harley and John Dugan, *Your Heritage of Freedom—Suggestions for Teachers* (New York: McGraw-Hill Book Company, Inc., 1948); "Here Are the Tools You Can Use for Freedom, A Catalogue of New Publications," NYPL; "School Study Guide and Suggestions for Teachers" called "Your Heritage of Freedom," edited by William Lewin, National Education Association, NYPL.

23. Frank Monaghan, *Heritage of Freedom: The History and Significance of the Basic Documents of American Liberty* (Princeton, NJ: Princeton University Press, 1947).

24. American Heritage Foundation, *Good Citizen, the Rights and Duties of an American*, An Official Freedom Train Publication, American Heritage Foundation, 1948, 1, 11–15.

25. The council claimed that over two million "Good Citizen" brochures were distributed in total. See "How Business Helps Solve Public Problems," "A Report on the Eighth Year of the Advertising Council, March 1949 to March 1950," Advertising Council Annual Reports, ACA; "The Freedom Train," interim Report of Thomas D'Arcy Brophy, president of the American Heritage Foundation, November 4, 1948, NYPL; "What Helps People Helps Business," "The Seventh Year of the Advertising Council, March 1948–March 1949," 15, Advertising Council Annual Reports, ACA.

26. Gilbert Bailey, "Why They Throng to the Freedom Train," *New York Times*, January 25, 1948, 18.

27. "The American Heritage Program for Your Community," 11, NYPL; American Heritage Foundation, Inc., "Conference at the White House for the Purpose of Organizing the American Heritage Program, May 22, 1947," box 12, State Department of Overseas Information, Charles W. Jackson Files, SMOF, TPTL; Conference: The White House, September 17–18, 1946, 10, box 4, Ad Council 50th Anniversary File, 1943–1993, ACA.

28. The Advertising Council addressed civil rights almost from the beginning. The Negro Newspaper Publishers Association served on the council, and the council made civil rights an issue during the Freedom Train. In addition, it launched a campaign called the United America; see also Thomas Borstelmann, *The Cold War and the Color Line: American Race Relations in the Global Arena* (Cambridge, MA: Harvard University Press, 2001); Mary L. Dudziak, *Cold War Civil Rights, Race and the Image of American Democracy* (Princeton, NJ: Princeton University Press, 2000).

29. Rick Fantasia and Kim Voss, *Hard Work: Remaking the American Labor Movement* (Berkeley, CA: University of California Press, 2004); Nelson Lichtenstein, *State of the Union: A Century of American Labor* (Princeton, NJ: Princeton University Press, 2003); Robert H. Zieger and Gilbert J. Gall, *American Workers, American Unions: The Twentieth Century* (*Baltimore, MD*: John Hopkins University Press, 2002).

30. "Ceremony Slated for Freedom Train," *New York Times*, December 27, 1948, 5; "Queens Turns Out for Freedom Train," *New York Times*, September 29, 1947, 7; "What Helps People Helps Business," "The Sixth Year of the Advertising Council, March 1947–March 1948," 11, ACA; "Why Is There a Freedom Train? How It Started," 1948, NYPL; John White, "Civil Rights in Conflict: The 'Birmingham Plan' and the Freedom Train," *Alabama Review*, 52: 2 (April 1999), 2, 121–127.

31. "Birmingham Is Ruled Out," *New York Times*, December 25, 1947, 8; "Freedom Train to Skirt 2 Cities; Many in South Lift 'Jim Crowism,'" *New York Times*, December 25, 1947, 1; White, "Civil Rights in Conflict," 135–140.

32. Hartfield quoted in "Freedom Train Barred," *New York Times*, November 20, 1947, 31; "Against Racial Bias," *New York Times*, November 21, 1947, 26; "Segregation Plan Bars Freedom Train Showing," *New York Times*, November 18, 1947, 31.

33. "Aboard the Freedom Train," *New York Times*, December 26, 1947, 14; "Celebrating Freedom from Fear Day in Brooklyn," *New York Times*, December 2, 1948, 17; "For Gettysburg Event," *New York Times*, November 17, 1948, 20.

34. "A Campaign to Explain the American Economic System," 3, 5, 21, Miracle of America 1948, Historical Files 1941–97, ACA; " 'How Business Helps Solve Public Problems,' A Report on the Eighth Year of the Advertising Council, March 1949 to March 1950," "Advertising Council Annual Reports, ACA; " 'What Helps People Helps Business,' " "The Seventh Year of the Advertising Council, March 1948–March 1949," 14, Advertising Council Annual Reports, ACA; John Vianney McGinnis, "The Advertising Council and the Cold War," dissertation University of Syracuse, 1991, 51.

35. The Advertising Council, "A Campaign to Explain the American Economic System, "2, 4, 6, 16, Historical Files 1941–1947, ACA; Paul G. Hoffman, administrator, Economic Cooperation Administration, 1948–50, Oral History Interview, New York, New York, October 25, 1964, by Dr. Philip C. Brooks, TPTL; McGinnis, "The Advertising Council and the Cold War," 47, 52, 54–55; "What Helps People Helps Business," "The Seventh Year of the Advertising Council, March 1948–March 1949," 14, Advertising Council Annual Reports, ACA.

36. Cull, *The Cold War and the United States Information Agency*, 44

37. Paul G. Hoffman to Charles E Wilson, April 29, 1948, Miracle of America, Historical Files 1941–97, ACA.

38. The Advertising Council, "A Campaign to Explain the American Economic System," 1948, 3–5, Historical Files 1941–1947, ACA.

39. Ibid.,

40. Ibid.,

41. Ibid.,

42. McGinnis, "The Advertising Council and the Cold War," 51; The Advertising Council, "The Miracle of America," 1948, 1, 10–12, 19, Historical Files 1941–1947, ACA.

43. "What Helps People Helps Business," "The Sixth Year of the Advertising Council, March 1947–March 1, 1948," 10, Advertising Council Annual Reports, ACA.

Chapter 3

1. "Transcript Proceedings of the Public Relations Executives' Clinic; held as a part of the 'Brand Names Day' program," April 18, 1947, 4, Waldorf Astoria Hotel, UWML; Oscar Schisgall, *Eyes on Tomorrow: The Evolution of Procter & Gamble* (Chicago: J.G Ferguson Publishing Company, 1981).

2. Bristol-Myers Company secretary, George McMillan explained the mission of the BNF during the Brand Names Foundation; see "Transcript Proceedings of the Public Relations Executives' Clinic; held as a part of the 'Brand Names Day' program, April 18, 1947, 6, Waldorf Astoria Hotel, University of Wisconsin—Madison Library; Brand Names Foundation, "Transcript Proceedings of the Department Store Clinic Held as Part of the 'Brand Names' Day' Program," April 18, 1947, Waldorf-Astoria Hotel, NYC, UWML; "A.O Buckingham Quits as Director of Cluett Firm," *Times Record*, Troy, New York, July 21, 1949, 19; Brand Names Foundation, Incorporated, "43,000 Years of Public Service: A Roster of Product-identifying Names Used By the American Public for 50 Consecutive Years or More," June 1947; "Brands Preferred to U.S. Standard," *New York Times*, April 26, 1945, 27; "Council Is Formed to Spur Industry," *New York Times*, August 13, 1946, 34, 38; National Family Opinion, Incorporated, "The Importance of Brand Buying: Results of a survey conducted as a contribution to the continuing program of Brand Names Foundation, Incorporated," Cleveland Public Library, August 1950.

3. Very little evidence exists regarding the institutional history of the Brand Names Foundation, see "Brand Retailing Year Round Task," *Post-Register, Idaho Falls, Idaho*, April 22, 1958; "Foundation Established To Fight Federal Curbs," *The Lima News*, May 15, 1963, 11.

4. "Advertising News and Notes—Now Brand Names Foundation." *New York Times*, August 28, 1946, 47; Rader Winget, "And You Save Money, Brands Fighting It Out To Win Customer Nod," *The Amarillo Daily News*, March 29, 1949, 6; Brand Names Foundation, "How Greenfield Did It . . . A Comprehensive Guide to a Worthwhile Community Activity" (New York: Brand Names Foundation, Incorporated, 1947), 39.

5. Brand Names Foundation, "Transcript Proceedings of the Public Relations Executives' Clinic; held as a part of the 'Brand Names Day' program, April 18, 1947, 2; Cohen, *Consumer Republic*, 77, 83, 114.

6. "Advertising News and Notes," *New York Times*, April 17, 1947, 46; "Advertising News and Notes—Public Belief in Ads Damaged." *New York Times*, November 15, 1946, 41; "Brands Preferred to U.S. Standard," *New York Times*, April 26, 1945, 27; "Director Raps Ad Criticism," *Salt Lake City Tribune*, September 19, 1946, 13; "Fifty Brand Names Honored by Trade," *New York Times*, April 19, 1947, 32; "Hawkes Flays Bid To Destroy Brands—Senator Warns Foundation Aim Is to Upset American System for 'Economic Revolution,'" *New York Times*, February 6, 1946, 36.

7. Alfred Buckingham, Chairman of Brand Names Research Foundation, and VP of Cluett, Peabody & Co., quoted in "Hawkes Flays Bid To Destroy Brands—Senator Warns Foundation Aim Is to Upset American System for 'Economic Revolution,'" *New York Times*, February 6, 1946, 36; "Director Raps Ad Criticism," *Salt Lake City Tribune*, 19 September 1946, 13; "Sees Threats to Brands," *New York Times*, March 26, 1946, 44.

8. Brand Names Foundation, "How Greenfield Did It . . . A Comprehensive Guide to a Worthwhile Community Activity" (New York: Brand Names Foundation, Incorporated, 1947), 12; BNF, Transcript Proceedings of the Advertising Agencies' Clinic Held as Part of the 'Brand Names' Day' Program," April 18, 1947, 5, 17; BNF, Department Stores Clinic, 10; George McMillan, "Transcript Proceedings of the Public Relations Executives' Clinic; held as a part of the 'Brand Names Day' program, April 18, 1947, 20, UWML.

9. BNF, Advertising Agencies' Clinic, held as a part of the 'Brand Names Day' program, April 18, 1947, 1 UWML; Brand Names Foundation, Incorporated, "43,000 Years of Public Service: A Roster of Product-identifying Names Used By the American Public for 50 Consecutive Years or More," June 1947, ii; "Brand Names President Stresses Clerks' Role In Maintaining U.S. System," *Greenfield Recorder-Gazette*, October 21, 1947; National Family Opinion, Incorporated, "The Importance of Brand Buying: Results of a survey conducted as a contribution to the continuing program of Brand Names Foundation, Incorporated," Cleveland Public Library, August 1950, i.

10. Truman vetoed the bill, but it passed June 23, 1947; BNF, Dept Stores Clinic, 9; BNF, Adv Media Clinic, 2, 5; BNF, PR Clinic, 4, UWML.

11. Henry Abt, Director of the Brand Names Research Foundation in a speech to the American Association of Newspaper Representatives quoted in "New and Notes in the Advertising Field," *New York Times*, February 15, 1946, 41.

12. BNF, "43,000 Years of Public Service," i–ii.

13. "Hawkes Flays Bid To Destroy Brands—Senator Warns Foundation Aim Is to Upset American System for 'Economic Revolution,'" *New York Times*, February 6, 1946, 36.

14. "Good-Will Ads for Brand Names," *New York Times*, October 9, 1946, 40; Herbert Koshetz, "Battle of Brands Looms in History," *New York Times*, February 9, 1947, F6; "Sponsor Brand Name Contest," *New York Times*, March 5, 1947, 42; "Stress Dress Brand Name," *New York Times*, January 9, 1947, 39.

15. "Good-Will Ads for Brand Names," *New York Times*, October 9, 1946, 40; Herbert Koshetz, "Battle of Brands Looms in History," *New York Times*, February 9, 1947, F6; "Sponsor Brand Name Contest," *New York Times*, March 5, 1947, 42; "Stress Dress Brand Name," *New York Times*, January 9, 1947, 39.

16. "Advertising News and Notes," *New York Times*, June 13, 1947, 34; "Awards for Retail Stores," *New York Times*, April 7, 1947, 33; BNF, "43,000 Years of Public Service," ii; "80 Brand Names to Be Honored," *New York Times*, November 24, 1947, 40; "Store Cited for Brand Ads," *New York Times*, May 13, 1947.

17. Brand Names Foundation, "How Greenfield Did It . . . A Comprehensive Guide to a Worthwhile Community Activity," 5; "Expect National Business Heads Here For 'Greenfield Experiment,'" *Greenfield Recorder-Gazette*, October 17, 1947; "The Show is On," *Greenfield Recorder-Gazette*, October 19, 1947.

18. "Advertising News and Notes," *New York Times*, April 17, 1947, 46; BNF, "Transcript Proceedings of the Public Relations Executives' Clinic, Held as a part of the

'Brand Names Day' program, April 18, 1947, 2, UWML; "Fifty Brand Names Honored By Trade," *New York Times*, April 19, 1947, 32.

19. BNF, Advertising Agencies' Clinic, 5–8, 15; BNF, Advertising Media Clinic, 13, 17, 24; BNF, Public Relations Executives' Clinic, 2, Held as a part of the 'Brand Names Day' program, April 18, 1947, UWML.

20. BNF, "43,000 Years of Public Service: A Roster of Product-identifying Names Used By the American Public for 50 Consecutive Years or More," June 1947, i–ii.

21. BNF, "Transcript Proceedings of the Public Relations Executives' Clinic; Held as a part of the 'Brand Names Day' program, April 18, 1947, 6–9, UWML.

22. Ibid., 1–3.

23. BNF, Advertising Media Clinic, 21–23; BNF, Public Relations Clinic, Held as a part of the 'Brand Names Day' program, April 18, 1947, 4–5, UWML.

24. BNF, Advertising Media Clinic, Held as a part of the 'Brand Names Day' program, April 18, 1947, 3–4, 8–9, 16–18, 25, UWML.

25. Ibid., 16–18.

26. BNF, Advertising Agencies Clinic, Held as a part of the 'Brand Names Day' program, April 18, 1947, 4, UWML; BNF, *43,000*, i.

27. BNF, Advertising Media Clinic, Held as a part of the 'Brand Names Day' program, April 18, 1947, 16, UWML.

28. Brand Names Foundation, Department Store Clinic, Held as Part of the 'Brand Names' Day' Program," April 18, 1947, 2, 4, 6–7, 12, UWML.

29. BNF, Advertising Agencies' Clinic, 15, UWML; Brand Names Foundation, "How Greenfield Did It," 12; "Expect Greenfield to Overflow During Brand Names Experiment," *Greenfield-Recorder Gazette*, October 9, 1947, 1.

30. "Brand Names President Stresses Clerks' Role In Maintaining U.S. System," *Greenfield Recorder Gazette*, October 21, 1947; Brand Names Foundation, "How Greenfield Did It," 8; "Expect Greenfield to Overflow During Brand Names Experiment," *Greenfield-Recorder Gazette*, October 9, 1947, 1; "Expect National Business Heads Here For 'Greenfield Experiment,'" *Greenfield Recorder-Gazette*, October 17, 1947.

31. Brand Names Foundation, "How Greenfield Did It," 9; "Expect Greenfield to Overflow During Brand Names Experiment," *Greenfield Recorder-Gazette*, October 9, 1947; "Greenfield's Brand Names Celebration," *Greenfield Recorder-Gazette*, October 18, 1947; "The Show Is On," *Greenfield Recorder-Gazette*, October 19, 1947.

32. Brand Names Foundation, "How Greenfield Did It," 9, 12; "Brand Names President Stresses Clerks' Role In Maintaining U.S. System," *Greenfield Recorder-Gazette*, October 21, 1947; "Campaign Boosted Brand Acceptance," *New York Times*, January 5, 1948, 27; "Expect National Business Heads Here For 'Greenfield Experiment,'" *Greenfield Recorder-Gazette*, October 17, 1947.

33. Brand Names Foundation, "How Greenfield Did It," 12; "Brand Names President Stresses Clerks' Role In Maintaining U.S. System," *Greenfield Recorder Gazette*, October 21, 1947; "Fashion Show Tonight, Autos Saturday Brand

Names Events," *Greenfield Recorder Gazette*, October 24, 1947; "Movies Will Assist Brand Names Show," *New York Times*, October 22, 1947, 43; "Two Good Names Are Better Than One," *Greenfield Recorder-Gazette*, October 30, 1947, 3.

34. BNF, "How Greenfield Did It," 5–6, 9, 33.

35. "The Beginning of the Story of Greenfield Brand Names," *Greenfield Recorder-Gazette*, October 14, 1947, 13; "The Eyes of the Nation are on You," *Greenfield Recorder-Gazette*, October 31, 1947, 27; "The Show is On," *Greenfield Recorder-Gazette*, October 19, 1947.

36. Hartley W. Barclay, "Heavy Sales Mark Brand Experiment," *New York Times*, October 28, 1947, 35, 40; Brand Names Foundation, "How Greenfield Did It," 18; "Business Writer Sees Promotion Long-Range Aid," *Greenfield Recorder-Gazette*, November 4, 1947; "Expect National Business Heads Here For 'Greenfield Experiment,'" *Greenfield Recorder Gazette*, October 17, 1947; "Two Good Names Are Better Than One," *Greenfield Recorder-Gazette*, October 30, 1947, 3.

37. Brand Names Foundation, "How Greenfield Did It," 22, 27.

38. Ibid., 26; "Expect National Business Heads Here For 'Greenfield Experiment'" *Greenfield Recorder-Gazette*, October 17, 1947; "Greenfield Sponsors America's Brand Names," *Greenfield Recorder-Gazette*, October 14, 1947, 13; "Two Good Names Are Better Than One," *Greenfield Recorder Gazette*, October 30, 1947, 3.

39. "Backed by 155 years of Service," *Greenfield Recorder-Gazette*, October 1, 1947, 21; "Greenfield Sponsors America's Brand Names," *Greenfield Recorder-Gazette*, October 14, 1947, 13; "Re-Elected! Today and Every Day, A Vote For Brand Names," *Greenfield Recorder Gazette*, October 28, 1947, 11.

40. "The Beginning o f the Story of Greenfield Brand Names," *Greenfield Recorder-Gazette*, October 14, 1947, 13; "...Symbols of Many Accomplishments," *Greenfield Recorder-Gazette*, October 24, 1947; "When Greenfield Goes Traveling," *Greenfield Recorder-Gazette*, October 18, 1947.

41. BNF, "43,000 Years of Public Service: A Roster of Product-identifying Names Used By the American Public for 50 Consecutive Years or More," June 1947, 1–2.

42. BNF, "How Greenfield Did It," 12, 14–15, 22; "Brand Names President Stresses Clerks' Role In Maintaining U.S. System," *Greenfield Recorder-Gazette*, October 21, 1947.

43. "Brand Experiment on in Bay State Area," *New York Times*, October 22, 1947, 50; "How Greenfield Did It," 28, 30

44. "Goddard & Wallner's Old Home Day Events," *Greenfield Recorder-Gazette*, October 30, 1947, 17.

45. "How Greenfield Did It," 20, 22–23, 41.

46. "Backed by 155 years of Service," *Greenfield Recorder-Gazette*, October 1, 1947, 21; "Fashion Show Tonight, Autos Saturday Brand Names Events," *Greenfield Recorder Gazette*, October 24, 1947; "How Greenfield Did It," 18, 20, 22–23, 41; "Movies Will Assist Brand Names Show," *New York Times*, October 22, 1947, 43.

47. "Expect Greenfield to Overflow During Brand Names Experiment," *Greenfield Recorder-Gazette*, October 9, 1947; "Fashion Show Tonight, Autos Saturday Brand Names Events," *Greenfield Recorder-Gazette*, October 24, 1947.

48. "How Greenfield Did It," 12, 21.

49. "To Justify Your Faith." *Greenfield Recorder-Gazette*, October 29, 1947, 13; Garvey, *the Adman in the Parlor.*

50. "Brand Names Queen Contest Starts Tonight, Consumer School Monday Next Promotion Event," *Greenfield Recorder-Gazette*, October 25, 1947; " 'Brand Names Queen' Selection to Commence Monday Morning," *Greenfield Recorder-Gazette*, October 10, 1947, 12.

51. "You Can Be Greenfield's Brand Names Queen," *Greenfield Recorder-Gazette*, October 27, 1947.

52. " 'Brand Names Queen' Selection to Commence Monday Morning," *Greenfield Recorder-Gazette*, October 10, 1947, 12; "How Greenfield Did It," 17, 19; "Ready to Search For 'Brand Names Queen,' " *Greenfield Recorder-Gazette*, October 18, 1947.

53. "County Town Women Enter Queen Finals," *Greenfield Recorder-Gazette*, October 30, 1947, 1; "How Greenfield Did It," 12.

54. "County Town Women Enter Queen Finals," *Greenfield Recorder-Gazette*, October 30, 1947, 1; "How Greenfield Did It," 12, 20, 41; "Schoolgirls Start 'Good Buymanship' Courses," *Greenfield Recorder-Gazette*, October 24, 1947.

55. "Billy Brand, Stories of How Names Helped Make American Great." *Greenfield Recorder-Gazette*, October 29, 1947, 12.

56. Hartley W. Barclay, "Heavy Sales Mark Brand Experiment," *New York Times*, October 28, 1947, 35, 40; "Campaign Boosted Brand Acceptance," *New York Times*, January 5, 1948, 27; "How Greenfield Did It," 35–36.

57. "Advertising News," *New York Times*, October 31, 1947, 41; "Campaign Boosted Brand Acceptance," *New York Times*, January 5, 1948, 27; "How Greenfield Did It," 40–41; "Movies Will Assist Brand Names Show," *New York Times*, October 22, 1947, 43.

58. "How Greenfield Did It," 22, 41; "Schoolgirls Start 'Good Buymanship' Courses," *Greenfield Recorder-Gazette*, October 24, 1947.

59. "How Greenfield Did It," 22–23, 33, 41–42.

60. "How Greenfield Did It," 33, 43, 50, 52; "White Plains 'Experiment' Slated," *New York Times*, February 5, 1948, 31.

61. "FYI," *Syracuse Herald-Journal*, April 14, 1948, 34; " 'National Brands Week' Set," *New York Times*, March 1, 1948, 34; "Way Pointed to Aid Public Relations," *New York Times*, March 31, 1948, 37.

62. "Paper Official Named To Board of Advertisers," *The Kingsport News*, April 13, 1949, 3.

63. John Foster Dulles, "Reputation and Performance in World Affairs," Brand Names Foundation, NYC, April 11, 1949, "The North Atlantic Treaty and the United Nations," Department of State Overseas Broadcast April 29, 1949 (Based

upon a speech, Brand Names Foundation April 11, 1949), Seeley G. Mudd Manuscript Library, Princeton University Archives.

64. National Family Opinion, Incorporated, "The Importance of Brand Buying: Results of a survey conducted as a contribution to the continuing program of Brand Names Foundation, Incorporated," Cleveland Public Library, August 1950, v.

65. "Brand Names Meet Is Set Here Monday," *The Burlington (NC) Daily Times-News*, April 22, 1950, 7; "Brand Retailing Year Round Task," *The Post-Register, Idaho Falls, Idaho*, April 22, 1958; "Local Store Owner To Get High Award," *The Daily Review*, April 11, 1955, 10.

66. The Brand Names Foundation, "Roster of the Sponsors of Brand Names Foundation, Incorporated, Their Brands, Products and Services," April 18, 1956, Baker Library, Harvard Business School.

67. Ad inserts, Brand Names Foundation, Inc., *Parade*, December 11, 1960, 24; "Foundation Established To Fight Federal Curbs," *The Lima News*, May 15, 1963, 11.

Chapter 4

1. The term "nation branding" did not enter the general vernacular until the twenty-first century, but its practice in the United States began in the 1940s, see Keith Dinnie, *Nation Branding: Concepts, Issues, Practice* (London, Great Britain: Elsevier, LTD., 2008), 13–17.

2. Nicholas John Cull, *The Cold War and the United States Information Agency: American Propaganda and Public Diplomacy, 1945–1989* (New York: Cambridge University Press, 2008), 36, 39–41.

3. Robert E. Herzstein, *Henry R. Luce, A Political Portrait of the Man Who Created The American Century* (New York: Macmillan Publishing, 1994), xi, 35, 137, 301, 310.

4. Carroll L. Wilson, "The International Operations of the J. Walter Thompson Company, Analysis of and Expanding Venture With Policy Recommendations," December 15, 1945, i–ii, vi, 2, 8, Samuel W. Meeks Papers, International Offices, JWTCA, HCAMR.

5. Shirley Woodell to Jane Rutherford, NY Office, January 25, 1950; Report of the Caribbean, February 1950, Shirley Woodell to E.C. Sutter, J.B. Williams Company, April 16, 1951, box 2, Office File and Correspondence, 1950 January-March, Mexico, Panama, Colombia, Venezuela, Puerto Rico, Cuba; Shirley F. Woodell Papers, JWTCA, HCAMR.

6. Procter & Gamble, "A Company History" (Procter & Gamble, 2004), 9; Shirley Woodell to P.C. Smith, Caterpillar Tractor Company, July 14, 1948, box 1, Office and Correspondence, 1948, June 25–August, Mexico, Guatemala, Panama, Columbia, Venezuela, Puerto Rico, Cuba; Shirley Woodell to Miss Beck, Kingston (Jamaica) January 1, 1947, Shirley Woodell to Miss Beck,

Port of Spain (Trinidad, BWI) January 31, 1947, box 1, Office Files and Correspondence, 1947, January–February 3, Trinidad, Argentina, Peru, Colombia, Panama, Mexico; Shirley Woodell to Miss Beck, Sao Paulo, February 8, 1947; Shirley Woodell to Max Schmitt, September 24, 1947; Shirley Woodell to A.B. Reed, Eastman Kodak Company, September 25, 1947, box 1, Office Files and Correspondence, 1947, February 4–March 12, Cuba, Chili, Jamaica, Brazil, Trinidad, Argentina, Peru, Colombia, Panama, Mexico, Shirley F. Woodell Papers, JWTCA, HCAMR.

7. Shirley Woodell to J.S. Thomas, Readers Digest, September 30, 1947, Office Files and Correspondence, 1947, February 4–March 12, Cuba, Chili, Jamaica, Brazil, Trinidad, Argentina, Peru, Colombia, Panama, Mexico; Shirley Woodell to George Richardson, Jr. Detroit Office, July 14, 1948, File Office and Correspondence, 1948, June 25–August, Mexico, Guatemala, Panama, Columbia, Venezuela, Puerto Rico, Cuba, Shirley F. Woodell Papers, JWTCA, HCAMR.

8. Shirley Woodell to Adrian Head, February 1–2, 1950, box 2, Office File and Correspondence, 1950 January–March, Mexico, Panama, Colombia, Venezuela, Puerto Rico, Cuba, Shirley F. Woodell Papers; "Egyptian, A Report on Egypt by a Senior Executive of J.W.T. London," *JWT Bulletin*, May 18, 1949, 3:10, box 4, JWT Bulletin 1948–1950, JWT. Newsletter Collection; "How well do you know your JWT'ers?" December 5, 1949, box 14, India 1949–1950, 1962, JWT, Colin Dawkins Papers, JWTCA, HCAMR; Charles Sawyer, Secretary of Commerce, "American Business and World Development," April 24, 1949, 8, box 123, American Business World Development, Charles Sawyer, Secretary of Commerce, Speech File, SMOF, TPTL.

9. "Project: Promote Goodwill for the United States in Latin America," box 14, Colin Dawkins Papers, JWTCA, HCAMR; James L. Baughman, *Henry R. Luce and the Rise of the American News Media* (Boston, MA: Twayne Publishers, 1987), 103–104, 130–113; Herzstein, *Henry R. Luce*, xii; Robert E. Herzstein, *Henry R. Luce, Time, and the American Crusade in Asia* (Cambridge: Cambridge University Press, 2005), 2.

10. "Text of Policy Statement on Government Book and Library Program," *New York Times*, July 3, 1953, 10; See also Laura Belmonte, *Selling the American Way: U.S. Propaganda and the Cold War* (Philadelphia: University of Pennsylvania Press, 2008); Kenneth Osgood, *Total Cold War: Eisenhower's Secret Propaganda Battle at Home and Abroad* (Lawrence: University of Kansas Press, 2006).

11. In 1931, C.D. Jackson went on "secret mission to Turkey" during the war; See Herzstein, *Henry R. Luce, A Political Portrait*, 217–218, 269; "World Trade Meeting, Time–Life Building," July 25, 1946; "World Trade Campaign Meeting," August 15, 1946, box 7, Charles W. Jackson Files, SMOF, TPTL.

12. "World Trade Campaign—The Theme Problem," August 15, 1946; "Memorandum on World Trade," September 13, 1946, box 7, Charles W. Jackson Files, SMOF, TPTL.

13. "World Trade Meeting, Time-Life Building," July 25, 1946; "World Trade Campaign Meeting," August 15, 1946; "How Organizations Can Cooperate

With The Advertising Council's World Trade Campaign," nd, box 7, Charles W. Jackson Files, SMOF, TPTL; "What Helps People Helps Business, The Sixth Year of The Advertising Council March 1947–March 1948," 15, Advertising Council Annual Reports, ACA.

14. "Business Steps Up Its Candle Power, the Fifth Year of the Advertising Council March 1, 1946–March 1, 1947," 11, Advertising Council Annual Reports, ACA.

15. "Selling the U.S. System Abroad," *Tide*, November 21, 1947; Maurice F. Hanson to Charles W. Jackson, December 23, 1947, box 12, State Department of Overseas Information, Charles W. Jackson Files, SMOF, TPTL; "What Helps People Helps Business, The Sixth Year of The Advertising Council March 1947–March 1948," 2, Advertising Council Annual Reports, ACA.

16. "Recommendations on Greece and Turkey (Truman Doctrine), Message of the President to Congress, March 12, 1947," *Recent American Foreign Policy, Basic Documents 1941–1951*, ed. Francis Wilcox and Thorstein Kalijarvi (New York: Appleton Century Crofts, Inc., 1952), 817–818.

17. T.S. Repplier to Charles W. Jackson, December 24, 1947; William T. Stone to Charles Jackson, nd; Maurice F. Hanson to Charles W. Jackson, December 23, 1947, box 12, State Department of Overseas Information, Charles W. Jackson Files, SMOF, TPTL.

18. "What Helps People Helps Business, The Sixth Year of The Advertising Council March 1947–March 1948," 2–14; "What Helps People Helps Business, The Seventh Year of The Advertising Council March 1948–March 1949," 16; "How Business Helps Solve Public Problems, A Report on the Eighth Year of the Advertising Council, March 1949 to March 1950," Advertising Council Annual Reports, ACA; The Advertising Council, "Public Service by Radio Networks & Advertisers," nd, box 3, John T. Gibson Files, SMOF, TPTL.

19. Charles Sawyer, Secretary of Commerce, "American Business and World Development," April 24, 1949, 14, box 123, American Business World Development, Charles Sawyer, Secretary of Commerce, Speech File, SMOF, TPTL; "Economic Cooperation Administration, Office of the Administrator," Press Release for August 25 (nyear), box 9, Economic Cooperation Administration, Charles W. Jackson Files, SMOF, TPTL; "What Helps People Helps Business, The Seventh Year of The Advertising Council March 1948–March 1949," 4, Advertising Council Annual Reports, ACA; National Security Act of 1947, Act of July 26, 1947, http://www.intelligence.gov/0natsecact_1947.shtml.

20. Stanley E. Cohen, "This Week In Washington," *Advertising Age*, December 29, 1947, box 1, Ad Council 50th Anniversary Files, 1943–1993, ACA; "Ship Load of Food for Italy is Hailed," *New York Times*, December 19, 1947, 5; "Friendship Cargo Sails for Italy," *New York Times*, December 21, 1947, 5.

21. Charles W. Jackson to John Steelman, Subject ECA Information Program Overseas, April 9, 1948; "Conference Report, European Goodwill Program," February 6, 1948, box 12, State Department of Overseas Information, Charles W. Jackson Files, SMOF, TPTL; "What Helps People Helps Business, The

Seventh Year of The Advertising Council March 1948–March 1949," 16, 18–19, Advertising Council Annual Reports, ACA.

22. "Help of Business in Cold War Cited, Advertising Council Reviews Year's Campaigns Designed to Combat Communism," *New York Times*, August 25, 1949, 33, 38; "What Helps People Helps Business," The Seventh Year of The Advertising Council March 1948–March 1949," Advertising Council Annual Reports, ACA.

23. "U. S., Israel Agree on Refugee Funds," *New York Times*, February 28, 1952, 4.

24. The act remained the law of the land into the twenty-first century. In 2008, it covered the information produced by American Broadcasting Board of Governors and included the VOA, Alhurra, Radio Sawa, Radio Free Europe/ Radio Liberty, Radio Free Asia, Radio and TV Marti—The Office of Cuban Broadcasting.; for discussions of overseas broadcasting see Cull, *The Cold War and the United States Information Agency*; Richard Cummings, *Cold War Radio: The Dangerous History of American Broadcasting in Europe, 1950–1989* (Jefferson, NC: McFarland & Company, 2009); Cummings *Radio Free Europe's "Crusade for Freedom": Rallying Americans behind Cold War Broadcasting, 1950–1960* (Jefferson, NC: McFarland & Company, 2010); A. Ross Johnson, *Radio free Europe and Radio Liberty: The CIA Years and Beyond* (Washington, D.C.: Stanford, CA: Woodrow Wilson Center Press; Stanford University Press, 2010); Nancy Snow, *Propaganda, Inc.: Selling America's Culture to the World* (Emeryville, CA: Seven Stories Press; Distributed to the trade by Publishers Group West, 2002); Hans Tuch, *Communicating with the World: U.S. Public Diplomacy Overseas* (New York: St. Martin's Press, 1990).

25. Sam Pope Brewer, "Congressmen Pay Call Upon Franco," *New York Times*, October 9, 1947, 4; "Eisenhower's Remarks," *New York Times*, January 28, 1958, 8; "Europe's Collapse Called Complete," *New York Times* November 1, 1947, 7; "Self-Denial in U.S. Vital, Barkley Says," *New York Times*, October 7, 1947, 12; On Smith-Mundt the law into the twenty first century, see Michael, Z. Wise, "U.S. Writers Do Cultural Battle around the Globe," *New York Times*, December 7, 2002, B7.

26. Roland Marchand, *Creating the Corporate Soul: The Rise of Public Relations and Corporate Imagery in American Big Business* (Berkeley, CA: University of California Press, 1998); Robert David Johnson, *Congress and the Cold War* (Cambridge: Cambridge University Press, 2005), 11; Section 203, Title V, Sec 501–502, Title X—Loyalty Check on Personnel, Section 1001, Title X—Utilization of Private Agencies, Section 1005, United States Information and Educational Exchange Act of 1948, January 27, 1948 [H.R. 3342] [Public Law 402] http://www.ourstory.info/library/5-AFSIS/laws/Congress1.html.

27. Anthony Leviero, "Shake-up Is Urged in Psychology War," *New York Times*, July 9, 1953, 1; see Belmonte, *Selling the America Way*; Osgood, *Total Cold War*; William A. Rugh, *American Encounters with Arabs: The 'Soft Power' of U.S. Public Diplomacy in the Middle East* (Westport, CT: Praeger Security International, 2006), 27; http://www.voanews.com/english/about/OnlinePressKit.cfm, accessed June 30, 2008.

28. Jazz hour broadcasts began in 1955; "Battle for Men's Minds," *New York Times*, December 14, 1949, 24; Benjamin Fine, "Education in Review," *New York Times*, January 25, 1948, 7; Rugh, *American Encounters with Arabs*, 30; Reinhold Wagnleitner, *Coca-Colonization and the Cold War: The Cultural Mission of the United States in Austria after the Second World War*. Translated by Diana M. Wolf (Chapell Hill: University of North Carolina Press, 1994).

29. Charles A.H. Thomson, *Overseas Information Service of the United States Government* (Washington, D.C.: The Brookings Institute, 1948), 1, 10–13, 224, 321, 343, 360.

30. "Conference Report, European Goodwill Program," February 6, 1948; Charles W. Jackson to John Steelman, Subject ECA Information Program Overseas, April 9, 1948, box 12, State Department of Overseas Information, Charles W. Jackson Files, SMOF, TPTL; "What Helps People Helps Business, The Seventh Year of The Advertising Council March 1948–March 1949," 5, 15–16, 18, Advertising Council Annual Reports, ACA.

31. "What Helps People Helps Business, The Seventh Year of The Advertising Council March 1948–March 1949," 15–16, Advertising Council Annual Reports, ACA.

32. The Advertising Council, "Advertising A New Weapon in the World-Wide Fight for Freedom—A Guide for American Business Firms Advertising in Foreign Countries," 1948, 3, box 2, Misc.—National Safety, Guide for Advertising, Spencer R. Quick Files, SMOF, TPTL.

33. The Advertising Council, "Advertising A New Weapon in the World-Wide Fight," 1–3, 10.

34. Ibid., 2, 13.

35. Ibid.

36. Ibid., 2, 6, 9.

37. Ibid., 5, 7, 9.

38. Ibid., 4, 8.

39. Ibid., 7–8.

40. Ibid., 5, 9.

41. Ibid., 6.

42. Ibid.

43. Ibid., 3, 6, 13.

44. The Advertising Council, "Advertising A New Weapon in the World-Wide Fight," 8.

45. Ibid., 10.

46. Ibid., 11.

47. Ibid., 12; "How Business Helps Solve Public Problems," A Report on the Eighth Year of the Advertising Council, March 1949 to March 1950," Advertising Council Annual Reports, ACA.

48. "U.S. Ads Overseas to be Stepped Up," *New York Times*, January 30, 1950, 33.

49. "American Business In The Country's Service, A Report on the Ninth Year of the Advertising Council, March 1950 to March 1951," 6–7; "What Helps People

Helps Business, 10th Annual Report of the Advertising Council," Advertising Council Annual Reports, ACA; For an overview of information programs in support of the Korean War see Steven Casey, *Selling the Korean War: Propaganda, Politics, and Public Opinion in the United States, 1950–1953* (New York: Oxford University Press, 2008).

Chapter 5

1. The reported listed J. Walter Thompson Co. as the only agency involved in the Religion in American Life campaign see "How Business Helps Solve Public Problems," A Report on the Eighth Year of the Advertising Council, March 1949 to March 1950, Advertising Council Annual Reports, ACA.
2. Frederick C. Crawford, "ABC's of Economics," at Kodak Park, March 4, 1952, box Speeches 1952–1954; William S. Vaughn, "Our Increasing Responsibilities," October 15, 1951, KHC.
3. For discussion of Billy Graham see Steven Miller, *Billy Graham and the Rise of the Republican South* (Philadelphia, PA: University of Pennsylvania Press, 2009).
4. Volker R. Henning, "The Advertising Council and Its 'Religion in American Life Campaign,' " Dissertation, University of Tennessee, August 1996, v, 2.
5. Brendan M. Jones, "Go-to-Church Ads Win Wide Support," *New York Times*, December 25, 1949, 5; John Pollock, *The Billy Graham Story* (Grand Rapids, MI: Zondervan, 2003, 1985), 7; Henning, "The Advertising Council and Its 'Religion in American Life Campaign,' " v.
6. Edward B. Fiske, "Redefined Values in Religion Urged," *New York Times*, January 22, 1967, 54.
7. "Faith Campaign Planned," *New York Times*, October 19, 1949, 31; "Industries Advisory Committee, The Advertising Council, Inc.," August 10, 1950, box 1, Ad Council: Industry Advisory Committee, 1950, 1964, ACA; "Rabbis Acclaim Free Elections," *New York Times*, November 13, 1949, 59; Henning, "The Advertising Council and Its 'Religion in American Life Campaign,' " 75, 78, 108.
8. "320 Firms Help Council Expand Budget for 1949, *Advertising Age*, box November 15, 1948, 1, Ad Council 50th Anniversary Files 1943–1993; "Ad Council Issues Report on 8th Year," *Advertising Age*, September 11, 1950, 22; "How Business Helps Solve Public Problems, A Report on the Eighth Year of the Advertising Council, March 1949 to March 1950"; "The Advertising Council, 11th Annual Report, 1952–1953," 22; "Annual Report The Advertising Council, 1953–1954"; "Public Service Advertising Council, 1954–55," 11; Goes overseas "Annual Report Advertising Council 1955–56," 3, 21; "What Helps People . . . Helps Business, 15th Annual Report of The Advertising Council," 12; "The Advertising Council, Sixteenth Annual Report, 1957–58," 5; "The Advertising Council, 17th Annual Report, 1958–59"; "The Advertising Council Annual Report, 1960–1961," 7–8, Advertising Council Annual Reports, ACA.

9. Preston King Sheldon, "Church Going Urged by Laymen's Group," *New York Times*, November 3, 1951, 18; Sheldon, "Business Men Join in Religious Drive," *New York Times*, October 25, 1952, 18.

10. Frederick C. Crawford, "ABC's of Economics," at Kodak Park, March 4, 1952, box Speeches 1952–1954; William S. Vaughn, "Our Increasing Responsibilities," October 15, 1951, KHC.

11. The phrase "city upon the hill" regarding the United States was a common description of country's role in the world, as a religiously ordained model for other countries, see John Winthrop, *A Modell of Christian Charity (1630)*; Address of President-Elect John F. Kennedy Delivered to a Joint Convention of the General Court of the Commonwealth of Massachusetts The State House, Boston, January 9, 1961, http://www.jfklibrary.org/Historical+Resources/Archives/Reference+Desk/Speeches/JFK; Ronald Reagan's Farewell Address to the Nation, Oval Office, January 11, 1989, http://www.reaganlibrary.com/reagan/speeches/farewell.asp.

12. James Webb Young, Biographical Data," nd, box 2, Howard Henderson Papers; "Jim Young—Ad Man, Nomad," nd, box 6, Officers and Staff, Colin Dawkins Papers, JWTCA, HCAMR; Henning, "The Advertising Council and Its 'Religion in American Life Campaign,'" 109.

13. Regarding Luce see Robert E. Herzstein, *Henry R. Luce, Time, and the American Crusade in Asia* (Cambridge, UK: Cambridge University Press, 2005), 1–2. Herzstein argued that "Protestant Christianity and "a fervent faith in America's God-ordained global mission in Asia" were the dominant forces in Luce's "character and worldview." See also James L. Baughman, *Henry R. Luce and the Rise of the American News Media* (Boston, MA: Twayne Publishing, 1987), 8–10, 21, 155, 173; Robert E. Herzstein, *Henry R. Luce, A Political Portrait of the Man Who Created The American Century* (New York: Macmillan Publishing, 1994), xi, 35; Regarding Procter & Gamble see Dyer et al., *Rising Tide, Lessons for 165 Years of Brand Building at Procter & Gamble* (Boston, MA: Harvard Business School Press, 2004), 61; Alfred Lief, *"It Floats" The Story of Procter & Gamble* (New York: Rinehart & Company, Inc., 1958); Oscar Schisgall, *Eyes on Tomorrow: The Evolution of Procter & Gamble* (Chicago: J.G Ferguson Publishing Company, 1981).

14. Joseph J. Thorndike, Jr. and Joseph Kastner, eds., *Life's Picture History of Western Man* (New York: Time Incorporated, 1951), 1–5, 289–290.

15. Brendan M. Jones, "Go-to-Church Ads Win Wide Support," *New York Times*, December 25, 1949, 5; "How Business Helps Solve Public Problems," A Report on the Eighth Year of the Advertising Council, March 1949 to March 1950," ACA.

16. "Radio and Television," *New York Times*, October 26, 1949, 52; "Truman on Radio Sunday," *New York Times*, October 27, 1949, 29.

17. "Text of Truman Speech on Religious Faith," *New York Times*, October 31, 1949, 26; "Truman Acclaims Religion in Nation," *New York Times*, October 31, 1949, 26.

18. Mayor O'Dwyer quoted in "Reserve Corps Month," *New York Times*, November 1, 1949, 17; Brendan M. Jones, "Go-to-Church Ads Win Wide Support,"*New York Times*, December 25, 1949, 5.

19. "Wilson Renamed to Head Campaign," *New York Times*, January 9, 1950, 26; "Wilson Is Praised for Religious Gain," *New York Times*, January 19, 1951, 15.

20. "TV Programs This Week," *New York Times*, November 6, 1955, X12.

21. "American Business In The Country's Service, A Report on the Ninth Year of the Advertising Council, March 1950 to March 1951," 3, 13, 25, Advertising Council Annual Reports, ACA.

22. "Wilson Is Praised for Religious Gain," *New York Times*, January 19, 1951, 15; Preston King Sheldon, "Church Going Urged by Laymen's Group," *New York Times*, November 3, 1951, 18; "Business Financed 18 Major Drives," *New York Times*, August 2, 1951, 36.

23. "American Business In The Country's Service, A Report on the Ninth Year of the Advertising Council, March 1950 to March 1951," 25, ACA; Preston King Sheldon, "Cardinal Will Fly to South America," *New York Times*, November 17, 1951, 18; "What Helps People Helps Business, 10th Annual Report of the Advertising Council," 29, Advertising Council Annual Reports, ACA.

24. "The Advertising Council, 11th Annual Report, 1952–1953," 22, Advertising Council Annual Reports, ACA; "Jews to Observe Day of Atonement," *New York Times*, September 27, 1952, 12.

25. "Church Advertising Raises Attendance," *New York Times*, February 8, 1952, 15; "Digest of a few sample weekly columns and feature articles," December 31, 1952, box 1, Correspondence 1953, Files of Special Assistant Relating to the Office of Coordinator of Government Public Service Advertising, James M. Lambie Jr., Staff Files, EL; Preston King Sheldon, "Business Men Join in Religious Drive," *New York Times*, October 25, 1952, 18; "Cited for Religious Gains," *New York Times*, November 22, 1952, 14.

26. The Ford Foundation and John D. Rockefeller III funded the Round Tables, see The Advertising Council, Inc., "Report of the First Session of the American Round Table: The Moral and Religious Basis of the American Society," April 14, 1952, cover, 1–2, 17, box 4, Advertising Council General 1952, SMOF, Spencer R. Quick Files, TPTL.

27. For a history of Christina Free Enterprise in the United States see Bethany Moreton, *To Serve God and Wal-Mart: The Making of Christian Free Enterprise* (Cambridge, MA: Harvard University Press, 2009).

28. Brendan M. Jones, "Go-to-Church Ads Win Wide Support," *New York Times*, December 25, 1949, 5; Pollock, *The Billy Graham Story*, 7; Henning, "The Advertising Council and Its 'Religion in American Life Campaign,'" v.

29. Michael G. Long, *Billy Graham and the Beloved Community* (New York: Palgrave Macmillan, 2006), 73.

30. "Puff Graham" and Hearst promoting Graham in LA mentioned in *Time* magazine see "Heaven, Hell & Judgment Day," *Time*, March 20, 1950; Pollock, *The Billy Graham Story*, 47; For a good Review of Graham's relationship with the

American Presidents written by journalist see Nancy Gibbs and Michael Duffy, *The Preacher and the Presidents: Billy Graham in the White House* (New York, NY: Center Street, 2007).

31. Pollock, *The Billy Graham Story*, 7; For more on the career of Billy Graham see also Roger Bruns, *Billy Graham* (Westport, CT: Greenwood Press, 2004); John Charles Pollock, *The Billy Graham Story: The Authorized Biography* (Grand Rapids, MI: Zondervan, 2003); Sherwood Eliot Wirt, *Billy: A Personal Look at Billy Graham, the World's Best Loved Evangelist* (Wheaton, IL: Crossway Books), 1997.

32. "Sickle for the Harvest," *Time*, November 14, 1949; "Heaven, Hell & Judgment Day," *Time*, March 20, 1950; "A New Evangelist Arises, Billy Graham," *Life*, November 21, 1949, 97, 100.

33. "The Whiskey Rebellion," *Time*, February 20, 1950; "Heaven, Hell & Judgment Day," *Time*, March 20, 1950; "Billy Graham in Dixie," *Life*, March 27, 1950, 55; "Revival," *Time*, September 18, 1950; "Evangelism," November 13, 1950.

34. "50,000 on Boston Comm on Hear Pray-for-Peace Plea," *New York Times*, April 24, 1950, 6; Michael G. Long, *Billy Graham and the Beloved Community* (New York: Palgrave Macmillan, 2006), 81.

35. "The Kidding Stopped," *Time*, July 24, 1950; "President and Evangelist Pray in the White House," *New York Times*, July 15, 1950, 11.

36. "New Directions," *Time*, February 26, 1951; "First Christian Western," *Time*, October 8, 1951; "33-year-old Oral Roberts, revivalist," *Life*, May 7, 1951, 73.

37. BGEA: PENTAGON VISIT; 1952; 30 JAN 1952, Crusade Activities, 1950 Billy Graham Center Archives.

38. "Personality," *Time*, November 17, 1952; "God's Billy Pulpit," *Time*, November 15, 1993, http://205.188.238.109/time/magazine/article/0,9171,979573, 00.html; "Crusader in The Capital," *Time*, January 28, 1952; "An Evangelistic Meeting on the Steps of the Capitol," *New York Time*, February 4, 1952, 4.

39. C. L. Sulzberger, " 'Military Mind' Weighed as Political Question," *New York Times*, June 1, 1952, E3; "Eisenhower to See Committee Heads," *New York Times*, January 15, 1953, 18; "Billy Graham Sees President," *New York Times*, November 4, 1953, 24; "No Title," *Time*, November 16, 1953. *Time* has the same quote about "the nation is enjoying the greatest religious renaissance in history; "Crusader in the Capital," *Time*, January 28, 1952.

40. Ibid.,

41. Preston King Sheldon, "Survey Is Planned by Interfaith Unit," *New York Times*, January 24, 1953, 18; Charles E. Wilson to Publisher, October 22, 1953, box 7, "Religion in America" 1953, Files of Special Assistant Relating to the Office of Coordinator of Government Public Service Advertising, James M. Lambie Jr., Staff Files, EL.

42. "Spread of Religion Held Vital to Nation," *New York Times*, January 30, 1953, 10; "Program Preview," *Time*, November 2, 1953; "A Special Message for Religion in American Life by President Dwight D. Eisenhower," nd, box 1, Correspondence 1953; Henry C. Wehde, Jr., October 1953, box 7, "Religion

in America" 1953, Files of Special Assistant Relating to the Office of Coordinator of Government Public Service Advertising, James M. Lambie Jr., Staff Files, EL.; "A Special Message for Religion in American Life by President Dwight D. Eisenhower," nd, box 1, Correspondence 1953; "Good & Great," *Time*, November 9, 1953; Press Release, October 30, 1953, box 7, "Religion in America" 1953, Files of Special Assistant Relating to the Office of Coordinator of Government Public Service Advertising, James M. Lambie Jr., Staff Files, EL.

43. "Ad Council Plan 6th Annual Drive to Aid Religion," *Advertising Age*, November 1, 1954, 22, Advertising Age Clippings 1945–1959, Ad Council 50th Anniversary Files 1943–1993; "Public Service Advertising Council, 1954–55," Advertising Council Annual Reports, 1943–11, ACA; "Ad Council Will Urge Film TV Sponsors to Start using Public Service Messages," *Advertising Age*, June 1, 1953, 30, Advertising Age Clippings 1945–1959, Ad Council 50th Anniversary Files, 1943–1993, ACA; Press Release, October 30, 1953, box 7, "Religion in America" 1953, Files of Special Assistant Relating to the Office of Coordinator of Government Public Service Advertising, James M. Lambie Jr., Staff Files, EL; "Annual Report The Advertising Council, 1953–1954," 24, ACA.

44. Preston King Sheldon, "3 Faiths Will Join in Capital Parley," *New York Times*, November 6, 1954, 13.

45. "News of Advertising and Marketing," *New York Times*, October 7, 1955, 39; "Belief in God Is Vital to Americanism, Eisenhower Asserts in Filmed Talk Here," *New York Times*, February 21, 1955, 24; George Dugan, "TV Sponsors Ask for Billy Graham," *New York Times*, March 3, 1955, 37.

46. "Chairman Named by Religious Unit," *New York Times*, March 26, 1958, 50; George Dugan, "Call to Worship Going to Nation," *New York Times*, November 1, 1958, 22; "The Advertising Council, Sixteenth Annual Report, 1957–58," 5, Advertising Council Annual Reports, ACA.

47. Carl Spielvogel, "Critics Find a Need for More Realism," *New York Times*, October 22, 1959, 61; Spielvogel, "Advertising: Drive Held 'Phony,' " *New York Times*, November 19, 1959, 58.

48. "Advertising Council Releasing 12th Campaign Created by J. Walter Thompson for Religion in American Life," September 29, 1960; "A Special Message by President Dwight D. Eisenhower for Religion in American Life," nd, box 57, RIAL 1960, Files of Special Assistant Relating to the Office of Coordinator of Government Public Service Advertising, James M. Lambie Jr., Staff Files, EL.

49. George Dugan, "Mass to Be Sung for Civil Rights," *New York Times*, November 5, 1960, 26.

50. "Evangelist Draws 7,000," *New York Times*, March 17, 1952, 23; "Billy Graham Going to Korea," *New York Times*, December 2, 1952, 5; "Lights Fail Evangelist in Pusan," *New York Times*, December 17, 1952, 16; "Evangelist Reaches Formosa," *New York Times*, December 29, 1952, 3; "Korea Reds Said to Join Church," *New York Times*, December 31, 1952; "Two Visits to Korea," *Time*, January 5, 1953.

51. Richard J. Ellis, *To the Flag: The Unlikely History of the Pledge of Allegiance* (Lawrence: University of Kansas Press, 2005); "The Crusade for Britain," *Time* magazine, March 8, 1954; "U. S. Evangelist's 'Crusade' in Britain Is Criticized by Labor Party Leaders," *New York Times*, February 21, 1954, 33; "Billy Graham in Britain," *New York Times*, February 24, 1954, 2; Pollock, *The Billy Graham Story*, 64–71, 78.

52. "Billy's Britain," *Time*, 22 March 1954; "Revivalist Graham Fills London Arena at Opening of His 3 Months' 'Crusade,'" *New York Times*, March 2, 1954, 5; "10,000 in London Hear Graham," *New York Times*, March 3, 1954, 5.

53. Peter Whitney, "Evangelist Billy Graham London's Top Attraction," *New York Times*, March 7, 1954, E6; "Children at Graham Rally," *New York Times*, March 21, 1954, 17.

54. "Billy Graham Sets a Record," *New York Times*, May 10, 1954, 21; "Graham Hires Sports Stadium," *New York Times*, May 2, 1954, 84; "34,586 Decisions," *Time*, May 31, 1954; Peter D. Whitney, "Record 120,000 at London Arena Hear Billy Graham End Crusade," *New York Times*, May 23, 1954, 1, 14.

55. Peter D. Whitney, "Record 120,000 at London Arena Hear Billy Graham End Crusade," *New York Times*, May 23, 1954, 1, 14.

56. "Evangelist Billy Graham in Wembly Stadium," *Life*, June 7, 1954; "Billy Graham Visits Churchill," *New York Times*, May 26, 1954, 19.

57. "Billy in Germany," *Time* magazine, July 5, 1954; "The New Evangelist," *Time* magazine, October 25, 1954; "3,000 See Billy Graham Off"; *New York Times*, June 13, 1954, 14; "Billy Graham Criticized," *New York Times*, June 15, 1954, 2; "100,000 Swedes Hear Graham," *New York Times*, June 20, 1954, 28; "Graham Exhorts Berliners," *New York Times*, June 28, 1954, 14; "Billy Graham Sails for Home," *New York Times*, July 2, 1954, 4.

58. "Europe Seeks God, Evangelist Holds," *New York Times*, July 7, 1954, 28; "Evangelist Sees Eisenhower," *New York Times*, July 9, 1954, 15; "Graham Crusade Set for This City," *New York Times*, December 17, 1954, 28.

59. "The New Evangelist," *Time*, October 25, 1954.

60. Foster Hailey, "22,000 Jam Garden, 5,000 Outside, for Billy Graham," *New York Times*, March 4, 1955, 1; "Billy Graham in Britain," *New York Times*, March 19, 1955, 10; "Billy Graham Opens Crusade in Scotland," *New York Times*, March 22, 1955, 29.

61. Foster Hailey, "22,000 Jam Garden, 5,000 Outside, for Billy Graham," *New York Times*, March 4, 1955, 1; "Billy Graham in Britain," *New York Times*, March 19, 1955, 10; "Billy Graham Opens Crusade in Scotland," *New York Times*, March 22, 1955, 29.

62. "Billy Graham Back in London," *New York Times*, May 12, 1955, 11; "Billy Graham Opens Crusade In London," *New York Times*, May 15, 1955, 15; "Duchess Hears Billy Graham," *New York Times*, May 20, 1955, 2; "Britons Turn out for Billy Graham," *New York Times*, May 22, 1955, E4.

63. "Graham Ends Crusade," *New York Times*, May 22, 1955, 2; "Elizabeth Hears Graham Preach; Evangelist Lunches with Queen," *New York Times*, May 23, 1955, 1, 4.

64. "Billy Graham Opens Paris Drive Sunday; Stresses 'Crusade' Is Not Anti-Catholic," *New York Times*, June 3, 1955, 8; "Graham Speaks in Paris," *New York Times*, June 5, 1955, 7; Brady, Thomas F. "451 in Paris Heed Graham's Sermon," *New York Times*, June 6, 1955, 10; "Billy Graham Ends His 'Paris Crusade,'" *New York Times*, June 10, 1955, 2; "Swiss in 2 Arenas for Graham," *New York Times*, June 19, 1955, 10; "40,000 Germans Hear Graham," *New York Times*, June 22, 1955, 3.

65. "100,000 Indians Hear Graham," *New York Times*, January 30, 1956, 7; "New Delhi Hears Billy Graham," *New York Times*, February 5, 1956, 10; "Mme. Chiang Hears Graham," *New York Times*, February 18, 1956, 21; Pollock, *The Billy Graham Story*, 84.

66. "25,000 Filipinos Hear Graham," *New York Times*, February 13, 1956, 29; "Mme. Chiang Hears Graham," *New York Times*, February 18, 1956, 21; "Billy Graham in Tokyo," *New York Times*, February 19, 1956, 22; "Religious Drive Opening," *New York Times*, October 27, 1956, 10; "News of Advertising and Marketing," *New York Times*, October 7, 1955, 39.

67. "Ad Council Will Urge Film TV Sponsors to Start using Public Service Messages," *Advertising Age*, June 1, 1953, 30, Advertising Age Clippings 1945–1959, Ad Council 50th Anniversary Files, 1943–1993, ACA; Press Release, October 30, 1953, box 7, "Religion in America" 1953, Files of Special Assistant Relating to the Office of Coordinator of Government Public Service Advertising, James M. Lambie Jr., Staff Files, EL; "Annual Report The Advertising Council, 1953–1954," 24, ACA.

68. "Annual Report Advertising Council 1955–56," 13, ACA; "Ad Council Opens Overseas Aid Campaign For Churches," *Advertising Age*, March 5, 1956, 37, Advertising Age Clippings 1945–1959, Ad Council 50th Anniversary Files, 1943–1993, ACA; "Annual Report Advertising Council 1955–56," 21, Advertising Council Annual Reports, ACA.

69. William Inboden, *Religion and American Foreign Policy, 1945–1960, The Soul of Containment* (Cambridge, New York: Cambridge University Press, 2008).

70. "Launched in 2002, *My Hope* World Evangelism Through Television uses proven methods of evangelism and discipleship from more than 60 years of Crusade ministry to train believers around the world to open their homes and share their faith through Billy Graham Evangelistic Association (BGEA) TV broadcasts and videos" http://www.billygraham.org/IntlMin_WorldTVProject.asp; See also the Billy Graham organizations website http://www.billygraham.org/.

Chapter 6

1. Regarding the CIA, see Frances Stonor Saunders, *The Cultural Cold War: The CIA and the World of Arts and Letters* (New York: The New Press, 1999); Laura A. Belmonte, *Selling the American Way: U.S. Propaganda and the Cold War* (Philadelphia: University of Pennsylvania Press, 2008); Kenneth Osgood, *Total Cold War: Eisenhower's Secret Propaganda Battle at Home and Abroad* (Lawrence:

University of Kansas Press, 2006). See also A. Ross Johnson, *Radio Free Europe and Radio Liberty: The CIA Years and Beyond*, (Washington, D.C.: Stanford, CA: Woodrow Wilson Center Press; Stanford University Press), who argues that without the CIA support RFE/RL would notehave survived, x, 8–10, 200, 218, 224; See also Nicholas John Cull, *The Cold War and the United States Information Agency: American Propaganda and Public Diplomacy, 1945–1989* (New York: Cambridge University Press, 2008), 49–50; Richard Cummings, *Cold War Radio: The Dangerous History of American Broadcasting in Europe, 1950–1989* (Jefferson, N.C. McFarland & Company, 2009), 1, 28; Richard Cummings, *Radio Free Europe's Crusade for Freedom: Rallying Americans behind Cold War Broadcasting, 1950–1960* (Jefferson, N.C: McFarland & Company, 2010), 217; Reinhold Wagnleitner, *Coca-Colonization and the Cold War: The Cultural Mission of the United States in Austria after the Second World War.* Translated by Diana M. Wolf (Chapell Hill: University of North Carolina Press, 1994), xi.; Cissie Dore Hill, "Voices of Hope: The Story of Radio Free Europe and Radio Liberty," Hoover Digest, Hoover Institution, http://www.hoover.org/publications/digest/3475896.html, accessed October 28, 2008.

2. Cummings, *Cold War Radio*, 5–7; Cummings, *Radio Free Europe*, 5–6; Johnson, *Radio Free Europe and Radio Liberty*, 10–12.

3. Lt. General Willis D. Crittenberger to the Honorable Adolf A. Berle Jr. and others, April 21, 1958, box 54, CD Jackson Papers 1931–67, Eisenhower Library; "Gen. Clay To Help Free-Europe Drive," *New York Times*, April 27, 1950, 22; Crusade for Freedom, "Radio Free Europe—Fact Sheet," nd, 1, 5, box 166, Crusade for Freedom, HIWRP; Business Research Staff, General Motors Corp., "Radio Free Europe," December 15, 1952, 1, box 3, Citizens for Eisenhower Files of Young and Rubicam, 1952–61, EL.

4. Cummings, *Radio Free Europe*, 9; "Gen. Clay To Help Free-Europe Drive," *New York Times*, April 27, 1950, 22; Lucius D. Clay, Chairman, Crusade for Freedom to Regional Chairman, May 1, 1950; News Release, National Committee for A Free Europe, Inc., April 26, 1950, 1, box, 166, Crusade for Freedom, Hoover Institution on War, Revolution and Peace.

5. Johnson, *Radio Free Europe and Radio Liberty*, 13.

6. G.D. Crain Jr., "Footnotes," *Advertising Age*, September 11, 1950, 40, box 1, Advertising Age Clippings 1945–1959, Ad Council 50th Anniversary Files, 1943–1993; "Agenda: The Advertising Council, Inc. (Industries Advisory Committee) Dinner—Charles E. Wilson Presiding," September 20, 1950, box 1, Ad Council: Industry Advisory Committee File, 1950–1964, ACA.

7. Clay Chairman of Continental Can Company, Inc. see Business Advisory Council for the Department of Commerce, 1958, 23, box 3, Business Advisory Council, Neil McElroy Papers, 1948–62, Staff Files, EL; Regarding C.D. Jackson during WWII see Osgood, *Total Cold War*, 40.

8. James Webb, Young, Theodore Repplier, Phillip Graham from the Washington Post, and Sam Gale from General Mills worked on the ads on behalf of the Economic Cooperation Administration for western Europe, see "Ad Council Sells

ECA on Ad Effort in Foreign Media," *Advertising Age*, September 11, 1950, 71, box 1, Advertising Age Clippings, 1945–1959, Ad Council 50th Anniversary File, 1943–1993, ACA.

9. News Release, National Committee for A Free Europe, Inc., April 26, 1950, 1, box 166, Crusade for Freedom, HIWRP; "Gen. Clay To Help Free-Europe Drive," *New York Times*, April 27, 1950, 22; Business Research Staff, General Motors Corp., "Radio Free Europe," December 15, 1952, box 3, Citizens for Eisenhower Files of Young and Rubicam, 1952–61, EL.

10. News Release, National Committee for A Free Europe, Inc., April 26, 1950, 1; Harry Truman to Honorable Joseph C. Grew, National Committee for a Free Europe, May 1, 1950, box 166, Crusade for Freedom, HIWRP; "Truman Approves Free Europe Drive," *New York Times*, May 2, 1950, 19.

11. By 2011, RFE claimed to reach "nearly 20 million in 28 languages and 21 countries," http://www.rferl.org/info/about/176.html, accessed March 14, 2011.

12. "Ad Council Sets New Drive," *Advertising Age*, August 21, 1950, 17; "Ad Council Starts Crusade for Freedom," *Advertising Age*, September 4, 1950, 40, Ad Council 50th Anniversary File, 1943–1993, box 1, Advertising Age Clippings, 1945–1959, ACA.

13. Lt. General Willis D. Crittenberger to the Honorable Adolf A. Berle Jr. and others, April 21, 1958, box 54, CD Jackson Papers 1931–67, Eisenhower Library; "Gen. Clay To Help Free-Europe Drive," *New York Times*, April 27, 1950, 22; Crusade for Freedom, "Radio Free Europe—Fact Sheet," nd, 1, 5, box 166, Crusade for Freedom, HIWRP; Business Research Staff, General Motors Corp., "Radio Free Europe," December 15, 1952, 1, box 3, Citizens for Eisenhower Files of Young and Rubicam, 1952–61, EL.

14. Cummings, *Radio Free Europe*, 23–24; Cummings, *Cold War Radio*, 10.

15. Crusade for Freedom, "Radio Free Europe—Fact Sheet," box 166, Crusade for Freedom, HIWRP; "Help Truth Fight Communism . . . Join the Crusade for Freedom," 1951, 7, Historical File 1941–1997, ACA; Johnson, *Radio Free Europe and Radio Liberty*, 61.

16. Cummings *Cold War Radio*, 10; " 'Give us this day . . . our daily truth," Ad Mat, 1952, Historical File 1941–1997, ACA.

17. For an overview of RFE/ RL early history and impact data from 1962–1988 which shows that in Poland, Hungary, Czechoslovakia, Romania and Bulgaria Radio Free Europe reached millions more listeners than VOA, see "Cold War Broadcasting Impact," Report on a Conference by the Hoover Institution and the Cold War International History Project of the Woodrow Wilson International Center for Scholars at Stanford University, October 13–16, 2004, 5–6, 45–47; A. Ross Johnson and R. Eugene Parta, *Cold War Broadcasting: Impact on the Soviet Union and Eastern Europe* (Budaspest-New York: Central European University Press, 2010): see also Cull, *The Cold War and the United States Information Agency;* Cummings, *Cold War Radio* and *Radio Free Europe's "Crusade for Freedom"* ; Johnson, *Radio Free Europe and Radio Liberty*.

18. Lt. General Willis D. Crittenberger to the Honorable Adolf A. Berle Jr. and others, April 21, 1958, box 54, CD Jackson Papers 1931–67, EL; "Gen. Clay

To Help Free-Europe Drive," *New York Times*, April 27, 1950, 22; "Rumania," Item No. 03552/53, April 1, 1953; "A Young Austrian's Impressions of the Youth Festival," Item No. 8798/53, August 29, 1953, HU OSA 300–60–1 Records of the Research Institute of Radio Free Europe/Radio Liberty, Romanian Unit, 1953–1994, container no. 55, OSA.

19. "Bucharest Youth like RFE Newscasts," Item 7359/56, July 25, 195, Records of the Research Institute of Radio Free Europe/Radio Liberty, Romanian Unit, 1953–1994, container no. 55, OSA.

20. Crusade for Freedom, "Radio Free Europe—Fact Sheet," nd, 4, box 166, Crusade for Freedom, HIWRP; Hill, "Voices of Hope;" Analysis Reports, May 10, 1963, box 2, Records of the Research Institute of Radio Free Europe/Radio Liberty, Media and Opinion Research Administrative Files, OSA.

21. Lt. General Willis D. Crittenberger to the Honorable Adolf A. Berle Jr. and others, April 21, 1958, box 54, CD Jackson Papers 1931–67, EL; "Gen. Clay To Help Free-Europe Drive," *New York Times*, April 27, 1950, 22.

22. "Western Broadcasts Very Popular Only Source of Information," Item No. 8210/54, September 24, 1954; "A Young Austrian's Impressions of the Youth Festival," Item No. 8798/53, August 29, 1953; "Rumania," Item No. 8688/53, August 25, 1953; Item No. 8877/53, August 29, 1953; Item No. 279/54, January 14, 1954, "Audience Analysis with a Civil Engineer," Item 5630/56, June 1, 1956; "Audience Analysis Interview with an Intellectual," Item No. 5152/56, May 18, 1956, Records of the Research Institute of Radio Free Europe/Radio Liberty, Romanian Unit, 1953–1994, container no. 55; Analysis Reports, May 10, 1963, box 2, Records of the Research Institute of Radio Free Europe/Radio Liberty, Media and Opinion Research Administrative Files, box 2, OSA; Manager, Audience Research and Program Evaluation Department to Assistant to the Director, Radio Programming Division, Memorandum, February 12, 1957; Manager, Audience Research and Program Evaluation Department to Acting Director, Radio Programming Division, Memorandum, November 15, 1956; Manager, Audience Research and Program Evaluation Department to Acting Director, Radio Programming Division, Memorandum, November 15, 1956, box 1, Records of the Research Institute of Radio Free Europe/Radio Liberty, Media and Opinion Research Administrative Files, OSA.

23. "Source Munich," Item No. 3628/54, April 28, 1954; Item No. 8877/53, August 29, 1953, Records of the Research Institute of Radio Free Europe/Radio Liberty, Romanian Unit, 1953–1994, OSA.

24. Reports said audiences in Eastern Europe demonstrated little interest in Eisenhower's Christmas address, see "Audience Analysis Interview with an Intellectual," Item No. 5152/56, May 18, 1956; Item No. 3628/54, April 28, 1954; "Audience Analysis with Civil Engineer," Item No. 5630/56, June 1, 1956, 2, box 55, Records of the Research Institute of Radio Free Europe/Radio Liberty, Media and Opinion Research Administrative Files, OSA.

25. "Wired radio in the Satellite Nations," Item No. 279/54, January 14, 1954; "Rumania," Item No. 8688/53, August 25, 1953; Item No. 505/54, January 20,

1954; Item No. 3628/54, April 28, 1954, box 55; "Hungarians to see more Western Films," December 31, 1953, Hungary Cinema, 1950–1973, Hungary Subject Files, Records of the Research Institute of Radio Free Europe/Radio Liberty, Media and Opinion Research Administrative Files, OSA.

26. "Russia: East Germany All Satellites," Item No. 217/54, January 13, 1954; "Rumania—A Young Austrian's Impressions of the Youth Festival," Item No. 8798/53, August 28, 1953; Item No. 7359/56, July 25, 1956; "Bucharest Youth Likes RFE Newscasts," box 55, Records of the Research Institute of Radio Free Europe/Radio Liberty, Media and Opinion Research Administrative Files; "Seventh World Youth Festival, Vienna 1959," Analysis Report #5–1959, September 22, 1959, box 1, Analysis Reports, Records of the Research Institute of Radio Free Europe/Radio Liberty, OSA.

27. "One Year of the New Course: An Analytic Survey of Major Events in the Soviet Sphere," Free Europe Press Research and Analysis Department, 1954; "Second Analytic Survey of Major Trends in the Soviet Sphere," July 26, 1955, Box 102, HU OSA 300–8–3, Media and Opinion Research Administrative Files, OSA; Melvin L. De Fleur, "A Mass Communication Model of Stimulus Response Relationships: An Experiment in Leaflet Message Diffusion," *Sociometry*, 19, no. 1 (March, 1956), 12.

28. Howard S. Weaver, Speech delivered, October 17, 1955, 1, box 19, Crusade for Freedom 1955, Files of Special Assistant Relating to the Office of Coordinator of Government Public Service Advertising, James M. Lambie Jr., Staff Files, EL.

29. "Fig. 1: Balloon on Launching," "Fig. 2: Paper Release," nd, box 150, Balloons General 1951–1956, HIWRP.

30. "Printed Word Delivery by Balloon," March 7, 19?, box 150, Balloons General 1951–1956, HIWRP.

31. "Printed Word Operation Progress Report Free Europe Press," December 16, 1954, box 150, Balloons General 1951–1956, HIWRP; Cummings, *Radio Free Europe's "Crusade for Freedom,"* 56–57.

32. "Trial Balloons," Frank Altschul to C.D. Jackson, February 26, 1951, 1; Radio Free Europe, Division of the National Committee for a Free Europe, Inc. to Abbott Washburn, Crusade for Freedom, Inc., October 8, 1951, box 150, Balloons General 1951–1956, HIWRP; Procter & Gamble Company, "It Floats Behind the Iron Curtain," General Office *Moonbeams*, April 1952, 14; Procter & Gamble, "Soap to Russia on Easter," Manufacturing Department *Moonbeams*, April 1952, 2.

33. "Soviets Said to Be Outfitting Floating Jamming Station," Item No. 8128/52, June 18, 1952, Records of the Research Institute of Radio Free Europe/Radio Liberty, Romanian Unit, 1953–1994, OSA; C.D. Jackson to John (no last name), January 21, 1952, letter cc to "Messrs. Phenix, Lang, Washburn, Dolbeare, Tyson, HB Miller," 1; "Printed Word Operation Progress Report Free Europe Press," December 16, 1954, box 150, Balloons General 1951–1956, HIWRP.

34. "Balance Sheet of the People's Struggle," June 21, 195?, 1–2, box 150, Balloons General 1951–1956, HIWRP; Regarding leaflets dropped over 1953 Bucharest

Film Festival, "Audience Analysis with a Civil Engineer," Item 5630/56, June 1, 1956. Records of the Research Institute of Radio Free Europe/Radio Liberty, Romanian Unit, 1953–1994; "Audience Analysis with a Radio Technician," Item No. 11400/56, file 506 Communications/Radio 1955–56, Records of the Research Institute of Radio Free Europe/Radio Liberty, Romanian Unit, 1953–1994, OSA.

35. Osgood, *Total Cold War;* Ross, *Radio Free Europe and Radio Liberty*, Hoover Institute, http://hoorferl.stanford.edu/RFE_Register.pdf.

36. Cummings, James Webb, Young, Theodore Repplier, Phillip Graham from the Washington Post, and Sam Gale from General Mills worked on the ads on behalf of the Economic Cooperation Administration for western Europe, see "Ad Council Sells ECA on Ad Effort in Foreign Media," *Advertising Age*, September 11, 1950, 71, box 1, *Advertising Age Clippings*, 1945–1959, Ad Council 50th Anniversary File, 1943–1993; "Agenda: The Advertising Council, Inc. (Industries Advisory Committee) Dinner—Charles E. Wilson Presiding," September 20, 1950, box 1, Ad Council: Industry Advisory Committee File, 1950–1964; "Ad Council Starts Crusade for Freedom," *Advertising Age*, September 4, 1950, 40, box 1, Advertising Age Clippings, 1945–1959, Ad Council 50th Anniversary File, 1943–1993, ACA.

37. "American Business In The Country's Service, A Report on the Ninth Year of the Advertising Council, March 1950 to March 1951," 22, Advertising Council Annual Reports, ACA.

38. This articles states 26 "Everyone Urged to Ring Bell and Pray When Freedom bell Rings Next Tuesday," *The North Adams*, October 19, 1950, 12. This article claims 21 cities "Crusading Bell Arrives on Ship," *New York Times*, September 7, 1950, 35.

39. "10-Ton Freedom Bell On Way to America," *New York Times*, August 28, 1950, 14; "Crusading Bell Arrives on Ship," *New York Times*, September 7, 1950, 35; "Help Truth Fight Communism . . . Join the Crusade for Freedom," Historical File 1941–1997, ACA; "Eisenhower Opens War on 'The Big Lie'," *New York Times*, September 5, 1950, 1, "Text of Eisenhower Call for Crusade," 14.

40. "Heads Scroll Drive Here In Crusade for Freedom," *New York Times*, August 30, 1950, 11; "Crusading Bell Arrives on Ship," *New York Times*, September 7, 1950, 35; "City Hears Peals of Freedom Bell," *New York Times*, September 9, 1950, 32.

41. "Freedom Bell Arrival Greeted By Several Hundred in City, *Jefferson City Post-Tribune*, September 14, 1950, 1; "Area Eager to Sign Freedom Scrolls," *The Chillicothe Constitutional-Tribunal*, September 19, 1950, 4.

42. "Bronze Freedom Bell Starts Trip Across Missouri," *The Maryville Daily Forum*, September 13, 1950, 7; "Special Train Carries Freedom bell to El Paso," *El Paso Herald-Post*, September 22, 1950, 13; "Freedom Bell Replica Is Due Here Tomorrow," *The Anniston Star*, September 29, 1950, 1.

43. "Film Workers Hear Communism Assailed," *New York Times*, September 28, 1950, 37; Bob Colacello, *Ronnie & Nancy, Their Path to The White House—1911*

to 1980 (New York: Warner Books, 2004), 251. His quote is based on a SAG press release dated September 17, 1950.

44. "Sermons to Stress Religious Liberty," *New York Times*, October 8, 1950, 50; "Freedom Sunday Observed in City," *New York Times*, October 9, 1950, 11.

45. "Everyone Urged to Ring Bell and Pray When Freedom bell Rings Next Tuesday," *The North Adams*, October 19, 1950, 12; "1,000 Balloons To Soar," *New York Times*, October 10, 1950, 38; " 'Crusade for Freedom' Takes to the Air," *New York Times*, October 11, 1950, 19.

46. "Bell for Freedom Hoisted In Berlin," *New York Times*, October 22, 1950, 23; "Help Truth Fight Communism . . . Join the Crusade for Freedom," 1951, Historical File 1941–1997; "How Business Helps Solve Public Problems," A Report of the Eighth Year of the Advertising Council, March 1949–March 1950, Advertising Council Annual Reports, ACA.

47. "Ad Council Starts Crusade for Freedom," *Advertising Age*, September 4, 1950, 40, box 1, Advertising Age Clippings, 1945–1959, Ad Council 50th Anniversary File 1943–1993, ACA.

48. "Join the Crusade for Freedom and Back your Country's Cause!" Ad Mat; "If Communism Triumphs, Democracy will Die," Ad Mat; "The Big Truth is the best answer to the Big Lie of Communism," Ad Mat; "I Believe," Ad Mat; "Help Life the Iron Curtain everywhere," Ad Mat, Historical File 1941–1997 ACA.

49. "Here's How You can Help Truth Fight Communism," 1952, Historical File 1941–1997, ACA; Display Ad 69, *New York Times*, October 10, 1950, 12; "The Crusade for Freedom," *Oxnard Press-Courier*, September 2, 1950, 4; http://www.sujet.de/sign/doku/freiheitsglocke/s5_e.html, accessed July 15, 2008.

50. Flanley to Major General C. L. Adcock and Abbott Washburn, "Activities and cooperation—Women's—etc." August 1950, 1–3, box 168, RFE/RL, HIWRP; See Cumming in *Radio Free Europe, Crusade for Freedom* which provides an excellent overview of these campaigns, and highlight the grassroots activities associated the campaigns.

51. "What Helps People Helps Business, 10th Annual Report of the Advertising Council," 25, Advertising Council Annual Reports, ACA; Crusade for Freedom, "Radio Free Europe—Fact Sheet," 5, nd, box 166, Crusade for Freedom, HIWRP.

52. "Crusade for Freedom," Chevrolet Motor Division, Historical File 1941–1997, Advertising Council Archives; "Chevrolet Supports Crusade," *New York Times*, August 23, 1951, 41; "Importance of Ideological Warfare," nd, 3, box 168, RFE/RL, HIWRP.

53. "What Helps People Helps Business, 10th Annual Report of the Advertising Council," 25, Advertising Council Annual Reports; "Launching Crusade for Freedom," 1951; "Crusade for Freedom," Chevrolet Motor Division, 1951, Historical File 1941–1997, ACA; "Crusade for Freedom, Motorcade Due Here Tonight," *Blue Island Sun-Standard*, October 4, 1951, 1; see also Cummings, *Radio Free Europe's "Crusade for Freedom,"* 60–61, 65.

54. "Chevrolet To Participate In 'Crusade for Freedom' Drive," *Chevrolet News*, August 27, 1951, Detroit, Michigan; "Crusade for Freedom," Chevrolet Motor

Division, Historical File 1941–1997, ACA; "Freedom Balloons pierce Iron Curtain," *The Deming Headligt*, August 24, 1951; "Freedom Crusade to Re-Enact 'Balloon Barrage' in Moberly," *Moberly Monitor-Index and Democrat*, September 13, 1951, 16; "Freedom Crusade Drive Is Launched," *The Burlington (N.C.) Daily Times-News*, September 15, 1951, 5; "Crusade for Freedom Motorcade Leaves Today to Tour State," *The Daily Oklahoman*, September 17, 1950, 1; regarding balloons, see Cummings, *Radio Free Europe's "Crusade for Freedom,"* 56–57.

55. "Chevrolet To Participate In 'Crusade for Freedom' Drive," *Chevrolet News*, August 27, 1951, Detroit, Michigan; W.E. Fish to Chevrolet Dealers, August 17, 1951; "Launching Crusade for Freedom," 1951, Historical File 1941–1997; "What Helps People Helps Business, 10th Annual Report of the Advertising Council," 25, Advertising Council Annual Reports, ACA.

56. Haskin & Sells, Certified Public Accountants, to Crusade for Freedom, June 27, 1952, 1–2, box 168, RFE/RL, HIWRP; "Howard J. Morgens Elected Chairman of Advertising Council," *Advertising Age*, March 31, 1952, Advertising Age Clippings 1945–1959, Ad Council 50th Anniversary Files, 1943–1993, ACA.

57. "The Advertising Council: in 10 years it has become the major public relations force for all business," *Tide*, October 10, 1952, box 1, Correspondence 1953, Files of Special Assistant Relating to the Office of Coordinator of Government Public Service Advertising, James M. Lambie Jr., Staff Files, EL; "The Advertising Council, 11th Annual Report, 1952–1953," 18, Advertising Council Annual Reports, ACA.

58. Haskin & Sells, Certified Public Accountants, to Crusade for Freedom, June 27, 1952, 1, box 168, RFE/RL, HIWRP; Crusade for Freedom, Help Truth Fight Communism, November-December, 1952, Historical File 1941–1997, ACA.

59. "'Give us this day . . . our daily truth," Ad Mat, 1952; "A Plea to All Americans of All Faiths!" Ad Mat, 1952; "This 'Flying Saucer' carries Truth!" Ad Mat, 1952, Historical File 1941–1997; "The Advertising Council, 11th Annual Report, 1952–1953," 24, Advertising Council Annual Reports, ACA.

60. "Annual Report The Advertising Council, 1953–1954," 19–20, 13/2/202 Advertising Council Annual Reports, ACA; The American Heritage Foundation, "A Story of Citizenship In Action," box 2, American Heritage Foundation, Files of Special Assistant Relating to the Office of Coordinator of Government Public Service Advertising, James M. Lambie Jr., Staff Files, EL.

61. "Sign Up Today with Freedom Crusade," nd, box 1, Correspondence 1953; Press Release; "Crusade for Freedom Washington Conference of National Organizations, October 20–21, 1953, box 2, American Heritage Foundation, Files of Special Assistant Relating to the Office of Coordinator of Government Public Service Advertising, James M. Lambie Jr., Staff Files, EL.

62. John Foster Dulles, "Reputation and Performance in World Affairs," Address to the Brand Names Foundation, April 12, 1949, Press Release #597, April 11, 1949, Seeley G. Mudd Manuscript Library, Princeton University.

63. "How Business Helps Solve Public Problems," A Report of the Eighth Year of the Advertising Council, March 1949 to March 1950, Advertising Council Annual Reports, ACA.

64. "American Business In The Country's Service, A Report on the Ninth Year of the Advertising Council, March 1950 to March 1951," 22, 26–27, Advertising Council Annual Reports, ACA.

65. "Crusading Bell Arrives on Ship," *New York Times*, September 7, 1950, 35; "Berliners Weep At Clay's Praise," *New York Times*, October 25, 1950, 22; "Importance of Ideological Warfare," nd, 11, box 168, folder 2, RFE/RL, HIWRP.

66. "American Business In The Country's Service, A Report on the Ninth Year of the Advertising Council, March 1950 to March 1951," 26, Advertising Council Annual Reports, ACA; "Everyone Urged to Ring Bell and Pray When Freedom bell Rings Next Tuesday," *The North Adams*, October 19, 1950, 12.

67. "Statement by the President on the Violation of the 38th Parallel in Korea, June 26, 1950"; "Radio and Television Report to the American People on the Situation in Korea, September 1, 1950," *Public Papers of the President of the United States, Harry Truman, 1950* (Washington, D.C.: United States Government Printing Office, 1965), 491–492, 609–610.

68. "American Business In The Country's Service, A Report on the Ninth Year of the Advertising Council, March 1950 to March 1951," 27, Advertising Council Annual Reports; "Re-Arm Fast Is Message of Public Service Campaign by Ad Council," *Advertising Age*, December 11, 1950, 123, Advertising Age Clippings 1945–1959, Ad Council 50th Anniversary Files, 1943–1993, ACA.

69. All statistics from Osgood, *Total Cold War*, 43. See also, Walter L. Hixson, *Parting the Curtain: Propaganda, Culture, and the Cold War, 1945–1961* (Palgrave Macmillan, 1997).

70. The report lists specific figure at 299,542,672, see Free Europe Press monthly report, October 1956, box 151, Balloons General April 1956–1958; Whitney H. Shepardson, President Free Europe Committee, Inc., "Statement to the Press," January 28, 1956, 1; "Free Europe Press Operations," February 8, 1956, 1, box 150, Balloons General 1951–1956, HIWRP.

71. Crusade for Freedom, "Radio Free Europe—Fact Sheet," nd, 1, box 166, Crusade for Freedom; Whitney H. Shepardson, President Free Europe Committee, Inc., "Statement to the Press," January 28, 1956, 1, box 150, Balloons General 1951–1956, HIWRP.

72. "Soviets Said to Be Outfitting Floating Jamming Station," Item No. 8128/52, June 18, 1952, Records of the Research Institute of Radio Free Europe/Radio Liberty, Romanian Unit, 1953–1994, OSA.

73. Advertising Council campaign master list, ACA.

74. Allan Brown, Vice President, The Bakelite Company to Dear Sir," Advertising Council, 1953; "Radio Free Europe Crusade for Freedom Kit," 1953, Historical File 1941–1997, ACA.

75. Advertising Council campaign master list, ACA.

76. What has great meaning for local German population is part of a fund-raising campaign conducted by American advertisers, brand-name business, and the CIA. For a great example of how it is difficult to determine how people find

meaning see http://www.sujet.de/sign/doku/freiheitsglocke/s4_e.html, accessed July 15, 2008.

77. Broadcasting Board of Governors, http://www.bbg.gov/bbg_aboutus.cfm, accessed July 19, 2008.

Chapter 7

1. T.V Department Organization, November 7, 1956, 1, File Administrative Records, June 1955–April 1956, 2, box 1, Department Organization, Radio TV Department, JWT. Papers of the Administrator, John F. Devine; "Memorandum on the Relations between the Representative and the Media and TV-Radio Departments," March 4, 1957, 1–2, box 14, JWT TV-Radio Department, 1930–1964, Colin Dawkins Papers, JWTCA, HCAMR; For an excellent overview of television between 1948 and 1961, particularly the conflict over programming, see James L. Baughman, *Same Time, Same Station: Creating American Television, 1948–1961* (Baltimore: John Hopkins University Press, 2007), 11–16, 192.

2. "Memorandum of the work of The War Advertising Council, 1942–1943," 13–14; "Words That Work For Victory, The Third Year of the War Advertising Council, March 1, 1944–March 1, 1945," 12, Advertising Council Annual Reports, ACA; Baughman, *Same Time, Same Station*, 258.

3. "What Helps People Helps Business, The Sixth Year of The Advertising Council, March 1947–March 1948," 17; "What Helps People Helps Business, The Seventh Year of The Advertising Council, March 1948–March 1949," 23, Advertising Council Annual Reports, ACA.

4. "In the Wake of the War, The Fourth year of The Advertising Council, March 1, 1945 to March 1, 1946," 16, Advertising Council Annual Reports, ACA; John Devine to O'Neill Ryan, Jr. and Ruth Jones, July 10, 1958, box 5, Programming Records: Programming Talent, Showcase, Networks, General Files, Papers of the Administrator, John F. Devine, JWTCA, HCAMR.

5. "J.W.T. Stages the World's First Television Advertising Program," J.W.T. News, September 1930, 5, box 14, JWT TV-Radio Department, 1930–1964, Colin Dawkins Papers, JWTCA, HCAMR.

6. Research Department to Miss Nelson, July 1, 1946, box 14, JWT TV-Radio Department, 1930–1964, Colin Dawkins Papers, JWTCA, HCAMR.

7. William Hawes, *Live Television Drama, 1946–1951* (London: McFarland & Company, Inc, 2001), 14–15.

8. Fred H. Fidler, "Television: Synopsis of a Dream Which May at Last Come True," *People*, November 1937, 16–27, box 11, Broadcast Advertising—Television 1937–1979, Colin Dawkins Papers, JWTCA, HCAMR; Hawes, *Live Television Drama, 1946–1951*, 14–16, 19.

9. "Departments," J. Walter Thompson, July 28, 1947, box 14, JWT TV-Radio Department 1930–1964, Colin Dawkins Papers, JWTCA, HCAMR; "Television," *JWT News*, July 12, 1948, V III, N 28, box 2, Administrative Records

TV, JWT TV Firsts 1950, 1958, Administrative Records, TV Administration: International TV—Non–TV, Administration: Management Committee, Papers of the Administrator, John F. Devine, JWTCA, HCAMR.

10. Baughman, *Same Time, Same Station*, 195; Lawrence R. Samuel, *Brought to You By Postwar Television, Advertising and the American Dream* (Austin, TX: University of Texas Press, 2001), 15; "Departments," J. Walter Thompson, July 28, 1947; "Television," *JWT News*, July 12, 1948; Hawes, *Live Television Drama, 1946–1951*, 13, 15.

11. Statistics based on *Printers' Ink* analysis, cited in the Television Bureau of Advertising, *The Three "Hows" of Television* (New York: Television Bureau of Advertising, Inc, June 1955), 13, 17, 19; Baughman, *Same Time, Same Station*, 44.

12. "Departments," J. Walter Thompson, July 28, 1947; Baughman, *Same Time, Same Station*, 47, 57, 61, 63–65, 93–94; see also Gary R. Edgerton, *The Columbia History of American Television* (New York: Columbia University Press, 2007), 105; Samuel, *Brought to You By Postwar Television*, xiv, 48.

13. Baughman, *Same Time, Same Station*, 55, 202; Norman Bassett to All Directors, "T.V. in the U.S.," November 29, 1950, box 14, Offices London, Colin Dawkins Papers, JWTCA, HCAMR.

14. William Hawes, *Filmed Television Drama, 1952–1958* (London: McFarland, 2002), 5, 69; Baughman, *Same Time, Same Station*, 225.

15. Kerry Segrave, *American Television Abroad, Hollywood's Attempt to Dominate World Television* (London: McFarland & Company, Inc, 1998), 15; Hawes, *Live Television Drama, 1946–1951*; William Hawes, *Filmed Television Drama, 1952–1958* (North Carolina, London: McFarland & Company, Inc., 2002); "JWT: The Fleet-Footed Tortoise," *Broadcasting*, November 23, 1964, 46–48, box 14, JWT TV-Radio Department 1930–1964, Colin Dawkins Papers, JWTCA, HCAMR.

16. Baughman, *Same Time, Same Station*, 202; Segrave, *American Television Abroad*, 15; "Annual Report Advertising Council 1955–56," 28; "Public Service Advertising Council, 1954–55," 4, 6, 26, Advertising Council Annual Reports, ACA.

17. "The J. Walter Thompson, 'Local Live TV Group'"; "Television, Radio and Motion Pictures," January 17, 1957; "JWT's New Television Studio," *Printer's Ink*, January 31, 1955, box 14, JWT TV-Radio Department 1930–1964, Colin Dawkins Papers, JWTCA, HCAMR.

18. "Thompson Announces New Color activities for Its Television Workshop"; "Thompson Pioneers Color-Tape Commercials," *J. Walter Thompson Company News*, July 21, 1958 box 14, TV-Radio News, JWT TV-Radio Department 1930–1964, Colin Dawkins Papers; "Why J. Walter Thompson is Banking on Color," *Broadcasting Television*, February 4, 1957, 31, box 3, Norman H. Strouse Papers, JWTCA, HCAMR.

19. Lawrence M. Hughes, "Free Choice or Free TV? The Argument Up-to-Date," *SR/ Recordings Section*, February 22, 1958, box 2, Administrative Records, TV Pay TV, 1958, Department Organization, Radio TV Department; Warren

G. Magnusen to Dan Seymour, J. Walter Thompson Co., December 30, 1958, box 2, Administrative Records, TV Legislation 1958–1959, May 1960, Papers of the Administrator, John F. Devine, JWTCA, HCAMR.

20. Regarding Pay-TV Hearings, see Baughman, *Same Time, Same Station*, 78–79; Robert W. Sarnoff, "It would 'Cannibalize' Free TV, Network Presidents State Views Against Pay TV," *Television Digest*, January 25, 1958, 1–4, 8, box 2, Administrative Records, TV Pay TV, 1958, Radio TV Department, Papers of the Administrator, John F. Devine, JWTCA, HCAMR.

21. "Help of Business in Cold War Cited, Advertising Council Reviews Year's Campaigns Designed to Combat Communism," *New York Times*, August 25, 1949, 33, 38; Baughman, *Same Time, Same Station*, 26.

22. "Advertising Hall of Fame," nd, box 1, Ted Repplier letters, speech, report, article, obituary, 1944–45, 1955, 1966, Ad Council 50th Anniversary Files 1943–1993; "American Business In The Country's Service, A Report on the Ninth Year of the Advertising Council, March 1950 to March 1951," 7, Advertising Council Annual Reports, ACA.

23. "American Business In The Country's Service, A Report on the Ninth Year of the Advertising Council, March 1950 to March 1951," 7, 15, 26; "Public Service Advertising Council, 1954–55," 28, Advertising Council Annual Reports; "Ad Council 1950 Activities Hit New High Point," *Advertising Age*, August 6, 1951, 43, Advertising Age Clippings 1945–1959, Ad Council 50th Anniversary Files 1943–1993, ACA.

24. "What Helps People Helps Business, 10th Annual Report of the Advertising Council," 18, 22, Advertising Council Annual Reports; "Ad Council Will Urge Film TV Sponsors to Start using Public Service Messages," *Advertising Age*, June 1, 1953, 30, Advertising Age Clippings 1945–1959, Ad Council 50th Anniversary Files, 1943–1993, ACA.

25. "Annual Report Advertising Council 1955–56," 26; "The Advertising Council, 11th Annual Report, 1952–1953," 6, Advertising Council Annual Reports, ACA; On American fears of atomic energy, see Allan M. Winkler, *Life Under a Cloud: American Anxiety about the Atom* (New York: Oxford University Press, 1993).

26. "Public Service Advertising Council, 1954–55," 4, 28, Advertising Council Annual Reports, ACA.

27. Baughman, *Same Time, Same Station*, 202; Segrave, *American Television Abroad*, 15; "Annual Report Advertising Council 1955–56," 28; "Public Service Advertising Council, 1954–55," 4, 6, 26, Advertising Council Annual Reports, ACA

28. "Public Service Advertising Council, 1954–55," 29; The council's 1955–1956 report included a month by month schedule of TV campaigns, see "Annual Report Advertising Council 1955–56," 6, Advertising Council Annual Reports, ACA.

29. Baughman, *Same Time, Same Station*, 162–164; Hawes, *Filmed Television Drama, 1952–1958*, 170–172; On African-American advertising executives and television see, Jason Chambers, *Madison Avenue and the Color Line: African*

Americans in the Advertising Industry (Philadelphia: University of Pennsylvania Press, 2008).

30. "JWT: the fleet-footed tortoise," *Broadcasting*, November 23, 1964, 46–48, box 14, JWT TV-Radio Department, 1930–1964, Colin Dawkins Papers, JWTCA, HCAMR.

31. Baughman, *Same Time, Same Station*, 29–30; Samuel, *Brought to You By Postwar Television*, 4; Newsletter, June 10, 1946, box 14, JWT TV-Radio Department 1930–1964, Colin Dawkins Papers, JWTCA, HCAMR; Bulova corporate history, http://www.bulova.com/about/about.aspx#history.aspx.

32. Samuel, *Brought to You By Postwar Television*, 11; Baughman, *Same Time, Same Station*, 41, 46; "Departments," J. Walter Thompson, July 28, 1947; "Television," *JWT News*, July 12, 1948, JWT TV-Radio Department 1930–1964, Colin Dawkins Papers, JWTCA, HCAMR.

33. Regarding J Robinson and NBC, see Baughman, *Same Time, Same Station*, 162–164; Jackson, Mississippi, first TV station WJTV Jackson in 1953; Steven D. Classen, *Watching Jim Crow: The Struggles Over Mississippi TV, 1955–196* (Durham: Duke University Press, 2004), 34, 158; Lee Lowenfish, *Branch Rickey: Baseball's Ferocious Gentleman* (Lincoln: University of Nebraska Press, 2007), 351–352 356–357, 371–384; Hawes, *Filmed Television Drama, 1952–1958*, 170–172.

34. John Kelly, "Integrating America: Jackie Robinson, Critical Events and Baseball Black and White," *International Journal of the History of Sport*, 22, no. 6 (November, 2005), 1011–1035.

35. Regarding President Truman establishing White House and information departments to deliver news, see Nancy E. Bernhard, *U.S Television News and Cold War Propaganda, 1947–1960* (Cambridge: Cambridge University Press, 1999); Baughman, *Same Time, Same Station*, 43, 220, 224–225, 227–229.

36. Based on A.C. Nielsen ratings statistic, see the Television Bureau of Advertising, *The Three "Hows" of Television* (New York: Television Bureau of Advertising, Inc, June 1955.), 21; Baughman, *Same Time, Same Station*, 41, 232; Samuel, *Brought to You By Postwar Television*, 34.

37. See Darrell M. West, *Air Wars: Television Advertising in Election Campaigns, 1952–2004*, 4th ed. (Washington, D.C.: CQ Press, 2005); M.C. MacGregor, "Television's Impact on the 1952 Presidential Election and Influence on the Political Process," November 1986, 40–41 Thesis, Ohio University, MacGregor cites "The Networks' New Policy," *New York Times*, January 14, 1952, 12.

38. MacGregor, 80–81; MacGregor cites Melvyn H. Bloom, *Public Relations and Presidential Campaigns: A Crisis in Democracy* (New York: Thomas Y. Crowell CO., 1973), 43 and Steve M Barkin, "TV Planning in the 1952 Eisenhower Campaign," (AEJMC paper presented in August 1981), 3; also an Eisenhower archives report on meeting called "TV Plans Board" December 17, 1951; "What American Did to Swing the Vote," *Sponsor*, November 3, 1952; Robert Bendiner, "How Much Has TV Changed Campaigning?" *New York Times Magazine*, November 2, 1952, 13.

39. Advertising Council, "History's Greatest Register and Vote Campaign," box 2, Register and Vote Ad, Council 50th Anniversary File, 1943–1993 ACA; "Crusader in the Capital," *Time*, January 28, 1952, "An Evangelistic Meeting on the Steps of the Capitol," *New York Time*, February 4, 1952, 4; Stanley J. Quinn to John F. Devine, March 24, 1958, box 1 Administrative Records, TV Personnel, 1958, 1961, Administrative Records, Papers of the Administrator, John F. Devine, JWTCA, HCAMR.

40. Clyde Vandeburg, American Heritage Foundation Press Release, May 14, 1953; "Background of the American Heritage Foundation," box 2, American Heritage Foundation, Files of Special Assistant Relating to the Office of Coordinator of Government Public Service Advertising, James M. Lambie Jr., Staff Files, EL.

41. The American Heritage Foundation, "News Release," August 28, 1952; The American Heritage Foundation, "Feature Story for Release," box 7, Vote Campaign, Files of James M. Lambie Jr., Staff Files, EL.

42. The American Heritage Foundation, "Feature Story for Release;" "Background of the American Heritage Foundation," nd, 3, box 2, The American Heritage Foundation, "Feature Story for Release Files of James M. Lambie Jr., Staff Files, EL.

43. Bob Colacello, *Ronnie & Nancy, Their Path to the White House–1911 to 1980* (New York: Warner Books, 2004), 271–274; Frances Stonor Saunders, *The Cultural Cold War: The CIA and the World of Arts and Letters* (New York: The New Press, 1999), 132, 158, 422.

44. Carroll L. Wilson, "The International Operation of the J. Walter Thompson Company, Analysis of an Expanding Venture with Policy Recommendations," December 15, 1945, box 4, The International Operation of the J. Walter Thompson Company, Analysis of an Expanding Venture with Policy Recommendations, International Offices, International Department, International Marketing, Samuel W. Meek Papers, JWTCA, HCAMR.

45. "J. Walter Thompson, Television, Radio and Motion Pictures," 2, box 1, Administrative Records, June 1955–April 1956, Department Organization, Radio TV Department, Papers of the Administrator, John F. Devine, JWTCA, HCAMR.

46. "London Office," J. Walter Thompson Company, nd; J. Walter Thompson Company Limited, London, "A Technique of Planning applied to influencing Opinion and Behaviour" (Printed by Waterlow & Sons Limited, London, 1948), box 14, Offices London, Colin Dawkins Papers, JWTCA, HCAMR.

47. H.H. Wilson, "The Campaign for Commercial Television in England" (New Brunswick, NJ: Rutgers University Press, 1961), 1–3, 16, box 14, Offices London, Colin Dawkins Papers, JWTCA, HCAMR; Samuel, *Brought to You By Postwar Television*, 67.

48. In the 1920s, American movie studios successfully brought American movies to theaters in other countries often quashing local production efforts that could not compete with larger budget Hollywood productions, see Segrave, *American*

Television Abroad, 3–4, 7–9; Segrave cites a *Reader's Digest* article from 1955; see A. E. Hotchner, "Global TV is on the Way," *Reader's Digest* 66, May 1955, 61–63.

49. "J. Walter Thompson, Television, Radio and Motion Pictures," 2, box 1 Administrative Records, June 1955–April 1956, Department Organization, Radio TV Department; Renichi Yatsunami to Norman Strouse, December 1, 1956, box 2, Administrative Records, TV: International TV, 1956, Radio TV Department, Papers of the Administrator, John F. Devine, JWTCA, HCAMR; Samuel, *Brought to You By Postwar Television*, 67; Segrave, *American Television Abroad*, 19.

50. Thornton B. Wierum to Peter Dunham, December 11, 1956, RE: Lassie—Kellogg De Mexico, Administrative Records, TV: International TV, March 1957-November 1958; Virginia C. Spragle to Norma Kingsley, December 6, 1956, box 2, Administrative Records, TV: International TV, March 1957–November 1958, Radio TV Department: Papers of the Administrator, John F. Devine, JWTCA, HCAMR.

51. Sigrid H. Pedersen to Carroll Cartwright, June 29, 1956, "Re: Standard Brands—TV Bowling Game Program in Latin America"; Thornton B. Wierum to W. E. Hazard, November 20, 1956, box 2, Administrative Records, TV: International TV, 1956, Radio TV Department, Papers of the Administrator, John F. Devine, JWTCA, HCAMR.

52. "Theatre and Television Production and Distribution for Overseas Film Commercials," November 2, 1956, box 2, Administrative Records, TV: International TV, March 1957–November 1958, Radio TV Department, Papers of the Administrator, John F. Devine, JWTCA, HCAMR.

53. "Thompson is playing a leading part in the rapid TV development in Australia," JWT News, October 21, 1957, box 14, Offices Australia 1930, 1931, 1937, Colin Dawkins Papers, JWTCA, HCAMR.

54. Segrave, *American Television Abroad*, 6, 22, 34; John F. Devine to Virginia Spragle, April 2, 1956, box 2, Administrative Records, TV: International TV, 1956, Radio TV Department, Papers of the Administrator, John F. Devine, JWTCA, HCAMR.

55. Segrave, *American Television Abroad*, 10, 20–21, 26–27, 43–44.

56. USIA "Overseas Television Developments"; "Principal News Agencies of the World," box 1 Radio and Television; "Developments in the Field of Freedom of Information Liberation by the U.S," box 4 International Flow of News U.S. President's Committee on Information Activities Abroad (Sprague Committee) Records, 1959–61, EL.

57. Nancy E. Bernhard, *U.S. Television News and Cold War Propaganda, 1947–60* (Cambridge: Cambridge University Press, 1999), 186; Segrave, *American Television Abroad*, 33–35.

58. Nicholas John Cull, *The Cold War and the United States Information Agency: American Propaganda and Public Diplomacy, 1945–1989* (New York: Cambridge University Press, 2008), p. 111: Earl James Collins, "A History of The Creation, Development and Use of A Worldwide Military Non-Commercial Television

Network for the United States Military By the Armed Forces Radio and Television Service," Dissertation, Ohio State University, 1959, 1, 45, 49, 71, 75, map.

59. Television Bureau of Advertising, *The Three "Hows" of Television* (New York: Television Bureau of Advertising, Inc, June 1955), 6, 11, 53, 58.

60. Ibid., 1, 7–9, 11–12, 22–23, 63.

61. "Television's next five years," "News," October 1, 1956, box 14, TV-Radio Department, 1930–1964, Colin Dawkins Papers, JWTCA, HCAMR.

62. "What Helps People . . . Helps Business, 15th Annual Report of The Advertising Council," 20, Advertising Council Annual Reports, ACA; "The Top 40 Agencies In Broadcast Billings," *Broadcasting Telecasting, The Business Weekly of Radio and Television*, December 3, 1956, V. 51, N. 23, 27, box 2, Administrative Records—non-TV Management Committee, 1956, Papers of the Administrator, John F. Devine, JWTCA, HCAMR.

Chapter 8

1. "Cherry Blossom Time in Washington," confidential report, March 31, 1953, 6, box 1, Washington Conference 1953, Washington Conference File, 1949–59, ACA.

2. "Public Service Advertising Council, 1954–55," 4–6, Advertising Council Annual Reports, ACA.

3. Robert Kieve to Thomas E. Stephens, March 23, 1953; Dwight D. Eisenhower to T.S. Repplier, April 10, 1953, box 620, Advertising Council 1952–53, Official File 122–A–1, DDE Records as President, WHCF, EL.

4. C.D. Jackson, "Notes for Governor Adams," September 18, 1953, 2, box 2, Association of National Advertisers, 1953, Files of James M. Lambie Jr., Staff Files, EL.; See also Cull, Cummings, Johnson.

5. CD Jackson to Sinclair Weeks, Secretary of Commerce, March 30, 1953, box 620, Advertising Council 1952–53, Official File 122–A–1, DDE Records as President, WHCF, EL.

6. James M. Lambie, Jr. to The President, January 16, 1954, box 621, Advertising Council 1952–53,Official File 122–A–1, Box 621, DDE Records as President, WHCF, EL.

7. "Functions heretofore performed by the White House in connection with Government Information Campaigns," nd, box 1, Correspondence 1953, Files of Special Assistant Relating to the Office of Coordinator of Government Public Service Advertising, James M. Lambie Jr., Staff Files, EL.

8. "Advertising Council Releasing 12th Campaign Created by J. Walter Thompson for Religion in American Life," September 29, 1960; "A Special Message by President Dwight D. Eisenhower for Religion in American Life," nd, box 57, RIAL 1960, Files of James M. Lambie Jr., Staff Files, EL.

9. Press Release, October 30, 1953, 1; Henry C. Wehde, Jr., October 1953; "Light their life with Faith, Bring them to worship this week," nd; Charles E. Wilson to

Publisher, October 22, 1953, box 7, "Religion in America" 1953, Files of James M. Lambie Jr., Staff Files, EL.

10. "Ad Council Opens Overseas Aid Campaign For Churches," *Advertising Age*, March 5, 1956, 37, Advertising Age Clippings 1945–1959, Ad Council 50th Anniversary Files, 1943–1993; "Report of Public Policy Committee Meeting," November 20, 1957, 2, box 1, Reports for Public Policy Committee Meeting, 1956–1957, Public Policy Committee Meeting Reports and Minutes, 1954–1986, ACA; "Minutes of Public Policy Committee Meeting," November 13, 1958, 4, box 1, Reports for Public Policy Committee Meeting, 1958–1959; "Report of Public Policy Committee Meeting," November 18, 1960, 2, box 1, Reports for Public Policy Committee Meeting, 1960–1961, Public Policy Committee Meeting Reports and Minutes, 1954–1986, ACA.

11. "Senate Restricts Smokey Bear Symbol to Public Service," *Advertising Age*, March 10, 1952, 16; "Smokey Bear Products Get 1st Retail Push," *Advertising Age*, September 21, 1953, Advertising Age Clippings 1945–1959, Ad Council 50th Anniversary Files, 1943–1993; "Annual Report The Advertising Council, 1953–1954," 6, Advertising Council Annual Reports, ACA; "Smokey Bear," Senate Report 1128, Senate Calendar No. 1062, 82 Congress, January 28, 1952, 1–5; "Smokey Bear," House of Representatives, Report No. 1512, 82 Congress, March 12, 1952, 1–6.

12. Lisa McGirr, *Suburban Warriors: The Origins of the New American Right* (Princeton: Princeton University Press, 2001), 3–19.

13. "Reece Attacks Ad Council and Ford Foundation," *Advertising Age*, August 3, 1953; "Rep. Wilson, San Diego Agency Man Comes to Defense of the Ad Council," *Advertising Age*, August 10, 1953, box 2, Ad Council 50th Anniversary File, ACA; "The Advertising Council," Extension of Remarks of Hon. Bob Wilson of California in the House of Representatives, July 31, 1953, Congressional Record, Proceedings and Debates of the 83rd Congress First Session, Volume 99—Part 12, July 2, 1953–August 28, 1953, A4918–4919; A4955.

14. Two press releases were issued with the same title on May 14, 1950, see Clyde Vandeburg, American Heritage Foundation Press Release, May 14, 1953, box 2, American Heritage Foundation, Files of James M. Lambie Jr., Staff Files, EL.

15. The American Heritage Foundation, "A Story of Citizenship In Action," box 2, American Heritage Foundation, Files of James M. Lambie Jr., Staff Files, EL.

16. Kenneth Osgood, *Total Cold War: Eisenhower's Secret Propaganda Battle at Home and Abroad* (Lawrence: University of Kansas Press, 2006), 71–72; Stephen E. Ambrose, *Eisenhower: Soldier and President* (New York: Simon and Schuster, 1991); Stephen E. Ambrose, *Ike's Spies: Eisenhower and The Espionage Establishment* (Jackson University Press of Mississippi, Banner Books), 1999; Dwight D. Eisenhower, *The Papers of Dwight David Eisenhower*, edited by Jr. Alfred D. Chandler, Stephen E. Ambrose, associate editor [and others] (Baltimore: Johns Hopkins Press, 1984).

17. Eldridge Hiller, "For the Hearts and Souls of Men," nd., box 1, Advertising Council General 1953, Files of James M. Lambie Jr., Staff Files, EL.

18. Stalin died March 5, 1953; the hearings in question began March 6, 1953, see Osgood, *Total Cold War*, 89; "Overseas Information Programs of the United States," Hearings before a Subcommittee of the Committee on Foreign Relations United States Senate, Eighty-Third Congress, First Session on Overseas Information Programs of the United States, 1953; Harold B. Hinton, "U. S. Called Faulty in Propaganda Job?" *New York Times*, June 14, 1953, 31; Anthony Leviero, "Shake-up Is Urged in Psychology War," *New York Times*, July 9, 1953, 1.

19. Osgood, *Total Cold War*, 78–95; "Text of White House Statement on Committee Report," *New York Times*, July 9, 1953, 8; "The Overseas Information Program," U.S. Information Agency, U. S. Government Printing Office, July 1960.

20. "Overseas Information Programs of the United States," Hearings before a Subcommittee of the Committee on Foreign Relations United States Senate, Eighty-Third Congress, First Session on Overseas Information Programs of the United States, 1953, 229–243, 268–269.

21. Ibid., 352–353, 382.

22. Ibid., 709, 711–712, 721–727; see Roland Marchand, *Creating the Corporate Soul: The Rise of Public Relations and Corporate Imagery in American Big Business* (Berkeley: University of California Press, 1998); Stuart Ewen, *PR! A Social History of Spin* (New York: BasicBooks, 1996).

23. Ibid., 731–733, 735.

24. Ibid., 778.

25. Jay Walz, "New Information Unit Has Some Big Plans," *New York Times*, November 1, 1953, E6.

26. Osgood, *Total Cold War*, 89, 138; Harold B. Hinton, "U. S. Called Faulty in Propaganda Job," *New York Times*, June 14, 1953, 31; "Text of White House Statement on Committee Report," *New York Times*, July 9, 1953, 8; "Text of Policy Statement on Government Book and Library Program," *New York Times*, July 9, 1953, 10.

27. William H. McCahon to James M. Lambie, October 29, 1953; "Advisory Committee on Voluntary Foreign Aid Foreign Operations Administration," October 29, 1953, box 2, Advisory Committee on Voluntary Foreign Aid, Files of James M. Lambie Jr., Staff Files, EL.

28. Henry G. Little to Ted (Repplier), March 23, 1954, 1; "U.S. Information Agency Plans to Step Up Its Overseas PR Operations," reprinted from *Advertising Age*, January 4, 1954, box 15, U.S. Information Agency, Files of James M. Lambie Jr., Staff Files, EL.

29. T.S. Repplier to the Board of Directors, December 1, 1954, box 15, U.S. Information Agency, Files of James M. Lambie Jr., Staff Files, EL.

30. Osgood devotes a chapter to Atoms for Peace campaign called "Spinning the Friendly Atom, The Atom for Peace Campaign"; see Osgood, *Total Cold War*, 153–180.

31. "The Sixth White House Meeting for the Board of Directors and Committees of the Advertising Council, February 15 and 16, 1950;" "The Eighth White House Conference in cooperation with the Advertising Council," March

4–5, 1952; "The Eleventh Washington Conference," March 22, 1955; "The Fourteenth Washington Conference, the Advertising Council," May 6, 1958, box 1, Washington Conference Programs, Washington Conference File, 1944–1959, ACA.

32. "Talks in the Treaty Room," "Confidential Not For Publication, as reported by Leo Burnett, president, Leo Burnett Company, Inc., and director, The Advertising Council," February 15–16, 1950, 10, box 1, Washington Conference File, 1944–1959, ACA.

33. "The Advertising Council, 11th Annual Report, 1952–1953," 6, Advertising Council Annual Reports, ACA.

34. Osgood, *Total Cold War*, 154, 158–160, 163, 171–176; See also Ira Chernus, *Eisenhower's Atoms for Peace* (College Station: Texas A&M University Press, 2002).

35. Arthur Goodfriend, *What is America?* (New York: Simon and Schuster, 1954), 9, 16–17; "Ad Council Panel on America Bears Fruit in Book Marked for World Distribution," *Advertising Age*, November 23, 1954, 24, Advertising Age Clippings 1945–1959, Ad Council 50th Anniversary Files, 1943–1993, ACA.

36. Thomas Borstelmann, *The Cold War and the Color Line: American Race Relations in the Global Arena* (Cambridge, MA: Harvard University Press, 2001), 80–81, 91; Mary L. Dudziak, *Cold War Civil Rights: Race and the Image of American Democracy* (Princeton, NJ: Princeton University Press, 1998), 61, 93–95, 115–151. Report cited "Status Report on the National Psychological Effort and First Progress Report of the Psychological Strategy Board," August 1, 1952, box 22, Papers of the Psychological Strategy Board, TPTL.

37. "Admen in Europe Interested in Forming an International Advertising Council," *Advertising Age*, December 3, 1951, Advertising Age Clippings 1945–1959, Ad Council 50th Anniversary Files, 1943–1993, ACA.

38. Borstelmann, *The Cold War and the Color Line*, 77–79, 97; Dudziak, *Cold War Civil Rights*, 61–63, 71, 220; See also, David A. Nichols, *A Matter of Justice: Eisenhower and the Civil Rights Revolution* (Simon & Schuster, 2008).

39. Borstelmann, *The Cold War and the Color Line*, 103–106, 111; Dudziak, *Cold War Civil Rights*, 119–125, 143–145.

40. "Summary of Projects In Cooperation With Private Enterprise Initiated, Continued, or Completed from January 1, 1953 to June 30, 1953—ICO," box 7, State Overseas Information 1953; CD Jackson to Stuart Peabody, The Borden Company, April 15, 1955, box 23, North Atlantic Treaty Organization 1955; U.S. Information Agency, Press Release, November 10, 1955, box 24, U.S. Information Agency Correspondence 1955, Files of James M. Lambie Jr., Staff Files, EL; Shirley Woodell to Miss Glover, Bogota, February 26, 1954; Shirley Woodell to A.B. Reed, Eastman Kodak, March 22, 1954; Shirley Woodell to James F. Lewis, Jr., Champion Spark Plug Company, March 27, 1954; box 2, Office Files and Correspondence, 1954 February-March, Colombia, Venezuela, Puerto Rico, Shirley Woodell Papers, JWTCA, HCAMR.

41. Carroll B. Cartwright to Shirley Woodell, October 26, 1954, Re: Standard Brands, Puerto Rico; No name to Miss Glover, Caracas, November 16, 1954; Shirley Woodell to Frank W. Matthay, The Parker Pen Company, December 6, 1954; Shirley Woodell to C.J. Luten, Sylvania Electric Products, Inc., December 8, 1954; Shirley Woodell to J.C. Speirs, Standard Brands International, December 9, 1954; Shirley Woodell to Holbrook R. Davis, Aluminium [*sic*] Limited Sales, Inc., December 13, 1954; Shirley Woodell to E.H. Mirman, Kraft Foods Company, December 20, 1954; Shirley Woodell to John Russo, December 22, 1954, box 3, File Office Files and Correspondence, 1954 October–December, Cuba, Puerto Rico, Venezuela, Colombia, Peru; Shirley Woodell to Miss Fields, Rio de Janeiro, July 16, 1955, box 3, Office Files and Correspondence 1955, July–August 26, Puerto Rico, Venezuela, Brazil, Argentina, Chile, Colombia, Panama, Mexico, Cuba, Shirley Woodell Papers, JWTCA, HCAMR.

42. Sidney Olson to Robert Maitland, May 15, 1957; Sidney Olson to Robert Maitland, May 23, 1957; Sidney Olson to Robert Maitland, May 23, 1957; Sidney Olson to Robert Maitland, May 28, 1957; Sidney Olson to Robert Maitland, June 1, 1957; Sidney Olson to Robert Maitland, June 3, 1957, box 2, Sidney A. Olson Papers, JWTCA, HCAMR.

43. "A Company History" (Cincinnati, OH: Procter & Gamble, 2004), 9–10.

44. "Waging Peace in the Americas: Address by Secretary Acheson; September 19, 1949," *A Decade of Foreign Policy; Basic Documents, 1941–1949* (Washington, D.C.: Government Printing Office, 1950); http://avalon.law.yale.edu/20th_century/decad063.asp, accessed June 4, 2011.

45. *A Schedule of the Records of the Bancroft, Simpson, and Eddystone Textile Firms* (Delaware: Eleutherian Mills Historical Society, 1964), 1, The Hagley Museum and Library; "Patents in Brazil," April 22, 1957, Accession 1359, Box 166, Patents-South America, August 1951–August 1963, Bancroft Textile Collection, The Hagley Museum and Library.

46. For a history of the Miss America pageant see Armando Riverol, *Live From Atlantic City: The History of the Miss America Pageant Before, After and In Spite of Television* (Bowling Green, OH: Bowling Green State University, Popular Press, 1992), 9, 12, 1835, 41–42, 93; Official Year Book Of The Miss America Pageant, Atlantic City 1949, Accession 72.430, box 10, Pictorial Collection Department, HM&L.

47. Bancroft Textile to Mr. George B. Adams, John Gilbert Craig Advertising, November 21, 1950, Licensing and Licensees, Everfast Fabrics, Inc., Accession 1359, box 115, Bancroft Collection; Everfast Advertisement, Licensing and Licensees, Everfast Fabrics, Inc., Accession 1359, box 115, BTC, HM&L.

48. "Miss America, Everglaze Wardrobe by McCall's patterns in Fabrics by Everfast," 1955–1962, Accession 72.430, box 8, Pictorial Collection Department, HM&L.

49. Eric Kluger to E. J. Evans Baker, October 19, 1954, Foreign Offices and Agents, Bancroft-Brillotex International, Accession 1359, box 182, Bancroft Textile

Collection; Press Conference Release, November 14, 1956, Accession 1359, box 170, BTC, Pictorial Collection Department, HM&L.

50. Mrs. Lola Martin is the only woman's name, other than Miss America and references made by executives to their wives, that appears in the Bancroft correspondence. Mrs. Martin worked for the marketing division. She primarily worked on the Miss America campaign. She did not work for Bancroft-Brillotex. "Everfast Fabrics, Inc.," January 1960–1963, Accession 1359, box 115, BTC, HM&L.

51. "Everglaze" Bulletin, No. 1, 1954, Accession 1359, box 170, Pictorial Collection Department, BTC, HM&L.

52. Jack Barry to Mr. Mac, January 6, 1955, Bancroft-Brillotex International, September 1953–June 1961; Jack Berry to W.R. MacIntyre, August 11, 1955, Bancroft-Brillotex International, June 1952–February, 1962, Accession 1359, box 165, Bancroft Textile Collection; Eric Kluger to W.R. MacIntyre, May 12, 1955, "Everglaze" 1955, Accession 1359, box 177, BTC, HM&L.

53. Eric Kluger to W.R. MacIntyre, November 15, 1954, Bancroft-Brillotex International, June 1952–February 1962, Accession 1359, box 165, BTC, HM&L.

54. W.R. MacIntyre to Eric Kluger; Harvey Bounds to Andrew Klein, April 20, 1953, Foreign Offices and Agents, Bancroft-Brillotex, Middle & Near East, May 1952–April 1958; Eric Kruger to W.R. MacIntyre, February 16, 1955, Foreign Offices and Agents, Greece 1954–1955, Accession 1359, box 182; Eric Kruger to W.R. MacIntyre, March 21, 1957, Foreign Offices and Agents, Bancroft-Brillotex, Middle & Near East, May 1952–April 1958, Accession 1359, box 171, BTC, HM&L.

55. Eric Kluger to W.R. MacIntyre, August 5, 1954, Foreign Offices and Agents, Bancroft-Brillotex, Middle & Near East, May 1952–April 1958, Accession 1359, box 182; Eric Kluger to El Lewa George Naldrett-Jays Pacha, October 19, 1954, "Everglaze," Bancroft-Brillotex, April 1952–March 1960, Accession 1359, Box 182, BTC, HM&L.

56. W.R. MacIntyre to Mr. Max Held, June 11, 1953, "Everglaze," Bancroft-Brillotex International, April 1952–March 1960, Accession 1359, box 182, BTC, HM&L.

57. International Chamber of Commerce, "Promotion of Advertising Councils," June 16, 1954, Box 10, Files of James M. Lambie Jr., Staff Files, Eisenhower Library," Advertising Council General, 1954; "Annual Report The Advertising Council, 1953–1954," 8, Advertising Council Annual Reports, ACA.

58. "Ike Uses Ad Council Meeting to Promote Foreign Trade Plan," *Advertising Age*, March 28, 1955, 3, 28, Advertising Age Clippings 1945–1959, Ad Council 50th Anniversary Files, 1943–1993, ACA.

59. Joint ANA—AAAA Committee, "If We, as a People," February 9, 1955, box 21, Files of James M. Lambie Jr., Staff Files, EL.

60. "Sign Up Today with Freedom Crusade," nd; "This is Your Crusade," nd; Howard S. Weaver, October 17, 1955, box 19, Crusade for Freedom 1955, Files of James M. Lambie Jr., Staff Files, EL.

61. "The Crusader, News of the Crusade for Freedom," January 1955, 2:5, box 19, Crusade for Freedom 1955, Files of James M. Lambie Jr., Staff Files, EL.

62. Allan Brown, "An Urgent Message to America's Newspapers," The Advertising Council, Inc., 1957, Historical File 1941–1997, ACA; "1959 Crusade for Freedom, Radio Free Europe," Radio Fact Sheet, The Advertising Council, Inc., 1959, Historical File 1941–1997, ACA.

63. Lt. General Willis D. Crittenberger to the Honorable Adolf A. Berle Jr. and others, April 21, 1958, 2, box 54, CD Jackson Papers 1931–67, EL.

64. Osgood, *Total Cold War*, 271; James M. Lambie to President Eisenhower, August 3, 1955, nd., box 17, Ad Council Repplier Eisenhower Fellow 1955, Files of James M. Lambie Jr., Staff Files, EL; "Ad Council Names Committee to Help Build Trade Fairs," Advertising *Age*, March 12, 1955, 88, Advertising Age Clippings 1945–1959, Ad Council 50th Anniversary Files 1943–1993; Alberto Galindo, "A South American Journalist-Economist Looks at the United States People's Capitalism, The Process of Realization," distributed by The Advertising Council, Historical File, 1947–1997, ACA.

65. Paul Hoffman, "The Advertising Council Public Policy Committee Luncheon," December 1, 1955, Historical File, 1941–1997, ACA; Howard Pyle, March 19, 1955, box 622, Ad Council 1955, Official File 122–A–1, DDE Records as President, WHCF, EL.

66. Confidential report; Theodore S. Repplier, "Some Thoughts About American Propaganda," June 17, 1955, box 17, Ad Council Repplier Eisenhower Fellow 1955, Files of James M. Lambie Jr., Staff Files, EL; Theodore S. Repplier, "Persuasion Under the Cherry Blossoms," *Saturday Review*, October 1, 1955, 13, 44–46, Ad Council 50th Anniversary Files, 1943–1993, ACA; Theodore Repplier, "Transcript of Report on US Propaganda Overseas, Historical File, 1941–1997," Advertising Council Archives, June 30, 1955, 8–11, 17; Also found in the Eisenhower library, Theodore S. Repplier, "Transcript of Report on United States Propaganda Overseas," June 30, 1955, box 17, Ad Council Repplier Eisenhower Fellow 1955, Files of James M. Lambie Jr., Staff Files, EL; Congressional Record Appendix A5991, 1955; "Public Service Advertising Council, 1954–55," 7; "Annual Report Advertising Council 1955–56," 4, 9; "What Helps People ... Helps Business, 15th Annual Report of The Advertising Council," 4, ACA; Theodore S. Repplier, June 30, 1955, box 17, Ad Council Repplier Eisenhower Fellow 1955; Edited Transcript of "Report on U.S. Propaganda Overseas," Files of James M. Lambie Jr., Staff Files, EL.

67. Theodore S. Repplier, Confidential Memorandum, nd, box 23, People's Capitalism 1955; Theodore S. Repplier, "Some Thoughts About American Propaganda," June 17, 1955, box 17, Ad Council Repplier Eisenhower Fellow 1955, Files of James M. Lambie Jr., Staff Files, EL; For discussions of People's Capitalism, see also Belmonte, Cull, Osgood.

68. Theodore Repplier, "Transcript of Report on US Propaganda Overseas," June 30, 1955, 17, Historical File, 1941–1997, ACA; "Report of Public Policy Committee Meeting," December 1, 1955, 7–8, box 1, Reports for Public Policy Committee Meeting, 1954–1955, Public Policy Committee Meeting Reports and Minutes, 1954–1986, ACA; Memorandum of the Conversation Between the President and T.S. Repplier, August 3, 1955, box 23, People's Capitalism 1955, Files of James M. Lambie Jr., Staff Files, EL.

69. "Report of Public Policy Committee Meeting," December 1, 1955, 7–8, box 1, Reports for Public Policy Committee Meeting, 1954–1955, Public Policy Committee Meeting Reports and Minutes, 1954–1986, ACA; Theodore S. Repplier, June 30, 1955, 17; Theodore S. Repplier, "Some Thoughts About American Propaganda," June 17, 1955, box 17, Ad Council Repplier Eisenhower Fellow 1955, Files of James M. Lambie Jr., Staff Files, EL.

70. Theodore S. Repplier, "The Whisper that Should Be a Shout," November 2, 1955, 1, 4, 7, 8–9, 10, 13–14, box 19, Association of National Advertising ANA 1955, Files of James M. Lambie Jr., Staff Files, EL; "The Advertising Council, Sixteenth Annual Report, 1957–58," 2, Advertising Council Annual Reports, ACA.

71. "People's Capitalism" Exhibit Hailed as Ad Council's Top Overseas Effort," *Advertising Age*, February 20, 1956, Advertising Age Clippings 1945–1959, Ad Council 50th Anniversary Files, 1943–1993, ACA.

72. "Ad Council, Yale Sponsor "People's Capitalism' Study," *Advertising Age*, June 10, 1957, 20, Advertising Age Clippings 1945–1959, Ad Council 50th Anniversary Files, 1943–1993; "Report of Public Policy Meeting, November 28, 1956, box 1, Reports for Public Policy Committee Meeting, 1956–1957, Public Policy Committee Meeting Reports and Minutes, 1954–1986; David M. Potter, "The American Round Table, People's Capitalism Part 1," November 16–17, 1956 (The Advertising Council, 1957); Potter, "The American Round Table, People's Capitalism Part II," May 22, 1957 (The Advertising Council, 1957), Historical File, 1947–1997, ACA.

73. Dwight D. Eisenhower to Mr. Repplier, January 3, 1957, box 622, Ad Council 1957, Official File 122–A–1, DDE Records as President, WHCF, EL.

74. "Ike Praises As Council, "People's Capitalism Exhibit," *Advertising Age*, April 8, 1956, 1, 124, Advertising Age Clippings 1945–1959, Ad Council 50th Anniversary Files, 1943–1993, ACA.

75. Dwight D. Eisenhower to Mr. Repplier, January 3, 1957, box 622, Ad Council, 1957; Official File 122–A–1, DDE Records as President, WHCF, EL; "What Helps People . . . Helps Business, 15th Annual Report of The Advertising Council," 2, ACA; Osgood, *Total Cold War*, 216, 232–244, 252, 304, 313, 320, 366; The People to People International organization can be found at http://www.ptpi.org/about_us/.

76. Charles Wilson, http://www.defenselink.mil/specials/secdef_histories/bios/wilson.htm; accessed June 4, 2011.

77. Osgood, *Total Cold War*, 341; Alfred Lief, *"It Floats" The Story of Procter & Gamble* (New York: Rinehart & Company, Inc., 1958), 323–325; Neil McElroy, The Eisenhower Administration Project, New York Times Oral History Program, Columbia University Oral History Collection (Glen Rock, NJ: Microfilming Corporation of America, 1976), 32–33; For more on McElroy see also David Rothkopf, *Superclass: The Global Power Elite and the World they are Making* (New York: Farrar, Straus and Giroux, 2008), 190–191.

78. "The Advertising Council Public Service Award," 1960, 6, box 5, Speeches, Statements, Press Conferences, Neil McElroy Papers, 1948–62, Staff Files, EL;

"Nomination of Neil H. McElroy," Hearing before the Committee On Armed Services United States Senate, Eighty-Fifth Congress, First Session, August 15, 1957 (Washington, D.C.: Government Printing Office, 1957); Neil McElroy, http://www.defenselink.mil/specials/secdef_histories/bios/mcelroy.htm; accessed June 4, 2011.

79. "The Advertising Council Public Service Award," 1960, 6, box 5, Speeches, Statements, Press Conferences; Neil McElroy to Nikita Sergeevich Khrushchev, September 18, 1959, 2, box 1, Personal Letters; Prescott Bush to Neil McElroy, March 3, 1959, box 1, Congressional Letters 1958–59; Dinner in honor of Secretary of Defense and Mrs. McElroy, January 19, 1959, box 4, Guest List for Parties; "The Advertising Council Public Service Award," 1960, 6; Neil McElroy, "Staffing Out Government for World Leadership," Speech at Annual Award Dinner of Advertising Council, November 22, 1960, 7; Neil McElroy, "Some aspects of United State-Canadian Relations," February 13, 1961, 7, box 5, Speeches, Statements, Press Conference; Neil McElroy, "Education Our Ultimate Weapon," July 14, 1960, 7, box 5, Speeches, Statements, Press Conferences, Neil McElroy Papers, 1948–62, Staff Files, EL.

80. President Eisenhower, April 13, 1959, box 623, Ad Council, 1959–1960, Official File 122–A–1, DDE Records as President, WHCF, EL.

Conclusion

1. http://www.jwt.com/now/pdf/about/FAST_FACTS_p1_081016.pdf; accessed April 1, 2008; http://www.wpp.com/wpp/companies/company-list.htm#; accessed April 1, 2008; accessed June 4, 2011.

2. "Our Mission," Brandweek, http://www.brandweek.com/bw/contactus/aboutus. jsp, accessed April 1, 2008.

3. "Top 10 Advertisers—by U.S. Spending on Traditional Media," 2007, http:// www.nielsen.com/media/toptens_yearend_v2007.html, accessed January 10, 2008 and March 28, 2008. "Nielsen: Ad Spend Up 0.6% in 2007," Brandweek, March 31, 2008. http://www.brandweek.com/bw/news/recent_display.jsp?vnu_ content_id=1003783003, accessed April 1, 2008; "US Advertising Spending Down 0.1% in First Three Quarters, Online Up 16%," http://www.marketing charts.com/television/us-advertising-spending-down-01-in-first-three-quarters-online-up-16-2844/, accessed March 28, 2008. Jack Neff, "P&G Hikes Ad Spending by $1 Billion to Grow Share, Sales," Advertising Age, August 3, 2010.

4. For a complete list of the Ad Council Board of Directors, see http://www. adcouncil.org/default.aspx?id=78; accessed September 5, 2008.

5. Michael Z. Wise, "U.S. Writers Do Cultural Battle around the Globe," New York Times, December 7, 2002; William A. Rugh, American Encounters with Arabs: The 'Soft Power' of U.S. Public Diplomacy in the Middle East (Westport, CT: Praeger Security International, 2006); Juliana G. Pilon, "Obsolete Restrictions on Public Diplomacy Hurt U.S. Outreach and Strategy," Heritage Foundation, December 3, 2007.

6. Wise, "U.S. Writers Do Cultural Battle around the Globe," *New York Times*, December 7, 2002; Rugh, *American Encounters with Arabs*, 27; Pilon, "Obsolete Restrictions on Public Diplomacy Hurt U.S. Outreach and Strategy," *Heritage Foundation*, December 3, 2007, http://www.heritage.org/research/NationalSecurity/bg2089.cfm; accessed June 4, 2011.

7. Alvin A. Snyder, *Warriors of Disinformation: How Charles Wick, the USIA, and Videotape Won the Cold War* (New York: Arcade Publishing, 1995); see also University of Southern Center on Public Diplomacy, http://uscpublicdiplomacy.org; accessed June4, 2011; the Heritage Foundation, http://www.heritage.org/research/NationalSecurity/em1029.cfm; accessed June 4, 2011.

8. http://www.supportamericaunited.com/; http://www.americasupportsyou.org/AmericaSupportsYou/about.html; http://www.americasupportsyou.org/americasupportsyou/press_releases/adcouncil_press.html; http://www.defenselink.mil/news/newsarticle.aspx?id=15033; all accessed September 7, 2008.

9. Karl Rove, *Courage and Consequences* (New York: Threshold Editions, 2010), 48–49; White House Office of Global Communications, http://www.whitehouse.gov/news/releases/2003/01/20030121-3.html, accessed April 3, 2008.

10. Department of Defense, "Information Operations Roadmap," October 30, 2003, Secret. National Security Archives, George Washington University; "Statement of Kenneth Y. Tomlinson Chairman, Broadcasting Board of Governors, August 23, 2004," Capitol Hill Hearing Testimony, 9/11 Commission Report: Public Diplomacy, Committee on House Government Reform Subcommittee on National Security, Emerging Threats, and International Relations.

11. For the official government website on USAID, see http://www.usaid.gov/branding/, accessed May 4, 2008.

12. Stuart Elliott, "Campaign for Tsunami Aid Assembled in What May Be Record Time," *New York Times*, January 7, 2005.

13. http://www.usaid.gov/branding/, accessed May 4, 2008.

14. Fact Sheet, Office of the Spokesman, U.S. Department of State, January 18, 2006, http://www.state.gov/r/pa/prs/ps/2006/59339.htm, accessed May 5, 2008.

15. Department of State and Other International Programs, the Budget for Fiscal Year 2009, 91–92, 95.

16. Patricia Harrison, Corporation for Public Broadcasting president and chief executive officer, "Sesame Street Diplomacy," http://www.cpb.org/features/sesamestreetdiplomacy/index.html, accessed May 1, 2008.

17. "Public Diplomacy Open Forum Muppet Diplomacy with Gary Knell," March 25, 2004, http://uscpublicdiplomacy.com/index.php/events/events_detail/217/, accessed April 1, 2008.

18. Sian Powell, "Open Sesame on Condi's Puppet Diplomacy," *Australian*, March 15, 2006, http://www.seasite.niu.edu/flin/rice-elmo-15mar06.htm; accessed June 4, 2011; "Secretary Rice Announces U.S. Funded 'Indonesian Sesame Street' Program," March 14, 2006, http://www.state.gov/r/pa/ei/pix/2006/63130.htm; http://future.state.gov/what/special/63144.htm; accessed June 4, 2011.

19. Keith Dinnie, *Nation Branding: Concepts, Issues, Practice* (Oxford: Butterworth-Heinemann, 2008), 13–15; see also http://USCPublicDiplomacy.org; accessed June 4, 2011.

20. Naomi Klein, "Brand USA: America's Attempt to Market Itself Abroad Using Advertising Principles Is Destined to Fail," *Los Angeles Times*, March 10, 2002; see also http://www.commondreams.org/views02/0310-06.htm; accessed June 4, 2011.

21. Dick Martin, *Rebuilding Brand American: What We Must Do to Restore Our Reputation and Safeguard the Future of American Business Abroad* (New York: American Management Association, 2007), 86–87.

22. Ibid., 169, 241–242.

23. Jesse Kornbluth, "A Religious Experience, Marketing to Muslims in America and Britain: JWT Accepts the Challenge," JWT NOW SUMMER 2007, 49, http://www.jwt.com/now/pdf/JWT_NOW_A_Religous_Experience.pdf; accessed November 11, 2008.

24. Regarding Norman Pattiz see http://people.forbes.com/profile/norman-j-pattiz/86314; June 4, 2011.

25. David Barstow and Robin Stein, "Under Bush, a New Age of Prepackaged TV News," *New York Times*, March 13, 2005.

26. David Barstow, "Behind TV Analysts, Pentagon's Hidden Hand," *New York Times*, April 20, 2008.

27. "About the BBG," http://www.bbg.gov/bbg_aboutus.cfm, accessed May 6, 2008.

28. United States Advisory Commission on Public Diplomacy. *Consolidation of USIA into the State Department: An Assessment after One Year* (Washington, D.C.: U.S. Advisory Commission on Public Diplomacy, 2000); see also "Strategic Plan," for the Broadcasting Board of Governors, http://www.bbg.gov/about/plan/; accessed June 7, 2011.

29. Department of State and Other International Programs, the Budget for Fiscal Year 2009, 91–92, 95.

30. Department of Commerce, the Budget for Fiscal Year 2009, 44: "Commerce Department Issues Final Rule to Launch Digital-to-Analog Converter Box Coupon Program, Full-Power TV Stations to Cease Analog Broadcasts after February 17, 2009, All U.S. Households Eligible to Apply For Up to Two, $40 Coupons toward the Purchase of Digital-to-Analog Converter Boxes Starting January 2008," Media Release, NTIA, National Telecommunications and Information Administration, March 12, 2007, http://www.ntia.doc.gov/ntiahome/press/2007/DTVfinalrule_031207.htm, https://www.dtv2009.gov/, accessed September 10, 2007, May 5, 2008.

31. Regarding the Left Behind Video and the *Left Behind* series, see http://www.leftbehindgames.com/free/index.html; http://www.eternalforces.com/, accessed April 2, 2008; http://www.eternalforces.com/features.aspx, accessed April 2, 2008; Tim LaHaye and Jerry B. Jenkins, *Left Behind, Left Behind Series* (Carol Stream, IL: Tyndale House Publishers, 1995).

Bibliography

Manuscript Sources

Advertising Council Archives, University of Illinois Archives, Urbana, Illinois
Dwight D. Eisenhower Presidential Library and Museum, Abilene, Kansas
    Citizens for Eisenhower, Young & Rubicam Files
    Dwight D. Eisenhower, Records as President [White House Central Files]
    Charles D. Jackson Papers
    James M. Lambie Jr. Papers
    Neil McElroy Papers
Hagley Museum and Library, Wilmington, Delaware
    Bancroft Textile Collection
J. Walter Thompson Company Archives,
Hartman Center for Sales, Advertising, and Market Research,
Rare Book, Manuscript, and Special Collections Library,
Duke University, Durham, North Carolina
    John Devine Papers
    Howard Henderson Papers
    Kenneth Webb Hinks Papers
    Samuel W. Meek Papers
    Sidney Olsen Papers
    Norman Strouse Papers
    Granger Tripp Papers
    Shirley Woodell Papers
    James Webb Young Papers
Hoover Institution on War, Revolution and Peace,
Stanford University, Stanford, California
    Radio Free Europe/Radio Liberty
Department of Rare Books and Special Collections
Rush Rhees Library of the University of Rochester, Rochester, New York
    Kodak Historical Collection
New York Public Library, New York, New York
    A Collection of Pamphlets, Clippings, Postcards,
    Relating to the Freedom Train, 1947–1948

Open Society Archives, Central European University, Budapest, Hungary
    Records of Radio Free Europe/Radio Liberty Research Institute
Seeley G. Mudd Manuscript Library, Princeton University, Princeton, New Jersey
    John Foster Dulles Collection
Harry S. Truman Library & Museum, Independence, Missouri
    Tom C. Clark Papers
    Dick Dickson Papers
    John T. Gibson Papers
    Dallas C. Halverstadt Papers
    Charles W. Jackson Papers
    Spencer R. Quick Papers
    Charles Sawyer Papers
    Harry S. Truman Papers

Newspapers

Amarillo Daily News
Anniston Star
Blue Island Sun-Standard
Burlington (N.C.) Daily Times-News
Chillicothe Constitutional-Tribunal
Daily Oklahoman
Deming Headligt
El Paso Herald-Post
Greenfield-Recorder Gazette
Jefferson City Post-Tribune
Lima News
Los Angeles Times
Maryville Daily Forum
Moberly Monitor-Index and Democrat
New York Times
The North Adams
Oxnard Press-Courier
Post-Register, Idaho Falls
Salt Lake City Tribune
Washington Post

Periodicals

Advertising Age
Life
Newsweek
Tide
Time

Oral Histories

Prescott Bush, Columbia Oral History Project
Neil McElroy, Columbia Oral History Project

Electronic Resources

Ad Council
  http://www.adcouncil.org/
America Supports You
  http://www.americasupportsyou.org
Broadcasting Board of Governors
  http://www.bbg.gov/
Emergence of Advertising in America: 1850–1920, Duke University, Rare Book,
  Manuscript, and Special Collections Library. Edited by Manuscript and Special
  Collections Library Duke University http://library.duke.edu/digitalcollections/eaa/
The Freedom Train
  http://www.freedomtrain.org/
  http://www.lincoln-highway-museum.org/FT/FT-Index.html
The Heritage Foundation
  http://www.heritage.org/research/NationalSecurity/bg2089.cfm
The J. Walter Thompson Company
  http://www.jwt.com/
Left Behind: Eternal Forces
  http://www.eternalforces.com/features.aspx
United States Information Agency USIA
  http://dosfan.lib.uic.edu/usia/
USAID
  http://www.usaid.gov/
The White House
  http://www.whitehouse.gov/
WPP
  http://www.wpp.com/wpp/

Secondary Sources

Ailes, Roger. *You Are the Message: Secrets of the Master Communicators.* Homewood,
  IL: Dow Jones-Irwin, 1988.
Ambrose, Stephen E. *Eisenhower: Soldier and President.* New York: Simon and
  Schuster, 1991.
Ambrose, Stephen E. *Ike's Spies: Eisenhower and the Espionage Establishment.* Jackson:
  University Press of Mississippi, Banner Books, 1999.
Anholt, Simon, and Hildreth, Jeremy. *Brand America: The Mother of All Brands.*
  London: Cyan, 2004.

Augspurger, Michael. *An Economy of Abundant Beauty: Fortune Magazine and the Depression.* Ithaca, NY: Cornell University Press, 2004.

Axelrod, Alan. *Selling the Great War: The Making of American Propaganda.* New York: Palgrave Macmillan, 2009.

Baughman, James L. *Henry R. Luce and the Rise of the American News Media.* Boston, MA: Twayne Publishing, 1987.

———*Same Time, Same Station: Creating American Television, 1948–1961.* Baltimore, MD: John Hopkins University Press, 2007.

Bell, Jonathan. *The Liberal State on Trial: The Cold War and American Politics in the Truman Years.* New York: Columbia University Press, 2004.

Belmonte, Laura A. *Selling the American Way: U.S. Propaganda and the Cold War.* Philadelphia, PA: University of Pennsylvania Press, 2008.

Bernays, Edward. *Propaganda,* edited by Mark Crispin Miller. Brooklyn, NY: Ig Publishing, 2005.

Bernhard, Nancy E. *U.S. Television News and Cold War Propaganda, 1947–1960.* New York: Cambridge University Press, 1999.

Borstelmann, Thomas. *The Cold War and the Color Line: American Race Relations in the Global Arena.* Cambridge, MA: Harvard University Press, 2001.

Brewer, Susan A. *Why America Fights: Patriotism and War Propaganda from the Philippines to Iraq.* Oxford, New York: Oxford University Press, 2009.

Brinson, Susan L. *The Red Scare, Politics, and the Federal Communications Commission, 1941–1960.* Westport, CT: Praeger, 2004.

Bruns, Roger. *Billy Graham: A Biography.* Westport, CT: Greenwood Press, 2004.

Calder, Lendol Glen. *Financing the American Dream: A Cultural History of Consumer Credit.* Princeton, NJ: Princeton University Press, 2006.

Casey, Steven. *Selling the Korean War: Propaganda, Politics, and Public Opinion in the United States, 1950–1953.* New York: Oxford University Press, 2008.

Castillo, Greg. *Cold War on the Home Front: The Soft Power of Midcentury Design,* Minneapolis, MN: University of Minnesota Press, 2010.

Chambers, Jason. *Madison Avenue and the Color Line: African Americans in the Advertising Industry.* Philadelphia, PA: University of Pennsylvania Press, 2008.

Chandler Jr., Alfred DuPont. *The Visible Hand: The Managerial Revolution in American Business.* Cambridge: Belknap Press of Harvard University Press, 1977.

Chernus, Ira. *Eisenhower's Atoms for Peace.* College Station: Texas A&M University Press, 2002.

Classen, Steven D. *Watching Jim Crow: The Struggles over Mississippi TV, 1955–1969.* Durham, North Carolina: Duke University Press, 2004.

Cohen, Lizabeth *Making a New Deal: Industrial Workers in Chicago, 1919–1939.* Cambridge, UK: Cambridge University Press, 1991.

———*A Consumer's Republic: The Politics of Mass Consumption in Postwar America.* New York: Knopf, 2003.

Colacello, Bob. *Ronnie & Nancy, Their Path to the White House–1911 to 1980.* New York: Warner Books, 2004.

Collins, Douglas. *The Story of Kodak.* New York: H.N. Abrams, 1990.

Cox, Jim. *Sold on Radio: Advertising in the Golden Age of Broadcasting*. Jefferson, North Carolina: McFarland & Company Inc., 2008.

Craig, Douglas B. *Fireside Politics: Radio and Political Culture in the United States, 1920–1940*. Baltimore, MD: Johns Hopkins University Press, 2006.

Creel, George. *How We Advertised America*. New York: Harper & Brothers, 1920.

Cull, Nicholas John. *The Cold War and the United States information Agency: American Propaganda and Public Diplomacy, 1945–1989*. New York: Cambridge University Press, 2008.

Cummings, Richard. *Cold War Radio: The Dangerous History of American Broadcasting in Europe, 1950–1989*. Jefferson, NC: McFarland & Company, 2009.

———*Radio Free Europe's "Crusade for Freedom": Rallying Americans behind Cold War Broadcasting, 1950–1960*. Jefferson, NC: McFarland & Company, 2010.

Delmendo, Sharon. *The Star-Entangled Banner: One Hundred Years of America in the Philippines*. New Brunswick, NJ: Rutgers University Press, 2004.

Dinnie, Keith. *Nation Branding: Concepts, Issues, Practice*. London: Butterworth-Heinemann, 2008.

Dizard, Wilson. *Inventing Public Diplomacy: The Story of the U.S. Information Agency*. Boulder, CO: Lynne Rienner Publishers, 2004.

Doherty, Thomas Patrick. *Cold War, Cool Medium: Television, McCarthyism, and American Culture*. New York: Columbia University Press, 2003.

Donohue, Kathleen G. *Freedom from Want: American Liberalism and the Idea of the Consumer*. Baltimore, MD: Johns Hopkins University Press, 2003.

Dudziak, Mary L. *Cold War Civil Rights: Race and the Image of American Democracy*. Princeton, NJ: Princeton University Press, 1998.

Dyer, Davis, Dalzell, Frederick, and Olegarion, Rowena. *Rising Tide, Lessons for 165 Years of Brand Building at Procter & Gamble*. Boston, MA: Harvard Business School Press, 2004.

Edgerton, Gary R. *The Columbia History of American Television*. New York: Columbia University Press, 2007.

Eisenhower, Dwight D. *The Papers of Dwight David Eisenhower*, edited by Jr. Alfred D. Chandler, editor. Stephen E. Ambrose, associate editor [and others]. Baltimore, MD: Johns Hopkins University Press, 1984.

Ellis, Richard J. *To the Flag: The Unlikely History of the Pledge of Allegiance*. Lawrence: University of Kansas Press, 2005.

Endy, Christopher. *Cold War Holidays: American Tourism in France*. Chapel Hill: University of North Carolina Press, 2004.

Ewen, Stuart. *Pr! A Social History of Spin*. New York: BasicBooks, 1996.

Fones-Wolf, Elizabeth A. *Selling Free Enterprise: The Business Assault on Labor and Liberalism, 1945–60*. Urbana: University of Illinois Press, 1994.

Fox, Frank W. *Madison Avenue Goes to War: The Strange Military Career of American Advertising, 1941–45*. Utah: Brigham Young University Press, 1975.

Fox, Richard Wightman and Lears, T. J. Jackson. *The Power of Culture: Critical Essays in American History*. New York: Pantheon Books, 1983.

Fox, Stephen R. *The Mirror Maker: A History of American Advertising and Its Creators.* New York: Morrow, 1984.

Fried, Richard. *The Russians Are Coming! The Russians Are Coming! Pageantry and Patriotism in Cold War America.* New York: Oxford University Press, 1998.

Friedman, Walter A. "Buyways: Billboards, Automobiles, and the American Landscape." *American Historical Review* 111, no. 2 (2006): 527–528.

Gaddis, John Lewis *We Now Know: Rethinking Cold War History.* Oxford: Oxford University Press, 1997.

————*Surprise, Security, and the American Experience.* Cambridge: Harvard University Press, 2004.

————*The Cold War, A New History.* New York: Penguin Press, 2005.

Garvey, Ellen Gruber. *The Adman in the Parlor: Magazines and the Gendering of Consumer Culture, 1880s to 1910s.* New York: Oxford University Press, 1999.

Glickman, Lawrence B. *Consumer Society in American History: A Reader.* Ithaca, NY: Cornell University Press, 1999.

Graham, Allison. *Framing the South: Hollywood, Television and Race during the Civil Rights Struggle,* Baltimore, MD: John Hopkins University Press, 2001.

Grazia, Victoria de. *Irresistible Empire: America's Advance through Twentieth-Century Europe.* Cambridge, MA: The Belknap Press of Harvard University Press, 2005.

Griffith, Robert. "The Selling of America: The Advertising Council and American Politics, 1942–1960." *Business History Review* 57, no. 3 (1983): 388–412.

Gudis, Catherine. *Buyways: Billboards, Automobiles, and the American Landscape.* New York: Routledge, 2004.

Hawes, William. *Live Television Drama, 1946–1951.* London: McFarland & Company, Inc., 2001.

————*Filmed Television Drama, 1952–1958.* London: McFarland, 2002.

Herzstein, Robert E. *Henry R. Luce.* New York: Charles Scribner's Sons, 1994.

————*Henry R. Luce, Time, and the American Crusade in Asia.* Cambridge, UK: Cambridge University Press, 2005.

Hixson, Walter L. *Parting the Curtain: Propaganda, Culture, and the Cold War, 1945–1961.* New York: Palgrave Macmillan, 1997.

Inboden, William. *Religion and American Foreign Policy, 1945–1960, the Soul of Containment.* Cambridge, New York: Cambridge University Press, 2008.

Jackall, Robert and Hirota, Janice M. *Image Makers: Advertising, Public Relations, and the Ethos of Advocacy.* Chicago: University of Chicago Press, 2003.

Jackson, Kenneth T. *Crabgrass Frontier: The Suburbanization of the United States.* New York: Oxford University Press, 1987.

Jacobs, Meg. *Pocketbook Politics: Economic Citizenship in Twentieth-Century American.* Princeton, NJ: Princeton University Press, 2005.

Jacobson, Lisa. *Raising Consumers: Children and the American Mass Market in the Early Twentieth Century.* New York: Columbia University Press, 2004.

Jeffreys-Jones, Rhodri. *The CIA and American Democracy.* New Haven: Yale University Press, 1998.

Johnson, A. Ross, *Radio Free Europe and Radio Liberty: The CIA years and Beyond.* Washington, D.C., Stanford, CA: Woodrow Wilson Center Press, Stanford University Press, 2010.

Johnson, A. Ross and Parta, Eugene (eds). *Cold War Broadcasting: Impact on the Soviet Union and Eastern Europe.* Budaspest-New York: Central European University Press, 2010.

Kackman, Michael. *Citizen Spy: Television, Espionage, and Cold War Culture.* Minneapolis, MN: University of Minnesota Press, 2005.

Kammen, Michael. *Mystic Chords of Memory: The Transformation of Tradition in American Culture.* New York: Alfred Knopf, 1991.

Kaplan, Amy and Pease, Donald E. (eds). *Cultures of United States Imperialism.* Durham: Duke University Press, 1993.

Kelly, John. "Integrating America: Jackie Robinson, Critical Events and Baseball Black and White." *International Journal of the History of Sport* 22, no. 6 (November 2005): 1011–1035.

Kennedy, David M. *Freedom from Fear: The American People in Depression and War, 1929–1945.* New York: Oxford University Press, 2001.

Kline, Ronald R. *Consumers in the Country: Technology and Social Change in Rural America.* Baltimore, MD: John Hopkins University Press, 2000.

Kunz, Diane B. *Butter and Guns: America's Cold War Economic Diplomacy.* New York: Free Press, 2005.

LaHaye, Tim and Jenkins, Jerry B. *Left Behind.* Wheaton, IL: Tyndale House, 1995.

Laird, Pamela Walker. *Advertising Progress: American Business and the Rise of Consumer Marketing.* Baltimore, MD: Johns Hopkins University Press, 1998.

Langley, Lester D. *The Banana War: United States Intervention in the Caribbean, 1898–1934.* Wilmington, Delaware: SR Books, 2002.

Langley, Lester D. and Schoonover, Thomas. *The Banana Men: American Mercenaries and Entrepreneurs in Central America, 1880–1930.* Lexington, KY: The University Press of Kentucky, 1995.

Lears, T. J. Jackson. *Fables of Abundance: A Cultural History of Advertising in America.* New York: Basic Books, 1994.

Lichtenstein, Nelson. *State of the Union: A Century of American Labor.* Princeton, NJ: Princeton University Press, 2003.

Lief, Alfred. *"It Floats" The Story of Procter & Gamble.* New York: Rinehart & Company, Inc., 1958.

Little, Stuart Jon. "The Freedom Train and the Formation of National Political Culture." University of Kansas, 1989.

———"The Freedom Train: Citizenship and Postwar Political Culture 1946–1949." *American Studies* 34, no. 1 (Spring 1993): 35–67.

Long, Michael G. *Billy Graham and the Beloved Community.* New York: Palgrave Macmillan, 2006.

Lowenfish, Lee. *Branch Rickey: Baseball's Ferocious Gentleman.* Lincoln: University of Nebraska Press, 2007.

Lykins, Daniel L. *From Total War to Total Diplomacy: The Advertising Council and the Construction of the Cold War Consensus.* Westport, CT: Praeger, 2003.

MacGregor, M.C. "Television's Impact on the 1952 Presidential Election and Influence on the Political Process." Ohio University, 1986.

Mann, Arthur. *The Jackie Robinson Story.* New York: Grosset & Dunlap, 1951.

Manring, M. M. *Slave in a Box: The Strange Career of Aunt Jemima.* Charlottesville, VA: University Press of Virginia, 1998.

Marchand, Roland. *Advertising the American Dream: Making Way for Modernity, 1920–1940.* Berkeley, CA: University of California Press, 1985.

———*Creating the Corporate Soul: The Rise of Public Relations and Corporate Imagery in American Big Business.* Berkeley, CA: University of California Press, 1998.

Martin, Dick. *Rebuilding Brand America: What We Must Do to Restore Our Reputation and Safeguard the Future of American Business Abroad.* New York: American Management Association, 2007.

May, Elaine Tyler. *Homeward Bound: American Families in the Cold War Era.* New York: Basic Books, 1999.

May, Lary. *The Big Tomorrow: Hollywood and the Politics of the American Way.* Chicago: University of Chicago Press, 2000.

McChesney, Robert W. *Telecommunications, Mass Media and Democracy: The Battle for the Control of U.S. Broadcasting, 1928–1935.* New York: Oxford University Press, 1994.

McCormick, Thomas J. *America's Half-Century: United States Foreign Policy in the Cold War.* Baltimore, MD: Johns Hopkins University Press, 1986.

———*China Market: America's Quest for Informal Empire, 1893–1901.* Chicago: I.R. Dee, 1993.

McGinnis, John Vianney. "The Advertising Council and the Cold War." Syracuse University, 1991.

McGirr, Lisa. *Suburban Warriors: The Origins of the New American Right.* Princeton, NJ: Princeton University Press, 2001.

McGovern, Charles F. *Sold American: Consumption and Citizenship, 1890–1945.* Chapell Hill: The University of North Carolina Press, 2006.

McKenzie, Brian Angus. *Remaking France: Americanization, Public Diplomacy, and the Marshall Plan.* New York: Berghahn Books, 2005.

Mickelson, Sig. *America's Other Voice: The Story of Radio Free Europe and Radio Liberty.* New York: Praeger, 1983.

Miller, Patrick B. and Wiggins, David Kenneth. *Sport and the Color Line: Black Athletes and Race Relations in Twentieth-Century America.* New York: Routledge, 2004.

Miller, Steven. *Billy Graham and the Rise of the Republican South.* Philadelphia, PA: University of Pennsylvania Press, 2009.

Monaghan, Frank. *Heritage of Freedom: The History & Significance of the Basic Documents of American Liberty.* Princeton, NJ: Princeton University Press; The American Heritage Foundation, 1947.

Moreno, Julio. *Yankee Don't Go Home! Mexican Nationalism, American Business Culture, and the Shaping of Modern Mexico, 1920–1950.* Chapel Hill: University of North Carolina Press, 2003.

Moreton, Bethany. *To Serve God and Wal-Mart: The Making of Christian Free Enterprise.* Cambridge, MA: Harvard University Press, 2009.

Mugridge, Ian. *The View from Xanadu: William Randolph Hearst and United States Foreign Policy.* Montreal: McGill-Queen's University Press, 1995.

Nichols, David A. *A Matter of Justice: Eisenhower and the Civil Rights Revolution.* New York: Simon & Schuster, 2008.

Olegario, Rowena, Dyer, Davis and Dalzell, Frederick. *Rising Tide: Lessons from 165 Years of Brand Building at Procter & Gamble.* Boston, MA: Harvard Business School Press, 2004.

Osgood, Kenneth. *Total Cold War: Eisenhower's Secret Propaganda Battle at Home and Abroad.* Lawrence: University of Kansas Press, 2006.

Oshinsky, David M. *A Conspiracy So Immense: The World of Joe McCarthy.* New York: Oxford University Press, 2005.

Parkin, Katherine J. *Food Is Love: Food Advertising and Gender Roles in Modern America.* Philadelphia, PA: University of Pennsylvania Press, 2007.

Pendergrast, Mark. *For God, Country, and Coca-Cola: The Unauthorized History of the Great American Soft Drink and the Company That Makes It.* New York: Maxwell Macmillan, 1993.

Perez Jr., Louis A. *The War of 1898: The United States and Cuba in History and Historiography.* Chapel Hill: The University of North Carolina, 1998.

Perlstein, Rick. *Nixonland: The Rise of a President and the Fracturing of America.* New York: Scribner, 2008.

Pisani, Sallie. *The CIA and the Marshall Plan.* Lawrence Kansas: University of Kansas, 1991.

Pollock, John. *The Billy Graham Story.* Grand Rapids, MI: Zondervan, 2003, 1985.

Puddington, Arch. *Broadcasting Freedom: The Cold War Triumph of Radio Free Europe and Radio Liberty.* Lexington: University Press of Kentucky, 2000.

Rawnsley, Gary D. *Radio Diplomacy and Propaganda: The BBC and VOA in International Politics, 1956–64.* New York: Macmillan, 1996.

Reynolds, David. *From World War to Cold War: Churchill, Roosevelt, and the International History of the 1940s.* New York: Oxford University Press, 2006.

Richmond, Yale. *Cultural Exchange & the Cold War: Raising the Iron Curtain.* University Park: Pennsylvania State University Press, 2003.

———*Practicing Public Diplomacy: A Cold War Odyssey, Explorations in Culture and International History.* New York: Berghahn Books, 2008.

Ritchie, Donald A. *Reporting from Washington: The History of the Washington Press Corps.* New York: Oxford University Press, 2005.

Riverol, Armando. *Live from Atlantic City: The History of the Miss America Pageant before, after and in Spite of Television.* Bowling Green, OH: Bowling Green State University, Popular Press, 1992.

Robin, Ron Theodore. *The Making of the Cold War Enemy: Culture and Politics in the Military-Intellectual Complex.* Princeton, NJ: Princeton University Press, 2001.

Rose, Lisle A. *The Cold War Comes to Main Street, America in 1950.* Lawrence: University Press of Kansas, 1999.

Rosenberg, Emily S. *Spreading the American Dream: American Economic & Cultural Expansion, 1890–1945.* New York: Hill and Wang, 1982.

———*Financial Missionaries to the World: The Politics and Culture of Dollar Diplomacy, 1900–1930.* Durham: Duke University Press, 2003.

Rosenberg, Jonathan. *How Far the Promised Land? World Affairs and the American Civil Rights Movement from the First World War to Vietnam.* Princeton, NJ: Princeton University Press, 2006.

Rothkopf, David J. *Superclass: The Global Power Elite and the World They are Making.* New York: Farrar, Straus and Giroux, 2008.

Rove, Karl. *Courage and Consequence.* New York: Threshold Editions, 2010.

Rudgers, David F. *Creating the Secret State: The Origins of the Central Intelligence Agency, 1943–1947.* Lawrence: University Press of Kansas, 2000.

Rugh, William A. *American Encounters with Arabs: The "Soft Power" Of U.S. Public Diplomacy in the Middle East.* Westport, CT: Praeger Security International, 2006.

Sammond, Nicholas. *Babes in Tomorrowland: Walt Disney and the Making of the American Child, 1930–1960.* Durham: Duke University Press, 2005.

Samuel, Lawrence R. *Brought to You By: Postwar Television Advertising and the American Dream.* Austin: University of Texas Press, 2001.

Sandage, C. H. *The Promise of Advertising.* Homewood, IL: R.D. Irwin, 1961.

Saunders, Frances Stonor. *The Cultural Cold War: The CIA and the World of Arts and Letters.* New York: The New Press, 1999.

Scanlon, Jennifer. *Inarticulate Longings: The Ladies' Home Journal, Gender, and the Promises of Consumer Culture.* New York: Routledge, 1995.

Schisgall, Oscar. *Eyes on Tomorrow: The Evolution of Procter & Gamble.* Chicago: J.G Ferguson Publishing Company, 1981.

Schmitz, David F. *Thank God They're on Our Side: The United States and Right-Wing Dictatorships, 1921–1965.* Chapel Hill: University of North Carolina Press, 1999.

Schwartz, Rosalie. *Flying Down to Rio: Hollywood, Tourists, and Yankee Clippers.* College Station: Texas A & M University Press, 2004.

Scott-Smith, Giles. *The Cultural Cold War in Western Europe, 1945–1960.* New York: Routledge, 2004.

Segrave, Kerry. *American Television Abroad, Hollywood's Attempt to Dominate World Television.* London: McFarland & Company, Inc., 1998.

Shank, Barry. *A Token of My Affection: Greeting Cards and American Business Culture.* New York: Columbia University Press, 2004.

Shulman, Holly Cowan. *VOA: Propaganda and Democracy, 1941–1945.* Madison: University of Wisconsin Press, 1991.

Sivulka, Juliann. *Stronger Than Dirt: A Cultural History of Advertising Personal Hygiene in America, 1875–1940.* Amherst, NY: Humanity Books, 2001.

Slotten, Hugh Richard. *Radio and Television Regulation: Broadcast Technology in the United States, 1920–1960.* Baltimore, MD: Johns Hopkins University Press, 2000.

Smith, Adam. *Wealth of Nations, Great Mind Series.* New York: Prometheus Books, 1991 (1776).

Smulyan, Susan. *Selling Radio: The Commercialization of American Broadcasting.* Washington, D. C.: The Smithsonian Institution Press, 1994.

Snow, Nancy, *Propaganda, Inc.: Selling America's Culture to the World*. Emeryville, CA: Seven Stories Press, Distributed to the trade by Publishers Group West, 2002.

Snyder, Alvin A. *Warriors of Disinformation: How Charles Wick, the USIA, and Videotape Won the Cold War*. New York: Arcade Publishing, 1995.

Sosin, Gene. *Sparks of Liberty: An Insider's Memoir of Radio Liberty*. University Park: Pennsylvania State University Press, 1999.

Spalding, Elizabeth Edwards. *The First Cold Warriors: Harry Truman, Containment, and the Remaking of Liberal Internationalism*. Lexington: University Press of Kentucky, 2006.

Spring, Joel H. *Educating the Consumer-Citizen: A History of the Marriage of Schools, Advertising, and Media*. Mahwah, NJ: Lawrence Erlbaum, 2003.

Steigerwald, David. "All Hail the Republic of Choice: Consumer History as Contemporary Thought." *Journal of American History* 93, no. 2 (2006): 385–403.

Stole, Inger L. *Advertising on Trial: Consumer Activism and Corporate Public Relations in the 1930s*. Urbana, IL: University of Illinois Press, 2006.

Strasser, Susan. *Satisfaction Guaranteed: The Making of the American Mass Market*. Washington, D.C.: Smithsonian Institution Press, 1995.

Sugrue, Thomas. *The Origins of Urban Crisis: Race and Inequality in Postwar Detroit*. Princeton, NJ: Princeton University Press, 1996.

Swasy, Alecia. *Soap Opera: The Inside Story of Procter & Gamble*. New York: Times Books, 1993.

Swint, Kerwin. *Dark Genius: The Influential Career of Legendary Political Operative and Fox News Founder Roger Ailes*. New York: Sterling Publishing, 2008.

Taubman, Philip. *Secret Empire: Eisenhower, the CIA, and the Hidden Story of America's Space Espionage*. New York: Simon & Schuster, 2003.

Tedlow, Richard S. *New and Improved: The Story of Mass Marketing in America*. Boston, MA: Harvard Business School Press, 1996.

Torres, Sasha. *Black, White, and in Color: Television and Black Civil Rights*. Princeton, NJ: Princeton University Press, 2003.

Tuch, Hans. *Communicating with the World: U.S. Public Diplomacy Overseas*. New York: St. Martin's Press, 1990.

Urban, G. R. *Radio Free Europe and the Pursuit of Democracy: My War within the Cold War*. New Haven: Yale University Press, 1997.

Vaughn, Stephen. *Ronald Reagan in Hollywood: Movies and Politics*. Cambridge: Cambridge University Press, 1994.

Vinikas, Vincent. *Soft Soap, Hard Sell: American Hygiene in an Age of Advertisement*. Ames, IA: Iowa State University Press, 1992.

VOA. *The Department of State, 1930–1955 [Expanding Functions and Responsibilities Prepared by the Historical Division of the Dept. Of State, with the Cooperation of Major Units of the Dept.]*. Washington: U.S. Govt. Print. Off., 1955.

Wagnleitner, Reinhold. *Coca-Colonization and the Cold War: The Cultural Mission of the United States in Austria after the Second World War*. Translated by Diana M. Wolf. Chapell Hill: University of North Carolina Press, 1994.

Wall, Wendy. *Inventing the "American Way": The Politics of Consensus from the New Deal to the Civil Rights Movement,* New York, Oxford: Oxford University Press, 2009.

Waltenburg, Eric N. *Choosing Where to Fight: Organized Labor and the Modern Regulatory State, 1947–1987.* Albany: State University of New York Press, 2002.

Watts, Steven. *The Magic Kingdom: Walt Disney and the American Way of Life.* Columbia, MO: University of Missouri Press, 2001.

———*The People's Tycoon Henry Ford and the American Century.* New York: Alfred A. Knopf, 2005.

West, Darrell M. *Air Wars: Television Advertising in Election Campaigns, 1952–2004.* 4th ed. Washington, D.C.: CQ Press, 2005.

Wharton, Annabel Jane. *Building the Cold War: Hilton International Hotels and Modern Architecture.* Chicago: University of Chicago, 2001.

White, John. "Civil Rights in Conflict: The 'Birmingham Plan' and the Freedom Train." *Alabama Review* 52, no. 2 (April 1999): 121–141.

Whitfield, Stephen J. *The Culture of the Cold War.* Baltimore, MD: Johns Hopkins University Press, 1991.

Williams, William Appleman. *The Tragedy of American Diplomacy.* 1st ed. New York: World Pub. Co., 1959.

Winkler, Allan M. *Life Under a Cloud: American Anxiety About the Atom.* New York: Oxford University Press, 1993.

Wirt, Sherwood Eliot. *Bill: A Personal Look at Billy Graham, the World's Best-Loved Evangelist.* Wheaton, IL: Crossway Books, 1997.

Yaqub, Salim. *Containing Arab Nationalism: The Eisenhower Doctrine and the Middle East* Chapel Hill: University of North Carolina Press, 2000.

Young, James Webb. *How to Become an Advertising Man.* Lincolnwood, IL: NTC Business Books, 1989.

———*The Diary of an Ad Man: The War Years, June 1, 1942-December 31, 1943.* Lincolnwood, IL: NTC Business Books, 1990.

———*A Technique for Producing Ideas.* New York: McGraw-Hill, 2003.

Zieger, Robert H. and Gall, Gilbert J. *American Workers, American Unions: The Twentieth Century.* Baltimore, MD: John Hopkins University Press, 2002.

Index

Note: Letter 'n' following the locators refer to notes cited in the text.

HF
5415
.1255
.S67
2011